How To Think Like a Programmer: Problem Solving for the Bewildered

By

Paul Vickers

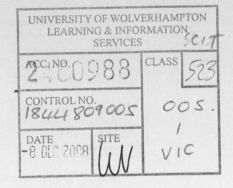
COURSE TECHNOLOGY
CENGAGE Learning

Australia • Brazil • Japan • Korea • Mexico • Singapore • Spain • United Kingdom • United States

COURSE TECHNOLOGY
CENGAGE Learning™

How to Think Like a Programmer:
Problem Solving for the Bewildered
Paul Vickers

Publishing Director: John Yates

Publisher: Gaynor Redvers-Mutton

Editorial Assistant: Matthew Lane

Production Manager: Alissa Chappell

Senior Production Controller: Maeve Healy

Manufacturing Manager: Helen Mason

Marketing Manager: Jason Bennett

Typesetter: Integra, India

Cover design: Jackie Wrout

For product information and technology assistance, contact **emea.info@cengage.com.**

For permission to use material from this text or product, and for permission queries, email **clsuk.permissions@cengage.com**

Products and services that are referred to in this book may be either trademarks and/or registered trademarks of their respective owners. The publishers and author/s make no claim to these trademarks.

British Library Cataloguing-in-Publication Data
A catalogue record for this book is available from the British Library.

ISBN: 978-1-84480-900-4

Cengage Learning EMEA
High Holborn House,
50-51 Bedford Row
London WC1R 4LR

Cengage Learning products are represented in Canada by Nelson Education Ltd.

For your lifelong learning solutions, visit **www.cengage.co.uk** and **www.course.cengage.com**

Printed by C&C Offset Printing, China
1 2 3 4 5 6 7 8 9 10 – 10 09 08

For Gina, a truly remarkable woman and a blessing beyond measure.

Contents

Contents vii

Preface xii

1 Introduction: Starting to Think Like a Programmer 1

   1.1 Who Is This Book For? 3

   1.2 Conventions and Learning Aids Used in This Book 3

      Think Spots 3

      In-text Exercises 4

      Key Terms and Important Points 4

      Brian Wildebeest FAQ 4

      End-of-Chapter Exercises 5

      Projects 5

      Layout 6

   1.3 Why Do We Write Programs and What *Are* They? 6

   1.4 Teaching Approach 8

      Algorithms 8

      Abstraction: Taking a Higher View 8

      Heuristic 10

      Getting the Most from This Book 11

   1.5 Structure of the Book 11

      Pseudo-code: An Algorithmic Language 12

   1.6 Coding Versus Problem Solving 12

   1.7 Chapter Summary 13

   1.8 Exercises 13

   1.9 Projects 14

      StockSnackz Vending Machine 14

      Stocksfield Fire Service: Hazchem Signs 14

      Puzzle world: Roman Numerals & Chronograms 15

      Pangrams: Holoalphabetic Sentences 16

2 A Strategy for Solving Problems 19

   2.1 Introduction 21

   2.2 What is a Problem? 21

   2.3 The Problem with Problem Solving 22

      Problem Domain Versus Programming Language Domain 22

2.4   A Strategy for Problem Solving 24

The Stages of Problem Solving 24

Understanding the Problem (Step 1) 25

Devising and Carrying Out the Plan (Steps 2 and 3) 26

Assessing the Results (Step 4) 29

Describing What We Have Learned (Step 5) 29

Documenting the Solution (Step 6) 30

2.5   Applying the Strategy 31

2.6   Chapter Summary 31

2.7   Exercises 31

2.8   Projects 32

StockSnackz Vending Machine 32

Stocksfield Fire Service 33

Puzzle World: Roman Numerals and Chrongrams 33

Pangrams: Holoalphabetic Sentences 34

Online Bookstore: ISBNs 34

2.9   "How To Think Like A Programmer" 34

3   Description Languages and Representations 37

3.1   Description Languages and Representations 39

Natural Language 39

Diagrams, Pictures, and Visual Thinking 39

Ant and Sugar 43

Mathematics 47

Physical Models 48

3.2   Pseudo-code – A Language for Solution Description 49

3.3   Chapter Summary 52

3.4   Exercises 53

3.5   Projects 54

StockSnackz Vending Machine 54

Stocksfield Fire Service 54

Puzzle World: Roman Numerals and Chronograms 54

Pangrams: Holoalphabetic Sentences 54

Online Bookstore: ISBNs 54

4   Problems of Choices and Repeated Actions 55

4.1   Making Coffee 57

4.2   Making Choices 61

4.3   Making It Again: Repeated Actions 65

4.4   Chapter Summary 78

4.5   Exercises 78

4.6   Projects 80
       StockSnackz Vending Machine 80
       Stocksfield Fire Service 80
       Puzzle World: Roman Numerals and Chronograms 80
       Pangrams: Holoalphabetic Sentences 81
       Online Bookstore: ISBNs 81

5   Calculating and Keeping Track of Things 83

5.1   Problems Involving Working Storage 85
       Understanding the Problem 87
       Devising a Plan to Solve the Problem 88
       Carrying Out the Plan 89
       Assessing the Result 94
       Finding the Variables 97
       Naming Conventions 98
       Problems Involving Arithmetic 102
       Understanding the Problem 103
       Devising a Plan to Solve the Problem 104
       Carrying Out the Plan 105
       Assessing the Result 110
       Loading More Than One Van 111
       Assessing the Result 117
       Describing What We Have Learned 118
       Documenting the Solution 119

5.2   Chapter Summary 121

5.3   Exercises 121

5.4   Projects 124
       StockSnackz Vending Machine 124
       Stocksfield Fire Service 125
       Puzzle World: Roman Numerals and Chronograms 125
       Pangrams: Holoalphabetic Sentences 125
       Online Bookstore: ISBNs 125

**6   Extending Our Vocabulary: Data and Control
       Abstractions 127**

6.1   Data Abstractions 129

6.2   Sequence 134

6.3   More Selections 134
       Simple and Extended Selections 134
       Extended Selections 135
       Multi-part Selections 136
       Writing Selection Conditions 139

6.4   Iteration   144
    Determinate Iterations   144
    Indeterminate Iterations   146
    Count-controlled Iterations   148
    At-least-once Indeterminate Loops   150

6.5   Applications of the WHILE and DO . . . WHILE Loops   152
    Sentinel-controlled Loops   152

6.6   Chapter Summary   156

6.7   Exercises   156

6.8   Projects   160
    StockSnackz Vending Machine   160
    Stocksfield Fire Service   161
    Puzzle World: Roman Numerals and Chronograms   161
    Pangrams: Holoalphabetic Sentences   161
    Online Bookstore: ISBNs   161

7   Object Orientation: Taking a Different View   163

7.1   The Procedural Paradigm   165

7.2   Objects and Classes, Properties and Methods   165
    Classes   167
    Getting Up in the Morning   169

7.3   Chapter Summary   178

7.4   Exercises   178

7.5   Projects   179
    StockSnackz Vending Machine   179
    Stocksfield Fire Service   179
    Puzzle World: Roman Numerals and Chronograms   179
    Pangrams: Holoalphabetic Sentences   179
    Online Bookstore: ISBNs   179

8   Looking Forward to Program Design   181

8.1   Algorithms   183

8.2   *HTTLAP* is **not** a Program Design Method   183

8.3   Program Design Methods   185
    Top-down Design: "Dysfunctional Decomposition"   185
    Bottom-up Design   187
    Data-structure Approaches   187
    Data-flow Approaches   188
    Object-oriented Approaches   189

8.4   Graphical Notations   189
    Flowcharts   190

Tree Diagrams 191
State Transition Diagrams 197
Data Flow Diagrams 200
UML-the Unified Modeling Language 202
Summary of Diagramming Techniques 203

8.5 Exercises 204
8.6 Projects 205
StockSnackz Vending Machine 205
Stocksfield Fire Service 205
Puzzle World: Roman Numerals and Chronograms 205
Pangrams: Holoalphabetic Sentences 205
Online Bookstore: ISBNs 205

Reflections 207

Abstract Data Type 207
Abstraction 207
Acronym 208
Assumptions 208
Computer Error 209
Documentation 209
Dysfunctional Decomposition 209
Heuristic 211
Initialization of Variables 211
Natural Numbers 212
George Pólya 213
Reusability 213
Small Capital Letters 214
Software Maintenance 214
Top Down 215
John von Neumann 217

References 219

Appendices

A **Pseudo-code 221**
B **Glossary 225**
C **Solutions to Selected Exercises 229**

Index 255

Preface

> Nothing is more important than to see the sources of invention which are, in
> my opinion, more interesting than the inventions themselves.
>
> *H. Gottfried Leibnitz (1646–1716)*

It is a fact of modern technology that what appears fantastical and wondrous today will, in a very short time indeed seem vulgar and commonplace. However, it is reassuring that in the discipline of computing the fundamental principles remain unchanged regardless of the technology used to implement them. Thus it is with computer programming. Whether we are talking about the punched-card systems of the 1970s or the interactive graphical user interface compilers of today (another technology that will doubtless seem quaint in a few years), the underlying concepts of data, data types and structures, sequence, iteration, selection, and abstraction remain stable. One can argue that the sophistication of modern technology has removed us from the heart of the computer to such a degree that programming skill is now harder to acquire than previously.

And so to the subject matter of this book. No matter what tools and technologies have been made available to assist the programmer in his task (including first course texts), the fact remains that too often the student of programming remains utterly bewildered and unable to complete his apprenticeship. The purpose of this book is to present the concepts and practices of computer programming in ways that will enable the bewildered novice to grasp just what is required. Using real-world examples and example algorithms (rather than the more traditional technical explanations followed by worked examples), I hope that upon completion of this study the reader will have picked up the essence of the discipline and will even feel the joy that comes with successfully constructing a machine (for that is what a program is) that correctly carries out its makers intentions and instructions. Programming really is fun but only if you are not bewildered.

So, this is a book about computer programming. But it is mostly a book on problem solving. Without the ability to do the latter, the former is very difficult indeed (if not impossible). Unfortunately, introductory programming books and university courses often ignore this fact. As far back as 1971 Gerald Weinberg complained that instead of *"trying to teach principles, ... schools seem devoted to teaching how to program in a single ... language. The objective seems to be to get the student writing some kind of program as soon as possible ... at the expense of limiting the future growth of the programmer"* (Weinberg, 1971). Many beginners come away from programming courses thinking that they're no good at programming and then look for ways in which to avoid all further contact with the subject (even to the extent of changing their university course!). As someone who enjoys programming I find this very sad, especially given that it is my belief that the bewildered student's perception is misplaced. I do not think it is programming they cannot do, rather, they have simply not learned basic principles of problem solving. Without this one will always struggle with writing a computer program because writing a program requires one to understand how to solve problems. I have seen too many pained faces in programming laboratories as the bewildered struggle to write a relatively straightforward program. When questioned they say that they do not know which bit of programming language code to use. Further questioning reveals the real difficulty: too often they simply do not understand the problem they are trying to solve. Hence their attempts to describe a solution to the problem in programming language code (for that is all a program is, a formalized, structured description of a solution to a problem) take them nowhere. Because they only encounter their difficulty when they try to write the solution as a program, the bewildered learner concludes that programming is hard and that he or she cannot do it. But until you have learned to solve problems, you cannot really judge whether or not you can program a computer.

The ancient Greeks developed a systematic approach to solving mathematical problems. Pappus, a mathematician who lived in Alexandria in the early part of the fourth century wrote about this method, although it goes back even earlier to the likes of Euclid (around 300 B.C.). The underlying principle is that of *heuristic* (what Leibnitz called the art of invention) which is a way of discovering solutions to problems when we do not have complete certainty that we are making the right decisions. Some people unkindly call heuristic the process of trial and error. I would like to think that while it certainly involves lots of trial and some error, it is at least based upon reasonable or educated guesswork. In 1945 the Hungarian mathematician George Pólya wrote a marvellous book called *How to Solve It* (Pólya, 1990) in which he brought together the HEURISTIC principles of Euclid and Pappus, Descartes, and Leibnitz to help with the solving of mathematical problems. In a nutshell, Pólya's method offers four basic steps: understand the problem, make a plan for solving the problem, carry out the plan, and reflect upon the solution. For nearly sixty years Pólya has helped students of mathematics to prove theorems and find answers. Unfortunately, computing educators have been slow to realize that Pólya also offers the bewildered programmer a ray of hope. Most introductory text books dive straight into writing program code (usually with an example program that displays "Hello World!" on the screen) and mix problem solving with coding. A few have realized Pólya's approach applies well to programming problems. Geoff Dromey applied it to traditional problems in computer science (Dromey, 1982). Simon Thompson applied it to functional programming problems (Thompson, 1997), and Michael Jackson observed that Pólya's principles apply to software development generally (Jackson, 1995).

So, this book attempts to separate problem solving from code writing. I hope that by bringing Pólya's framework to the task of learning to program the learner will begin to see how to think about tackling programming problems: writing program code and the discipline of program design can only be undertaken once the problem has been well understood.

Finally, throughout the book at points where in the past I have found learners to have particular difficulty you will find some frequently-asked questions (FAQ) typical of the kind asked of me by bewildered students. To encourage a dynamic learning community the book's website (at http://www.cengage.co.uk/vickers) contains a section where readers can submit their own FAQs seeking answers to issues that still cause puzzlement. I would like to encourage readers to submit their own FAQs and I will then provide answers to these on the website as appropriate.

Structure of the Book

The view taken in this book is that there are three areas of essential study, each with its own set of basic principles to be learned:

1. **The real-world domain**: this is concerned with problem understanding and problem solving.
2. **Systematizing the solution**: this is really a process of formalizing and checking our solutions, and hence leads into program design.
3. **The computer domain**: this is concerned with programming language syntax, programming concepts and techniques, and data structures. In other words, how to put our solutions into the computer.

This book deals with the first two areas, leaving issues of programming language syntax to other books. The expanded version of this book (*How to think like a programmer: Problem solving and program design solutions for the bewildered*) moves into the Computer Domain but only in terms of dealing with more specialized programming concepts and data structures. There are debates every year in university departments over what should be taught first, design or syntax. In this book I take the pragmatic view that problem solving should really come first as this feeds naturally into design which then feeds into the issues surrounding implementation using the chosen syntax (programming language).

To lessen the difficulty of doing 1 and 2 above without reference to a programming language, I have adopted the use of pseudo-code (structured English that is used to represent programming concepts) as a bridge to allow algorithm design without the messiness of an actual programming language.

We are not concerned here with how to get the computer to do things. We are interested only in making sure we understand the various aspects of real-world problems and then looking at how to get answers to those problems. Chapter 1 serves as an introduction to the book. Chapter 2 introduces the discipline of problem solving and shows how it is a necessary skill for would-be computer programmers. Chapter 3 offers a number of different ways of viewing and understanding problems and introduces the pseudo-code notation. In Chapter 4 we deal with simple real-world problems and in Chapter 5 we move on to more complicated examples. In both Chapters 4 and 5 we solve problems and then reflect on our solutions. We then look at how those solutions could be expressed in such a way as to allow them to be used by other people to get answers to those problems and others of the same type. We call this aspect *systematizing* the solution and it is essentially the process of building *algorithms*. Chapter 6 takes the concepts and structures of the first five chapters and expands them to give a wider algorithmic vocabulary by looking at some lower level control abstractions (iteration and selection types) and the notion of data typing. Chapter 7 introduces some of the high-level techniques and terminology necessary for beginning to think about problems in an object-oriented manner. Chapter 8 completes the main text by providing an introduction to program design techniques and notations.

With the exception of Chapter 7, all the solutions to the problems are of a procedural (imperative) nature. It is my opinion that even when using an object-oriented language as a first language the programmer still needs to be able to write procedural code. I would go as far as to say that procedural programming is a foundational skill upon which object-oriented techniques can be built; after all, many class methods in Java still need to be coded procedurally.

I am not a fan of large programming texts as I get the impression that cramming every detail of the language into the book is seen somehow as evidence of high quality and good value. It is almost as if the authors feel they are cheating their readers if they do not present every aspect of the programming language in question. Learning to program is sometimes compared with learning a foreign language. Weinberg went as far as to describe programming as a *"communication between two alien species"* (Weinberg, 1971). When learning a foreign language, primer texts do not cover every aspect of the language, every permutation of tense-mood arrangements. Rather, they focus on getting the beginner up to a level of competence in the essential aspects, such as an understanding of word order, a grasp of the present tense, and a small but workable vocabulary. Thus, I have deliberately kept this book as short as possible. In this book I have tried to present some general principles and ways of thinking that can be applied to programming problems in the large and translated to whatever language the reader is eventually required to code the algorithms in.

Above all, enjoy!

Paul Vickers

Stocksfield, Northumberland, UK

June 2007

Acknowledgments

First of all I would like to thank all the students over the best part of the last twenty years who have shared their bewilderment with me. People who are bright and otherwise successful in their studies have struggled to grasp the basics of what lies at the core of computer science courses because of the common mistake of confusing programming with programming languages. I hope that by focusing on the fundamental skill of problem solving within an algorithmic context this book goes some way to removing the bewilderment and helping future students to think like programmers.

Thanks go also to my colleagues past and present whose opinions and insights have helped to mould my ideas. Special thanks must go to John Pardoe, Melv King, and Stu Wade who taught me to how program in the first place.

A big thank-you to the editorial and production team at Cengage Learning who have provided a model for author-publisher relationships. Special mentions must go to: Gaynor Redvers-Mutton who picked up the project and ran with it, and through patience and clever cajoling got me to deliver it on time – masterfully done! To Matthew Lane, who dealt with my frequent and pedantic queries with good grace. To Alissa Chappell for her support in aspects of technical production. And to the anonymous reviewers of the manuscript whose support for the project and incisive comments have improved the book – any faults that remain are entirely my own.

Finally, I must thank Gina, Caitlin, Carys, and Zachary who have tolerated too many evenings and weekends with me locked in my study. Gina: thanks for holding the fort and also for redrawing my scruffy diagrams.

1

Introduction: Starting to Think Like a Programmer

1.1 Who Is This Book For?

1.2 Conventions and Learning Aids Used in This Book

1.3 Why Do We Write Programs and What Are They?

1.4 Teaching Approach

1.5 Structure of the Book

1.6 Coding Versus Problem Solving

1.7 Chapter Summary

1.8 Exercises

1.9 Projects

Learning Objectives

- Understand how to use the book and its special features
- Understand how programs are structured recipes (algorithms) to calculate/compute the answer to a given problem
- See how using abstraction is necessary for solving problems
- Understand the difference between solving problems and writing computer programming language code

This chapter serves two purposes. First, it describes for whom the book is intended, how the book is structured, and how to use it. Secondly, you will learn what a computer program is, why programmers write programs, and what they use to write those programs. You will discover the difference between writing program code and solving problems and you will learn why good programmers are, primarily, good problem solvers.

1.1 Who Is This Book For?

This book has two main audiences. The first audience is those who are taking an introductory programming or computer science course in which the first four to six weeks are spent developing the skills necessary to think like a programmer (algorithmically) and the course follows a more traditional programming language text.[1] The second audience is the "bewildered" programmer. If you can identify yourself in one or more of the following descriptions, then this book is also intended for you:

■ You have just started to learn a programming language at a university or college. You are only a little way into the course, but already you are starting to feel lost and panicky and may even be falling behind.

■ You have tried to learn programming and have come away feeling that it is terribly difficult. You have either fallen at the first hurdle or have finished an introductory course, but in either case you are left feeling bewildered with a sense that you never really understood it. If someone were to ask you which aspects of the subject you were having particular difficulty with, you would reply "all of it".

■ You have not learned any programming before, but it is a mandatory part of your university or college degree (which may not even be in Computer Science or Engineering). You feel anxious about it.

■ You are taking, or are about to take, an introductory programming course. You have had a look at the set textbook and even the first few chapters seem too advanced for you.

■ You are a secondary/high school student and you need an introductory book to get you started with the basics.

■ You are a mature reader. You are not necessarily on a formal course of study (though you may be) and you would like to find out what computer programming is about. Perhaps you have had a look at some other books and they all seem too advanced, too technical (even the introductory ones). You do not think you are a dummy or even an idiot, but you would like to see if you can get a foothold on what appears to be an interesting subject.

If you have identified yourself in the above list then continue reading. If you have not, continue reading anyway so that you can recommend this book to people you know who need to read it (and who can then stop bugging you for help!).

1.2 Conventions and Learning Aids Used in This Book

This book uses a number of techniques that have been designed to help you get the most out of its content. These are explained below.

Think Spots

The Think Spot is a point in the text where a question (or a number of questions) is raised for you to think about. To get the most benefit you should take

---

[1] If this book is being used at pre college/university level then it might be used over an entire term or semester.

a little time to think about the questions rather than just reading them and moving straight on. The famous Kodak Picture Spot signs at Disney World are sited at places where a great photograph can be taken; similarly, the Think Spot is located at points where you will really benefit from some reflective thinking and so develop the bigger picture.

In-text Exercises

Throughout the book you will see a picture of a pencil in the margins alongside some text in a shaded box denoting a short exercise:

This is a short exercise.

As these exercises are intended to help you understand a particular concept, you should not really proceed beyond an exercise until you have had a reasonable attempt at solving it. The exercises are like the Think Spots inasmuch as you need to stop and think, but unlike the Think Spots, you also need to physically do something such as sketching a solution, walking through a problem, or discussing something with a friend.

If an in-text exercise looks like this with a key in the margin, then a solution is also available in Appendix C. Just go to the In-text exercises section for the corresponding chapter in Appendix C and then look for the number that appears next to the key.

This is a short exercise with a solution available in Appendix C.

Key Terms and Important Points

Key terms ▶ Key terms and important points appear in the margin next to the paragraph or section in which they are introduced or defined. Together with the index this feature should make it easier for you to find what you are looking for.

Brian Wildebeest FAQ

Meet Mr B. Wildebeest. Brian is a wildebeest (also known as a 'gnu' and pronounced 'will-dur-beest') and usually he is happy.

However, sometimes Brian is a bewildered wildebeest at which times he looks like this:

Throughout the book you will see pictures of Brian looking bewildered in the margin. He appears at points where beginning programmers often have trouble understanding the point being made. Further down the page (or possibly on the next page) after seeing Brian you will find a box like this:

I don't understand why you said . . .

This is a common misunderstanding which arises from . . .

In the box is a question Brian the bewildered programmer is asking about the material next to which his picture appeared. Brian's queries are the kinds of frequently-asked questions (FAQ) I have been asked over the years by beginning programmers. The answer to the FAQ usually appears in the box below the question, though sometimes you are required to try to answer Brian's FAQ yourself.

The book's accompanying website (at www.cengage.co.uk/vickers) contains a section where readers can submit their own FAQs seeking answers to issues that still cause puzzlement. I would like to encourage readers to submit their own FAQs and I will then provide answers to these on the website as appropriate.

End-of-chapter Exercises

Each chapter has exercises at the end. The exercises are designed to help you reflect on what has been covered in that chapter. Any time you cannot complete an exercise suggests that you would benefit from going over the material again. Some exercises may be based on a single section (identified by the heading number), others may require ideas from several sections, and a few bring together the whole chapter. Solutions to selected exercises are given in Appendix C.

Projects

After the normal end-of-chapter exercises you will find some longer project-style exercises. These longer exercises are themed and will give you practice in incrementally building larger and larger solutions to more complex problems. The initial themes are introduced in the exercises at the end of this chapter and are then developed with each subsequent chapter. In these projects, you will be working toward developing complete programs that make use of most of the programming techniques discussed in this book. The projects cover a range of different problem scenarios, such as constructing a vending machine algorithm, decoding hazchem signs, working with Roman numerals and dates, playing with sentences that use all the letters of the alphabet, and working with ISBNs for an online bookstore.

Layout

All programming language code, pseudo-code (Chapter 3), examples of text that would appear on a computer screen or in a file on the computer's hard disc (or removable diskette), and examples of text that would be entered into a computer via the keyboard will appear in `this monospaced typewriter-style font`.

Reflections

Sometimes you will see a word or phrase set in SMALL CAPITAL LETTERS. Such words and phrases are the titles of short reflective opinion pieces that appear in the Reflections chapter (immediately following Chapter 8). These *Reflections* are designed to introduce some more complicated ideas that the interested reader can use to deepen their understanding of some of the problems and issues faced by programmers today.

1.3 Why Do We Write Programs and What *Are* They?

People write programs for a number of reasons. Authors like to use computers to help with the jobs of typing in and laying out text, checking their spelling, and so forth. Scientists and mathematicians use computers to calculate the answers to complex problems. Musicians and composers use the signal processing capabilities of computers to manipulate sound. In all cases, before the computer can carry out these tasks we must first tell it how to perform them. We do this by first solving the problem of deciding how the task can be carried out, and then expressing that solution in a form that can be turned into something the computer can interpret. The first stage (deciding how the task can be carried out) is the really important part as without doing this well we cannot progress to feeding the information into the computer.

Many beginners approach computer programming with a sense of awe, as if a computer program is some mystical artefact that only those initiated into the secret and black arts of computer science can produce. It is true that some programs are phenomenally complex comprising tens of millions of lines of programming language code.[2] But, at its heart a computer program is nothing more than a sequence of instructions to tell a machine (the computer) to do something specific.[3] The word processor I used to write this book is a program running on my home computer. When I use an ATM (cash machine) I am interacting with a program that decides whether there is enough money in my account to meet my

---

[2] It has been estimated that some of today's very large computer systems are the most complex artefacts ever built.

[3] Actually, the program may itself be considered a machine, only one built from logic rather than metal and plastic. For a clear and concise discussion of the program as machine, see *Software Requirements and Specifications* (Jackson, 1995).

withdrawal request. When I select a hot wash to get my cotton shirts really clean I am telling my washing machine to use the program (set of instructions) that will draw and heat enough water, release the detergent at the right time, rinse with cool water, and so on.

If you think about it, a computer program is in many ways just like a recipe. If you have ever cooked a meal then you will recall having to carry out particular tasks in a certain order. Even something as simple as making buttered toast or muffins requires that you spread the butter *after* the bread/muffin has come out of the toaster. You successfully make buttered toast or muffins (and keep your toaster in good working order) when you carry out the steps in the right order.

If you have never done so, find a cookery book and look at some of the recipes. You will see all the things you have to do in order to prepare various meals.

A good recipe is one that clearly sets out all that you have to do and when, that gives precise quantities for the ingredients, and that tells you what temperature to use in the oven and for how long to cook the dish. If the instructions are well set out then it should be possible for anyone to follow them and produce the desired result.

A musical score is a bit like a program too. Over hundreds of years musicians and composers have developed formalized languages of notation that allow musical instructions to be communicated on paper. A music score indicates all the notes to be played including their durations and volumes. Sections of the score can be marked for repetition including alternate endings to repeated phrases. Other marks tell the musician to speed up, slow down, pause, play louder, play more softly, etc. As long as a musician knows how to read and interpret a score then he or she can play music written by somebody else. The score in Figure 1.1 is presented in Western musical notation and shows a simple piece of piano music. It has a repeated section and alternative endings for the repeated section.

FIGURE 1.1 **A simple musical score: In this piece of music the first two bars are played through three times. The first two times they are followed by the music in Bar 3, and by the fourth bar after the third play through. The dots before the third bar line indicate that the previous section is to be repeated. The brackets with numbers indicate what should be played and how many times.**

1.4 **Teaching Approach**

What is needed by the novice programmer before all else is an understanding of the processes involved in examining and analyzing problems, in understanding the component parts of a problem, and in understanding what is required. You, the learner, then need to be able to solve the problem and check your solution for mistakes, inconsistencies, and limitations. Then you must be able to write down your plan for solving the problem in such a way that your solution can be repeatedly applied to the problem even when some of its values are altered.[4] Once this ability is acquired then, and only then, should you concern yourself with the details of programming languages. There is little use trying to write programs in programming language code if you do not first know how to solve the underlying problem, or worse, even understand the problem you have been asked to write a program to solve.

The philosophy behind this book is that before we can write programs on a computer we must first learn to think like a programmer. This can be approached in three stages:

1. Problem understanding and problem solving
2. Writing solutions in a structured form (algorithms)
3. Writing algorithms in a programming language

This book deals with Stages 1 and 2 for it is only after achieving competence in these stages that one should approach a real programming language. Before starting to think about writing any programming code, we must first focus on the problem statement, that is, on the *real-world domain*. First we must *understand* the problem and then we try *solving* it. Once we think we have solved it we *systematize* our solution by writing it out in a more formal way as a series of steps (an *algorithm*) that can be followed by another person.

Algorithms

Algorithm is a common word in programming circles. An algorithm is a rule, or a finite set of steps, for solving a mathematical problem. In computing it means a set of procedures for solving a problem or computing a result. The word *algorithm* is a derivation of Al-Khwarizmi (native of Khwarizm), the name given to the ninth-century mathematician Abu Ja'far Mohammed ben Musa who came from Khwarizm (modern day Khiva in the south of Uzbekistan). Thus, this book is about learning how to understand problems and design algorithms that are solutions to those problems.

Abstraction: Taking a Higher View

One thing all programmers do, whether they realize it or not, is use something called ABSTRACTION. Abstraction happens when we view something in general

---

[4] For example, imagine if the problem were to calculate the monthly payments on a loan. Your solution should work for all the possible values of loan amount, loan duration, interest rate, and so on, and not just for the example numbers given in the problem specification.

FIGURE 1.2   **Abu Ja'far Mohammed, aka Al-Khwarizmi after whom the algorithm is named.**

terms without focusing on its concrete details. For example, if you talk about driving in your car, the word *car* is really an abstraction for the specific individual car you drive. Your car will be different from my car. Even two cars of the same make, model, year, and specification are still different from each other inasmuch as they are both *individuals. Person* is an abstraction, as are *man, woman, child, boy, girl*, and so on. We all use abstraction in our everyday lives; indeed, without it we would not be able to function for it enables us to ignore all the fine details that would otherwise overwhelm us. The money in my pocket (how much, what currency, how many coins, what year were they minted, how many notes, their serial numbers), the people in the shop (how many men, women, boys, girls, what are their names, nationalities, ethnic groups, ages, heights, educational qualifications, first languages, etc.), and the stars in the sky are all abstract ways of managing an otherwise unmanageable amount of information.

Programmers use abstraction as a way of simplifying and managing detail. However, unlike most of our everyday abstractions, programmers do not actually ignore the detail, instead they *defer* its consideration. At some point the detail will need to be considered. Part of being a programmer is learning how to juggle abstractions, ignoring the fine detail when it is appropriate to do so.

This book follows the practice of dealing with **control abstraction** and **data abstraction** separately. The algorithms you will learn to build in this book **control** and manipulate **data** in order to produce desired results. When you withdraw money from your bank you are performing control (the sequence of actions necessary to withdraw the money) to manipulate data (the amount of money in your account, the date it was withdrawn, and so forth). Regarding data, this book takes a highly abstract view treating all the data in the problems it presents simply as values. Our control abstractions take a fairly general form in the beginning but as the book progresses the level of abstraction is lowered as we consider more specialized ways of performing actions.

Heuristic

This book takes a HEURISTIC approach to solving problems and expressing those solutions as algorithms. Having solved the problem and produced a corresponding algorithm, the programmer would then translate the algorithm into programming language code (a lower level of abstraction). When presented with an algorithm in a computer programming language such as Java or BASIC, the computer can carry out the instructions in the algorithm many millions of times faster (and reliably and accurately) than any person could.

Most books jump right away into the specific requirements of a given programming language and the learner will, through no fault of his or her own, associate the art of programming with writing instructions in a programming language. But using a programming language is one of the final steps in the process of writing a program. This book focuses on teaching you to concentrate on the most important stages: understanding the problem at hand and solving it algorithmically.

Too many beginning programmers blend problem solving with coding and treat them as one activity and then (reasonably) see programming as hard. Problem solving requires thinking about the problem at a high level of abstraction while writing programming language code requires a very low level of abstraction. Inevitably, the learner starts trying to apply the very low level of abstractions in their thinking about the problem. In fact, if problem solving and coding are separated we discover that the coding aspects are reasonably straightforward while it is really problem solving where the difficulty lies.

FIGURE 1.3 **Abstraction in the programming process**

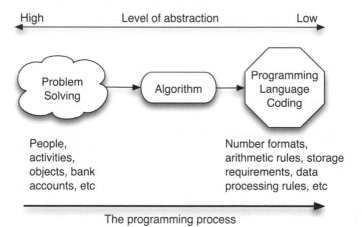

The programming process

One skill you will develop as a programmer is being able to think in terms of high-level abstractions (understanding and thinking about the problem at hand) and in terms of low level abstractions (individual data items, their format, and their status) simultaneously. However, having witnessed the confusion that can arise when a beginner is asked to do this from the very beginning, I decided in this book to make a clear separation between the high-level problem-solving skills and the low-level language-coding skills. Once you have become comfortable in approaching problems and producing algorithmic solutions, it is then time to think about translating the algorithms into a programming language. This book unashamedly deals with the high-level abstraction and leaves the translation exercise to other books that deal with specific programming languages. Eventually, after learning how to solve problems and then how to translate algorithms into programming language code you will find yourself able to mix the low-level abstractions with the high-level ones and the boundary between problem solving and writing in the chosen programming language will become more fluid.

Getting the Most from This Book

To get the most out of the book (and especially the exercises) you will find it helpful to get a willing friend or relative who can try out your solutions. If your friend can follow your instructions without seeking clarification from you and, using your instructions, can successfully complete the task or calculate the right answers, then you have begun to grasp problem solving and solution description. What you will have done is solve the general problem and create a set of steps and instructions that, when followed exactly, will allow you (or anybody else using the instructions) to solve any specific problem of the same type. In fact, the instructions are the solution to the problem and anyone using them no longer has to solve the problem, they simply have to follow some steps to calculate (or compute) the required answer.

1.5 Structure of the Book

The book is set out in the following way. In Chapter 2 we will look at what is meant by problem solving and how learning to solve problems will help us to become computer programmers. We will learn how to apply a structured strategy for problem solving. This strategy has steps dealing with understanding and describing the problem, planning how to solve it, and testing the solution.

Chapter 3 introduces different ways to think about problems and provides a form of structured English called *pseudo-code* that we will use to write down our algorithms (solutions to problems).

Chapters 4 and 5 are concerned with a few real-world problems that are used to develop skills in problem analysis and solution. The complexity of the problems gradually increases during the course of the two chapters to allow the introduction of basic programming concepts and techniques that you need in order to be able to think like a programmer, to solve problems, and to write down systematic solutions.

Chapter 6 takes our basic problem-solving skills and adds some more specialized vocabulary with which we will develop a repertoire of standard structures for implementing solutions to common programming problems.

Chapter 7 takes a small excursion into a different way of approaching programming and problem solving. Today object-oriented programming is very common and this chapter introduces some of the very basic concepts of this approach and shows how we can begin to think in object-oriented terms.

Solving the problem is the process of deriving a correct set of instructions that would enable us (or our friend) to calculate the right answer every time. By writing the instructions down in such a way that they are unambiguous and can be easily followed by anybody reading them, you have created an effective solution. If your solution does not involve unnecessary steps and is easily followed, then you have a good solution. A bad solution would be one that is hard to follow or is clumsy, or both (though this is a general rule that does not always apply – sometimes speed of execution is more important than elegance or comprehensibility). Therefore, in Chapter 8 we will look at some of the techniques available to you for designing good programs that are, after all, just solutions to problems.

Pseudo-code: An Algorithmic Language

As you probably have observed, people tend to use natural language (especially spoken language) imprecisely and meanings are often ambiguous.[5] Imagine the friend you have chosen to follow the instructions you will be writing down as you work through this book is unspeakably stupid and speaks only one language that has about thirty words in it. He is unable to interpret vague or woolly instructions and will reject any instructions that do not conform to the exact grammatical rules of his own, small language. Furthermore, he will slavishly obey everything you say to the letter. Imagine how careful you would have to be to write down your solution exactly right so that your friend could understand it and carry out your wishes. That is precisely how it is with a computer that cannot think for itself. For this reason, although this book does not deal with an actual programming language, it does use a form of structured English (called *pseudo-code*) for expressing solutions to problems. The pseudo-code used in this book is first introduced in Chapter 3. Learning to use pseudo-code provides a solid foundation for making the move to a computer programming language later on.

1.6 Coding Versus Problem Solving

We can say that a recipe is a solution to the problem of preparing a meal. Likewise, a computer program is a description of a solution to a computational or logic problem that is carried out by a computer rather than a person. The problem may be to work out the amount of tax we owe or to calculate the average mark of a university student. The problem may even be something as general as allowing a person to enter text, amend it, move it around, apply various formatting to it, save it, and print it out (just what a word processor does). However, in all these cases the program is the series of steps that, if followed, will lead to the desired outcome (assuming the program was correctly written). However, notice that the program does not actually solve the problem at hand,[6] rather it *calculates* (or computes) the *answer* to

---

[5] Take the following anonymous book dedication: "to my parents, George Pólya and God." What does that mean? Surely the author is not claiming that God is one of his parents? The sentence is syntactically (grammatically) correct though its meaning can be misunderstood. The addition of an extra comma makes things much clearer: "to my parents, George Pólya, and God." Most people are taught not to put a comma after the element that precedes the 'and' in a list, yet in this case adding the *serial comma* really helps to make the author's meaning crystal clear. You may be interested to know that the serial comma is also known as the Oxford comma as it is a stylistic practice of the Oxford University Press (OUP). The OUP uses it precisely because it removes ambiguity from lists. Most people do not use it, but I do. If you look closely you will see that it is used throughout this book. You hadn't noticed? Shame on you, programmers need to have an eye for detail you know.

[6] Certain problems in mathematics and engineering excepted.

the problem. That is, it calculates the correct tax or it correctly stores the text entered by the user of the word processor. The solution to the problem is provided by **you**, the programmer. It is you who solves the problem by deciding the correct series of instructions that, when followed, result in the desired outcome. The process of solving the problem is really the essence of computer programming. Many people are fooled into thinking that writing programming language code is what defines programming. Not so. Writing the code is merely the stage of expressing the solution to the problem in a way that it can be communicated to the computer. Once we have the solution, correctly expressing it in the chosen programming language does take skill and experience, but to be able to write the program code we must first solve the problem. Moreover, before we can solve the problem we must first understand it. It is one thing to try to write the program code for a problem we understand but have not completely solved yet (though this is still bad practice); it is quite another thing to try to write the code for a problem we do not even understand. Explaining tasks to a person and to a computer is essentially the same; the difference is the required level of precision, or un-ambiguity (abstraction), in the language used.

1.7 Chapter Summary

In addition to learning how this book is organized and the various ways it can be read, we also discussed what computer programs are, why we write them, and how good problem-solving skills are essential for successful programming. The programming process can be thought of as a two-stage activity: in the first stage, we work on understanding and solving the underlying problem. When that is accomplished we proceed to Stage 2, which is translating the problem solution into programming language code ready for compilation and execution on the computer.

Many beginners go astray because they start at Stage 2, that is, they read the problem definition and immediately try writing programming code. This is a major cause of bewilderment, hence the emphasis in this book is on doing Stage 1 properly. Before moving on to discussing the nature of problem solving in the next chapter, try the exercises below to make sure you have grasped the ideas presented in this chapter.

1.8 Exercises

1. What is an algorithm?

2. What is a program? Try giving an answer in no more than thirty words. Do you know someone who is very poor at understanding technology (usually they cannot program their video recorder or set the stations on their car radio)? If so, how would you explain to him or her what a computer program is?

3. Describe your wallet using three different levels of abstraction: low (as many details as you can think of), medium (the main points), and high (identifying characteristics only).

4. *Put on my shoes* is a highly abstract description of a common task. To describe the task at a lower level of abstraction requires some details to be known. Jot down some of the

main pieces of information that are needed to be able to describe step-by-step the process of putting on a pair of shoes.

5. Learning to write Java/C/Visual Basic/programming language of your choice is not the same thing as learning to program. Why not?

6. What were the causes of the First World War?

1.9 Projects

Below are the four themed projects that will be used to develop your programming skills throughout the rest of the book. After each set of end-of-chapter exercises you will find additional exercises related to one or more of these projects. As you progress through the book you will find yourself extending your solutions until you have outline algorithms for complete programs. Your task for this chapter is to read through the project descriptions and familiarize yourself with their contents. Try to identify what problems might exist.

StockSnackz Vending Machine

The University of Stocksfield has installed a StockSnackz brand vending machine in its staff common room for the benefit of the faculty. The University places a high value on its staff so the machine dispenses free snacks including chocolate, muesli bars, apples, popcorn, and cheese puffs. Drawing upon your own experiences of using vending machines, think about the problems associated with maintaining the StockSnackz machine: How will the user select an item? Which items should be dispensed? What happens when the machine runs out of an item? What information does the machine owner need to know about the number of dispensed snacks? If the snacks were not free, how is money taken and change given?

Stocksfield Fire Service: Hazchem Signs

Attached to the back of trucks transporting chemicals in many countries you will find a hazchem sign (Figure 1.4). The three-character code at the top is the EAC, or Emergency Action Code, which tells firefighters how to deal with a chemical spillage and fire.

FIGURE 1.4   **Hazchem sign**

The first character of the EAC is a number identifying the method to be used for fighting any fire. The second character is a letter identifying the safety precautions to be taken by firefighters, whether a violent or explosive reaction is possible, and whether to dilute or contain any spill. The third character is either blank or an E indicating the existence of a public safety hazard. The four-digit code is the United Nations substance identification number that is used to find out the exact name of the chemical. The hazard warning diamond gives specific information about the nature of the hazard. Table 1.1 shows how to decode the EAC.

Table 1.1   Emergency Action Code: required firefighting methods and precautions

1	Coarse spray	3	Foam
2	Fine spray	4	Dry agent

P	V	LTS(CPC)	Dilute spillage
R			
S	V	BA & fire kit	
T			
W	V	LTS(CPC)	Contain spillage
X			
Y	V	BA & fire kit	
Z			
E		Public safety hazard	

Key

V = Can be violently or explosively reactive

BA = Breathing apparatus

LTS = Liquid tight Suit/Chemical Protection Suit and BA required

DILUTE = Spillage may be washed away when greatly diluted with large quantities of water.

CONTAIN = Spillage must not enter water courses or drains.

DRY AGENT = Water must not be allowed to contact substance.

What patterns can you see in Table 1.1? How might these patterns help in solving problems related to the decoding of an Emergency Action Code?

Puzzle world: Roman Numerals and Chronograms

We express numbers in base 10 using digits derived from a Hindu-Arabic system. Arithmetic is straightforward in this system. However, consider the Roman

Empire that had an altogether different numbering system. In the Roman system, numbers are represented by combinations of the primitives given in Table 1.2 below. The number 51 is written as LI, the number 1,500 is written as MD, and so on. Further, the numbers 4, 9, 40, 90, 400, and 900 are written as IV, IX, XL, XC, CD, and CM respectively. Thus, 14 is XIV, 99 is XCIX, etc. (What is common to the numbers 9, 40, 90, and 900?). In this system, the year 1999 would be written as MCMXCIX and the year 2007 as MMVII.

Table 1.2 **The basic Roman Numerals**

Roman Numeral	Decimal Equivalent
I	1
V	5
X	10
L	50
C	100
D	500
M	1000

As you can imagine, arithmetic is not so simple using such numbers. For example, consider the simple sum 1,999 + 2,007 using Roman numerals:

$$MCMCXIX + MMVII = ?$$

The answer is MMMMVI. Why do we need to know about Roman numerals today? The media industry still uses them. TV shows have the year of production expressed in Roman numerals, as do some movies, books, and so on. The pages in the front matter of books (before the first chapter) are numbered using Roman numerals with Arabic digits being reserved for the main body (look at the page numbers for the preface in this book).

Imagine you are writing software for a media production company that needs a reliable way of dealing with translation of dates into Roman numerals. What sorts of problems might you face in converting between decimal numbers and Roman numerals?

Pangrams: Holoalphabetic Sentences

Pangrams are holoalphabetic, that is words or sentences that contain every letter in the alphabet. Here is a famous one used by computers to show how text looks in different fonts: *The quick brown fox jumps over the lazy dog*. Pangrams are useful in digital typography because they demonstrate all the letters in a font within a more meaningful context than just writing the alphabet – the interactions between the letters are also easier to see.

The "perfect" pangram is *isogrammatic*, that is, it uses each letter only once. It is extremely hard to produce meaningful isogrammatic pangrams in English. For example, here is one that uses only 26 letters:

Quartz glyph job vex'd cwm finks.

It is not terribly meaningful even if they are all real words. Most pangrams are not isogrammatic, so the next goal is to make them as close to being isogrammatic as possible. Here are some more pangrams with their letter count shown in parentheses.

Pack my box with five dozen liquor jugs (32, *e, i,* and *o* repeated).
Waltz, bad nymph, for quick jigs vex (28, only *a* and *i* repeated – not as meaningful though).
Six plump boys guzzled cheap raw vodka quite joyfully (46).
Sympathizing would fix Quaker objectives (36).
Quick waxy bugs jump the frozen veldt (31).
Brick quiz whangs jumpy veldt fox (27).

Think about what problems exist in constructing a pangram and in determining whether a sentence is a pangram. If it is, determine if it is isogrammatic.

Online Bookstore: ISBNs

The International Standard Book Number (ISBN) is a unique 10- or 13-digit number used to identify books. The system was invented in 1966 (then simply called SBN – Standard Book Numbering) by W.H. Smith (the U.K. bookseller and stationer) and was adopted as an international standard (ISO 2108) in 1970. Beginning in January 2007, ISBNs will have 13 rather than 10 digits.

FIGURE 1.5 **Anatomy of the International Standard Book Number (ISBN)**

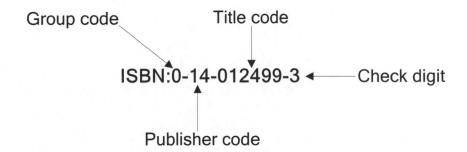

The number comprises four parts:

1. The country of origin or language code (called the group code)
2. The publisher's code
3. A number for the book title
4. A check digit

The different parts can have different lengths and usually are printed with hyphens separating the blocks (the hyphens are not part of the number). The check digit is introduced to ensure that the previous nine digits have been correctly transcribed. It can be a digit (0–9) or the character 'X' (representing the value 10 – it is not necessary yet to understand how the check digit is calculated).

Until January 2007 all ISBNs were 10 digits. A new 13-digit format was introduced in January 2007 (known as ISBN-13 or "Bookland EAN"). All 10-digit

ISBNs can be converted to ISBN-13 by adding a prefix of 978 and recalculating the check digit. The 10-digit ISBN 0-14-012499-3 becomes 978-0-14-012499-6 and 0-003-22371-X becomes 978-0-003-22371-2. In the following chapters, you will find exercises focusing on three specific problems related to ISBNs:

1. Validating an ISBN (checking it is correct)
2. Converting a 10-digit ISBN to ISBN-13 format
3. Displaying a raw ISBN such as 0140124993 with the correct hyphenation; Table 1.3 shows correct hyphenations for a few ISBNs

Table 1.3 **Hyphenating an ISBN**

Raw ISBN	Hyphenated ISBN	Book Title
0140124993	0-14-012499-3	How to Solve It
999361419X	99936-14-19-X	Gross National Happiness and Development.[7]
8466605037	84-666-0503-7	Los Simpson ¡Por Siempre!

Thinking of the three ISBN-related problems stated above, what sub-problems can you identify? That is, what things would you have to do to be able to solve the three problems for any ISBN?

[7] The book in question is Karma Ura and Karma Galay (eds), *Gross National Happiness and Development: Proceedings of the First International Seminar on Operationalization of Gross National Happiness*, The Centre for Bhutan Studies, Thimphu, Bhutan, 2004. However, you won't find it on Amazon. The group code is 99936 which is used for books published in the Kingdom of Bhutan.

2 A Strategy for Solving Problems

The sooner you start coding your program the longer it is going to take.

H. F. Ledgard (1975)

2.1   Introduction

2.2   What Is a Problem?

2.3   The Problem with Problem Solving

2.4   A Strategy for Problem Solving

2.5   Applying the Strategy

2.6   Chapter Summary

2.7   Exercises

2.8   Projects

2.9   "How To Think Like A Programmer"

Learning Objectives

- Understand what problems are and that they have several possible solutions
- Identify different types of problem
- Apply a strategy to help understand, solve, and evaluate the solution to a problem

This chapter is about problems and some of the many ways of going about solving them. It begins by considering the meaning of the word *problem* and then discusses some of the difficulties we have with solving problems. Section 2.4 presents a strategy for solving problems. This strategy is the cornerstone of the book, for it is the tool that you will use to solve the various problems presented in the remaining chapters. The rest of the chapter shows you how apply the strategy to real problems (Section 2.5).

2.1 Introduction

There is a great temptation among people starting to learn programming to use the computer far too early. Often they will quickly read over the task set by their teacher and then go to the computer and start typing in programming language code in a trial-and-error fashion in the hope that this will at some point result in a program that produces the right answers. Occasionally this works, but the resultant program is usually very badly constructed and hard to understand. More often, the student comes away from the experience feeling bewildered, feeling that programming is *very difficult*.

This is a natural temptation. When we buy a new gadget, how many of us really read the instructions before trying it out? We are used to learning through trial and error. While you may manage to make good use of a vacuum cleaner without reading its instructions, the same approach rarely works well with programming. Someone once said, "Hours spent using a new software program saves minutes reading the manual." With programming, it is vital to spend the majority of our time thinking about the problem and designing a solution to it. One of the very last stages of programming is actually turning on the computer, typing in, and running the program. When I began teaching programming to college students, this discipline was easier to instill because powerful personal computers and feature-rich program development environments were not commonly available. We used screen editors on terminals connected to a mainframe computer. Access to the terminals was restricted owing to their cost, so students had limited time in which to type in, compile, and test their programs. Programmers brought up on batch card readers would say they had it easy – at least they had direct access to the compiler while they waited overnight for the computer operators to compile their programs. Back then, you simply had to spend time poring over your code trying to ensure it was correct before approaching the computer because you had few other options. These days, the excellent integrated program development environments running on modern desktop machines provide too much temptation for the tentative novice programmer to resist. The belief is that the compiler will somehow help them to get their code right and that if a few half-understood lines of code are typed in, given enough attempts at compilation and execution, success is bound to follow. However, unless you have a good grasp of the problem you are trying to solve, and a good attempt at an outline solution to it, this try-it-and-see approach usually leads to many errors and even more frustration! In the sections that follow, we will focus on the core skill that a programmer needs: learning to solve problems.

2.2 What is a Problem?

There is an old story that illustrates a number of points about problem solving. Three students, one of physics, one of engineering, and one of business, were asked by a university professor how they would use a barometer to determine the height of a tall building. The physics student said he would find the atmospheric pressure at the top and the bottom of the building and, using a known formula, would convert the difference between the readings into the height.

The engineering student said that she would drop the barometer from the top of the building, time its descent to the ground, and thus calculate the height. The business student said he would offer the barometer to the building's caretaker as a gift in return for telling him the height.

What does this teach us about problem solving? Simply that most problems can be solved in a number of ways and it is not always clear which way is better. The problems that we solve in introductory programming courses are usually reasonably well defined in that the end or objective (also known as the program requirements) is often specified quite clearly, though this is not always the case. However, the ways of solving the problem vary. We want to choose the best way according to some list of recognized criteria. Our goal as professionals is to provide high-quality software solutions. We want to use a method of proceeding from problem specification to high-quality software solution in a reasonable manner.

2.3 The Problem with Problem Solving

We must be aware that no matter how systematic our approach, many problems will still contain aspects that simply require a lot of thinking and even some intuitive leaps. Take a crossword puzzle for instance. There are two principal types of crossword puzzles: those offering definitions of words that you have to find (e.g., "difficult question; something hard to understand – seven letters"),[1] and those that offer a cryptic puzzle that contains clues to the answer (e.g., "person startled by the parabolic spaceship perhaps? – nine letters").[2] The definition-type crossword puzzles are straightforward to solve: you just need a broad vocabulary and a good memory. Cryptic crosswords do not only require a good vocabulary, they also need an understanding of the different hints that cryptic clues contain and an ability to think laterally.

A problem-solving strategy provides a framework within which you are more likely to arrive at a good solution. Unfortunately, no programming method allows you to derive the correct solution merely by following a few simple rules; all programming problems require you to think for yourself.

Problem Domain Versus Programming Language Domain

When we move from solving problems in the real world to expressing those solutions in a form that a computer can process, we discover a second class of problem introduced by computer programming languages. For example, take the following problem of calculation. Suppose a certain car has a fuel tank with a capacity of 60 litres and an average fuel consumption of 14 km/l. How far can the car travel on one tank of fuel, and how many litres are needed to travel 650 km?

---

[1] What is the answer? Why, "problem," of course!

[2] OK, so that is just a nonsense clue that was made up, but surely you have seen similar clues. The famous crossword puzzle in *The Times* of London is an example of the cryptic genre.

This is a straightforward problem in arithmetic. We could make it slightly trickier: Assuming you start with a full tank, how many times must you refuel to travel 2000 km? Trickier still is to find how many *miles* can you travel on 10 *gallons* of fuel using the same car. The last two are each refinements of the first problem. How can we solve such problems? How can we write an algorithm to solve the problem? Can you then write an algorithm that provides a general solution to all problems of this type where the car's fuel tank capacity and fuel consumption can vary?[3]

Let us say we have solved the first problem by discovering that the range of the car equals its fuel capacity multiplied by its fuel consumption and that the amount of fuel required for a journey is the distance divided by the car's fuel consumption. We may be feeling confident that all that remains is the simple matter of translating the solution into our chosen programming language. In principle, this stage is straightforward but we will often discover that the language introduces subproblems. Using a calculator we find that the range of our car is 840 km (60×14) and that the amount of fuel needed to travel 650 km is $650 \div 14 = 46.428571$ litres. Now two questions arise: should the range (840 km) be displayed as a whole number, and how many digits should be used to display the fuel needed? What if the fuel consumption of the car were 14.6 km/l and its tank capacity 60.3 l? In this case, its range would be 880.38 km and the amount of fuel needed to travel 650 km would be 44.520547 l. Now the range is also a fractional number. Should we round everything up to the nearest whole number? Or should we display everything to two decimal places? Or three decimal places? The answers to these questions are important because you will discover that programming languages treat different kinds of numeric values in different ways and that displaying numbers in different formats can be a tricky business. Some programming languages make it very easy to display fractional numbers to a specified number of decimal places while others make it less straightforward. The point is that we need to be aware that the translation of a solution into programming language code can raise a further set of difficulties that should be treated as problems in their own right. We must distinguish between those subproblems that belong to the problem itself and those that belong to the programming language syntax (or our incomplete knowledge and/or misunderstanding of it). For example, discovering that the distance travelled must be divided by the fuel consumption to find the fuel needed for a journey belongs in the domain of the problem itself while displaying the answer to two decimal places is a problem in the domain of the programming language. In this book, we will predominantly be dealing with problems of the former type.

---

[3] Also, what do we mean by a gallon? In the United Kingdom, a gallon is 160 fluid ounces, there being eight pints in a gallon and 20 ounces in a pint. However, in the United States there are only 16 ounces in a U.S. pint, so a gallon there contains only 128 fluid ounces. That means that a U.K. (Imperial) gallon is (on these terms) 1.25 times the size of a U.S. gallon, or a U.S. gallon is 80% of the size of an Imperial one. And then we learn that the U.S. fluid ounce is 1.04 imperial fluid ounces, so 1 Imperial gallon is really 1.20 U.S. gallons. Sigh.

2.4 A Strategy for Problem Solving

In *How to Solve It*, GEORGE PÓLYA wrote, *"It is foolish to answer a question that you do not understand"* (Pólya, 1990). While this sounds like a self-evident truth, time after time I have witnessed confused beginners sitting at their computers chewing their pens in frustration because they cannot get their program to work. When faced with a programming problem, many novices begin by looking over the requirements to find out what they have to do. After some head scratching, accompanied by a general feeling of unease or bewilderment, they head for the computer, fire up the compiler, and start writing down some code in the hope that they will eventually hit upon a sequence of instructions that will solve the problem. The main difficulty here is that they are mixing the final language of the

Description ▶ vs. solution

problem description (the programming language code) with the task of *problem solving*. It is very much like trying to tell a friend how to bake a cake before you know how to do it yourself. In all likelihood, you will give your friend many false starts, contradictory instructions, tell him or her to do things in the wrong order, and generally end up with a big mess and wasted ingredients.

The Stages of Problem Solving

To make progress in programming you *must* begin by making sure you understand the problem – you need a strategy for solving problems. The first decision we will make in our strategy is to separate the task of solving the problem from the task of writing down the solution. Pólya (1990) proposed a strategy for solving mathematical problems that runs roughly as follows:

1. Understand the problem
2. Devise a plan to solve the problem
3. Carry out the plan
4. Look back (check the result and reflect upon it)

This is a good foundation for a programming strategy, and we shall adopt it with a couple of additions. Part of learning to think like a programmer involves reflecting upon what you have done. By describing what you have learned from each programming task, you begin to develop a repertoire of experience and knowledge about problems that will help you to solve similar or related problems in the future. While thinking about what you have learned is certainly useful,

Write it down ▶

writing it down is even more so for two reasons. First, once an idea is written down it can be retrieved later (otherwise, you may forget it). The second reason is that writing something down requires thinking very clearly about it. Before we can express something in writing, we must first have a good understanding of it. Often I will think I have understood something but it is not until I try writing down my explanation that I discover my understanding was not as clear as I thought. We will add a step to our strategy that deals with describing what we have learned:

1. Understand the problem
2. Devise a plan to solve the problem
3. Carry out the plan

4. Look back (check the result and reflect upon it)

5. Describe what we have learned from the process

Finally, as good programmers we should always assume that at some time in the future another programmer will need to pick up our programs and modify them. The act of changing a program after it has been finished is called SOFTWARE

Software ▶
maintenance

MAINTENANCE and it is estimated to consume anywhere between 70% and 90% of the total cost of a software system. That is, more money is spent on changing a program after it has been released for use than is spent on developing it in the first place. One obvious reason for carrying out maintenance is to remove errors that were not spotted during its development. Another reason is to update the software to increase its capabilities or to make it compatible with a newer version of an operating system. Whatever the reason, it is quite likely that a program written by one programmer will be maintained by a different person. As professionals, we must strive to ensure that our program is as easy to understand as possible so that the maintenance programmer does not have to waste a lot of time trying to figure out what we have done. So, as well as writing clearly laid-out and well-structured programs, we also need to provide good DOCUMENTATION that explains them. Documentation can be *internal* (comments within the program code to explain certain points) and *external* (general statements about the whole program, including design documents, requirements specifications, and so on). Therefore, we shall add a final stage to our problem-solving strategy that deals with explaining our results and documenting the program. Our outline framework for problem solving now looks like this:

1. Understand the problem
2. Devise a plan to solve the problem (plan an attack)
3. Carry out the plan/attack
4. Assess the result (i.e., look back – check the result and reflect upon it)
5. Describe what we have learned from the process
6. Explain our results (and document our program)

The complete strategy is given at the end of this chapter (after the exercises and projects) as Table 2.2. The following sections explain each element of the strategy.

Understanding the Problem (Step 1)

The first task is to understand the problem. Some problems will be very easy to understand, others harder. We must become familiar with the language of the problem, read it several times, and become aware of its principal parts. Sometimes rephrasing the problem or describing it with a different representation from the original can be useful. For example, drawing a picture or a diagram may shed light on what is required. In Chapter 3, we will look at using alternative representations to help us in describing problems and solutions.

When you have familiarized yourself with the problem, you can start digging out the details. What do we know for sure, and what is unknown? Look at the different parts of the problem and consider them individually. Then think about how they relate to each other. What effect would a change in one aspect have on the other parts and on the problem as a whole? For instance, going back to our earlier car example, we can say that we know the car's fuel capacity (60 litres) and we know its average fuel consumption (14 km/l). The *unknown* is the car's range as that is what the problem statement asks us to find out. Changes in either the fuel capacity or fuel consumption will affect the car's range so we see that the three values are related.

Devising and Carrying Out the Plan (Steps 2 and 3)

For Steps 2 and 3 we can use analogy, that is, we can draw upon our repertoire of similar problems that we have met in the past. If the current problem resembles a problem you have seen before, write down how it is similar and, just as important, write down how it differs. It is vital to record the differences also, for ignoring them may lead you to make unjustified ASSUMPTIONS about the current problem.

For those aspects that are similar, can you use the same solution techniques that you used in the past problems? Many programming problems fall into well-understood patterns that can be reused. All that is required is to adapt one of the standard solutions to the particular circumstances of your problem. As you continue you will learn that a great many programming problems are variations on a smaller number of previously solved problems.

Standard ▶ solutions

What do the following real-world problems have in common?

1. Put together a self-assembly wardrobe.
2. Hang a new door in the kitchen.
3. Fix a small bookshelf to the bedroom wall.
4. Put a new hard drive inside the computer.

One answer is that they may all require you to use a screwdriver. What other answers did you come up with?

Devise a Plan

All but the most trivial programming tasks will usually comprise a number of smaller subproblems. Even simple programs typically require you to solve the related problems of

■ providing your program with the data it needs (input);
■ processing the data; and
■ displaying the results or saving them to a file (output).

Exploring the second subproblem (processing the data) will likely yield a further set of subproblems. Each subproblem should be treated as a problem in its own right with its own structure and its own principal parts.[4]

---

[4] Michael Jackson deals with just this subject in his excellent book, *Problem Frames: Analyzing and Structuring Software Development Problems* (Jackson, 2001).

Try partitioning (separating out) the problem of getting up in the morning into a few simpler subproblems (or tasks).

Some subproblems may be easier to solve than others. Begin with them; their solution may give you clues to the remaining problems. If a particular problem is too difficult to solve immediately, can you extend the principle of analogy and solve a simpler version of it or a related problem? Doing so may just give you the inspiration you need.

In understanding the problem, I recommend making a drawing, or a sketch, or an alternative description of the problem. One technique I have observed to be very effective is to retell the problem in your own words to another person. Often, I have had a puzzled student approach me with a problem and the moment he or she explained it to me the penny dropped and the student answered his or her own question without me speaking a word. If you cannot find someone else, explain the problem to the wall, your teddy bear, or a mirror. Do not worry about feeling foolish – after all, there is nobody around to laugh or you would have used them instead.

Left over? ▶   Whenever I take apart a piece of machinery or an appliance in an attempt to fix it, I am always relieved when, having reassembled it, there are no parts left over. Sometimes, though, our problems have parts left over, pieces of information that we have overlooked or have not used. Check that you have not overlooked something. Is there a piece of information that did not seem important? If so, revisit it and see if it will help after all.

Although we should keep consideration of programming language details separate from understanding and solving the problem, this is not always possible. Michael Jackson (2001) gives the following advice:

> *When you structure a problem you can't avoid moving some way towards its solution – that is, towards talking about the computer and its software. . . . There is nothing wrong with that, provided that you don't neglect the problem world, and don't give a description of the computer and its software when you should be giving a description of the world. You always need to know clearly which one you are talking about. (p. 15)*

Carrying Out the Attack

Once you think you have a firm grasp on the solution, write down the sequence of actions necessary to solve the problem. Even if you have not worked everything out yet writing down the overall sequence of actions will help. The first question you can ask yourself is whether the ordering of the actions is correct. Does the order rely on certain conditions to be true? Have these conditions come from the problem statement or are they ASSUMPTIONS you have made? Is it possible to verify the assumptions?

Write down the sequence in which the various actions associated with getting up in the morning should be carried out.

If you are finding it too complicated to understand a problem, try removing some of the details to see if the simplification gives you a clearer understanding (though you must remember to deal with the details later on!).

Once you have a sequence of actions, check whether they all need to be carried out in all circumstances. Perhaps some of the actions only need to be carried out when certain conditions are met. For example, the sequence of actions involved in leaving the house and walking to the bus stop might involve putting up the umbrella. Unless you like permanent shade, you would probably only put up your umbrella if it is raining hard enough. So, although the solution to the problem of leaving the house and catching a bus contains the raise-umbrella action, whether or not the action is carried out depends on the circumstances that apply at the time; one day you may put up the umbrella, the next you may not.

Is it sufficient to carry out each action once only, or do some actions need to be repeated? For instance when mowing the lawn, whether or not I need to empty my lawn mower's grass box more than once depends on three things: the capacity of the grass box, the size of the garden, and the length of the grass. For my garden and my current mower two of these things are constant (lawn size and box capacity) but the length of the grass will be different each time I cut it.

Thinking back to getting up in the morning, are there any optional or conditional tasks involved in getting up in the morning?

Here is a tip that works well across Steps 1, 2, and 3. If you are having trouble understanding the problem, working out your plan, or carrying out your plan, then use the following technique. I have used it extensively and found **Sleep on it** ▶ to be an invaluable aid to problem solving: sleep on it. I often find that the answer to a problem that seemed intractable presents itself naturally if left alone for a while. As a student I used the following strategy for completing programming assignments: on the first day read through the assignment brief and take in the main points, then put it away. A couple of days later take out the brief and read it through again, but this time make some notes. Summarize the problem requirements, and then put it away. Two days later try designing an initial solution. Refine it a few times then put it away. Continuing in this way worked well for me most of the time. The trick was not to spend too long at any one time on the problem. There comes a point where no matter how long you stare at a problem you just cannot get the answer. It is best to put it away and come back to it fresh another day; often you will find that when you pick it up again the answer you were searching for comes more easily. Contrast this with the traditional student approach of leaving the assignment until the day before it is due and then working through the night to complete it. That is not a good strategy for programming because you are not leaving yourself enough reflection and background processing time. It is amazing what problems your brain can work through if you would stop bothering it and leave it alone to get on with the job.

Assessing the Results (Step 4)

When you have a solution that seems to be right then try it out. Ideally, you should get someone else to try out your solution. The problem with testing your own solutions is that you are likely to be blind to your own logical errors. You will intend a certain course of action and will interpret your instructions as meaning what you intended. But when you give your instructions to someone else they may just find instructions that mean something quite different from what you intended. It is the differences between what we intend, and how we actually express our intentions that result in bugs (defects) in our programs. Having a friend walk through your solution is a great way of ensuring that you learn to be more precise and unambiguous in your writing down of solutions. Did your friend manage to complete the task using your instructions? Did they manage to complete the task without asking for help or clarification? Did they misinterpret any of the instructions? If so, did they *really* misinterpret them or were they correct and you were wrong in the way you wrote the instruction? If you and your friend used the solution, did you both get the same answers? If not, who was wrong, and why? If you did get the same results, were they the correct ones?

Get your friend to evaluate/criticize your steps for getting up in the morning that you wrote down earlier.

Did your solution give the right outcome or the correct results? If so, well done, but are you sure it is correct? If you change some of the values and conditions, do you still get the correct answers? If you did get the right answers, did any parts of the solution seem cumbersome? With hindsight, is there a better way of doing things?

If you got the wrong answers, do you know why? Trace through your solution step-by-step to see if you can find where it is going wrong.

This step of assessing the result is very important as it will highlight errors in the solution and areas that could be improved. You should repeat Steps 2, 3, and 4 until you are as confident as you can reasonably be that your solution is the best one you can achieve. Only then should you move on to the following.

Describing What We Have Learned (Step 5)

Having gone through several cycles of devising a plan, carrying out the plan, and assessing the results, you should have a list of things you have learned. These lessons will form part of your problem-solving and programming repertoire of experience. When you first begin programming you will find that you have errors in your solutions that you just cannot get rid of. You approach your teacher, or another experienced programmer, and they spot in less than thirty seconds the fault that you have just spent several hours looking for. There is a temptation to feel foolish and to ascribe great intelligence to the person who spotted the error so quickly. However flattering that is, it is more likely that the experienced programmer just has a bigger repertoire of programming errors than you and has learned to recognize common symptoms. Programming teachers seem especially good at this, but only because they have used that programming task (or a variant) lots of times with lots of classes of many students. The first time they helped a student track down the error it may have taken them quite a few minutes. But each time after that they were able to spot the problem in just a few seconds. Writing down the lessons you learned from solving the problem will help you in fixing the lessons in your memory and will thus add to your programming repertoire. Where you encountered errors in your solution, making a note not just of the particular error, but also its symptoms is highly recommended; you never know when you might encounter the same symptom in the future. If you do not write it down you will probably forget it.

Documenting the Solution (Step 6)

Documenting solutions is a very important but much overlooked task. Once a problem has been solved and the solution handed in for grading there is a strong temptation to simply move on to the next piece of work. There are several reasons why documentation is so important. We noted earlier how SOFTWARE MAINTENANCE (changes made to programs after they have been completed) rather than new software development accounts for most programming activity. Watts Humphrey notes that the person best able to correct errors in a program is the person who wrote it in the first place (Humphrey, 1997). But the reality of the software industry is that people change jobs, get promotions, leave the company, etc., so it is not always possible for the original developer to carry out the maintenance. It is vital, therefore, that programmers learn the discipline of writing good, clear, and useful documentation that will help future programmers to read, understand, and maintain their programs (problem solutions). Even when you know you are going to maintain the program think about this: are you really sure that in six months you will still be able to understand the complex sequence of instructions that took you a week to construct? You see, you may understand your solution now but that is because you have spent a lot of time working with it. But it is likely that you will not understand it quite so well in the future. Now, if you could have trouble understanding your own solution in just a few months time, how do you think another programmer will approach it?

There are several types of documentation that programmers can produce. For now, we shall concentrate on explaining our solutions. Each solution should be preceded by a short statement of its purpose. For example, "this is a recipe for making bread," or "the following instructions will enable you to convert a temperature in degrees Fahrenheit to its equivalent in degrees Celsius." Then, look at the main body of your solution and list all the conditions that need to be true before the solution can be successfully applied. For example, a recipe for making bread will require that you have access to the necessary ingredients, a water supply, the right utensils, and a working oven with a temperature control. This sounds like the blindingly obvious, but it is a good discipline to get into because it will serve you well when you come to writing some real programs.

Look for ▶
assumptions
and
preconditions

A major cause of defects in programs is that the programmer has made ASSUMPTIONS that just are not true. They may seem to be very reasonable assumptions that are consistent with the problem statement, but they are assumptions nonetheless. Assumptions must be challenged to ensure that they are well-founded.

Documenting the conditions that must be met before your solution can be applied (sometimes known as preconditions) will help you to find some of your hidden assumptions. There is no point asking your friend to follow your bread-making recipe if the oven's electricity supply is not turned on – the oven will be cold and the dough will not bake. Your friend may have enough initiative to realize that the oven must first be turned on at the power socket before it can be used, but a computer does not have any initiative. If your program tells it to set the oven temperature and then put in the dough, that is exactly what it will do. If the electricity is not switched on, and you did not tell the computer to switch the electricity on, then it will not get switched on!

In documenting your solution you may find that you need to revisit Steps 2, 3, and 4 again to amend the instructions in the light of any assumptions you have found. This is good practice and it shows a commitment to getting things right.

2.5 Applying the Strategy

How can this strategy work in practice? That is what the rest of the book is about and we shall look at a number of problems together with solutions developed using this strategy. The complete strategy is provided as Table 2.2 at the end of this chapter, and again at the back of the book as a handy reference. Of course, we are doing this with the intention of eventually writing some computer programs, so we must take care that our solutions can eventually be translated into programming language code. Therefore, we will study how to *systematize* our solutions. That is, your solutions will be written down in a structured and consistent way using semi-formal language. Do not be frightened by this. We introduced ideas like this in Chapter 1 when we discussed musical scores and recipes. Remember, a good recipe is a set of straightforward and unambiguous instructions which, if repeated will lead to more or less the same results each time. The aim of the rest of the book is to get you to the point where you can analyze a problem, work out a solution, and write down the solution as a series of instructions in such a way that you could pass these instructions to the person sitting next to you and they could then use them to calculate the answer to the problem *without needing to clarify any matters with you.*

2.6 Chapter Summary

In this chapter we have looked at what it means to have a problem to solve and how problems can be broken down into smaller constituent parts. Understanding and solving problems lies at the heart of successful computer programming and so a strategy for solving problems was then introduced.

2.7 Exercises

The following exercises describe a problem situation. For each problem apply the *How To Think Like A Programmer (HTTLAP)* strategy (Table 2.2 at the end of this chapter) and devise a sequence of steps that will meet the requirements of the task. Be careful to look for hidden assumptions. To help, you can ask yourself, "If I specify it that way, will it still work in all cases?" Hint: In the example above we questioned whether it is possible to bathe after getting dressed. Pay close attention to Steps 4 and 5 "Assess the result" and "Describe what we have learned." Does your solution work well? What other valid ways are there to arrive at a correct outcome? What did any errors in your solution teach you a) about your understanding of the problem and b) about the problem-solving process? Solutions to a selection of the exercises can be found in Appendix C.

1. Suppose a certain car has a fuel tank with a capacity of 60 litres and an average fuel consumption of 14 km/l. How many times must you fill the tank to travel 2,000 km? How many miles can you travel on 10 gallons of fuel using the same car? You can answer this using imperial gallons (8 imperial pints, where 1 pint = 20 imperial fluid ounces) or U.S. gallons (8 U.S. pints, where 1 pint = 16 U.S. fluid ounces). 1 U.S. fluid ounce = 1.0408423 imperial fluid ounces. Thus, 1 litre = 0.219969157 imperial gallons = 0.264172051 U.S. gallons. Or, 1 imperial gallon = 4.54609 litres, and 1 U.S. gallon = 3.785411784 litres. 1 mile = 1.609344 km.

2. Getting dressed in the morning (that is, just the tasks associated with getting dressed; do not include getting up, washing, etc.).

3. Using an electric filter machine (also called a percolator) make a pot of coffee and pour a cup.

4. Filling a car with fuel.

5. Making a cheese and onion omelette.

6. Travelling from home to work/college.

7. Completing a piece of homework/college assignment.

8. A wedding ceremony. Note, this is very culturally dependent, so my solution may not resemble yours at all!

9. Choosing what to study at university.

10. Hanging a picture on the wall.

2.8 Projects

StockSnackz Vending Machine

A StockSnackz vending machine is being installed in the staff common room at the University of Stocksfield for the free use of the faculty. The machine has 10 numbered buttons. Pushing Button 1 dispenses a milk chocolate bar, Button 2 a muesli bar, Button 3 a pack of cheese puffs, Button 4 an apple, Button 5 a pack of popcorn, while pushing Button 6 displays on the machine's small screen a summary of how many of each item have been dispensed. Pushing the Buttons 0, 7, 8, or 9 has no effect.

Using the *HTTLAP* strategy write down the series of steps needed to install the new machine, fill it with supplies, and let people obtain snacks from it over the course of the first day. You may assume that the machine can store unlimited supplies of each item. At the end of the day, the dean of faculty will want to know how many snacks have been dispensed. For now, treat the problem of lots of people obtaining lots of snacks over the course of a day as a single abstract activity "Dispense snacks."

Stocksfield Fire Service

The Stocksfield Fire Service has asked you to write a program for identifying the precautions to take when dealing with chemical spillages. The program is to be installed on palm-top computers used by the fire fighters who will tap in the Emergence Action Code and be told what to do by the computer. For example, if they tapped in the code 2WE they would receive the instructions:

```
FIRE FIGHTING
~~~~~~~~~~~
Use Fine Spray.

PRECAUTIONS
~~~~~~~~~
Substance is prone to violent or explosive reaction.
Wear Liquid-tight suit/chemical protection clothing.
Contain the spillage.

PUBLIC SAFETY
~~~~~~~~~~~
Public safety hazard: Warn people to stay indoors with doors &
windows shut.
```

Use *HTTLAP* to write down the overall series of steps needed to translate each character of the three-character EAC.

Puzzle World: Roman Numerals and Chronograms

There are rules governing how Roman numerals can be written (though these rules are not universally applied). Look at the Roman numbers in Table 2.1 below and see how far you can get in inferring the rules. Use the questions in *HTTLAP* to structure your thinking.

Without any other information, what steps might you perform in the process of converting a decimal number to Roman numerals? Or a Roman number to decimal? Outline the overall stages of the process now.

Table 2.1 **Conversions of Some Numbers in Roman Numerals**

Roman Number	Decimal Equivalent
III	3
IV	4
CIX	109
LVIII	58
XCIX	99 (why not IC?)
D	500
M	1000
MCMC	Invalid

Pangrams: Holoalphabetic Sentences

Consider how you would go about systematically determining whether a sentence is a pangram. You might want to use a bag of Scrabble tiles as an aid. Write down the basic sequence of actions you would take. As before, make use of the *HTTLAP* questions to guide you.

Online Bookstore: ISBNs

To begin our investigation of ISBNs, think about how you would approach the problem of adding hyphens to an unformatted ISBN. Doing this makes them easier to read and so would make an Internet bookshop more user-friendly. Go back to the projects section in the Chapter 1 exercises and look again at Figure 1.5 and Table 1.3. What patterns you can spot in the way the numbers are hyphenated? Write down the sequence of actions necessary to write out the various parts of the ISBN with hyphens in between.

2.9 "How To Think Like A Programmer"

On the next two pages you will find a summary of our problem solving strategy given as Table 2.2 "How To Think Like A Programmer". Use it for the exercises in the coming chapters to help you arrive at solutions. The table is based upon Pólya's original list of questions and suggestions in *How to Solve It* (Pólya, 1990).

Table 2.2 *How To Think Like A Programmer (HTTLAP)*

1. Understanding the problem

You have to understand the problem. Do not go to the next stage until you have done this.	What are you being asked to do? What is required? Try restating the problem? Can the problem be better expressed by drawing a diagram or a picture? By using mathematical notation? By building a model out of wood, paper, or card?
	What is the *unknown*? Is finding the unknown part of the problem statement? Write down what you **do know** about the problem. Have you made any assumptions? If so, what can/should you do about it?
Sleep on the problem and come back to it fresh.	What are the principal parts of the problem? Are there several parts to the problem?

2. Devising a plan to solve the problem

Start thinking about the information you have and what the solution is required to do.	Have you solved this problem before (perhaps with different values/quantities)? Is this problem *similar* to one you have met before? If so, can you use any knowledge from that problem here? Does the solution to that problem apply to this one in any way?
	Are some parts of the problem more easily solved than others? If the problem is too hard, can you solve a simpler version of it, or a related problem?
	Does restating the problem (perhaps telling it in your own words to someone else) help you to get a grip on it? Try describing the problem in a different *language* (e.g., diagrammatically, pictorially, using mathematics, building a physical model or representation).

Stop bothering your brain and sleep on the problem.

Did you make use of all the information in the problem statement? Can you satisfy all the conditions of the problem? Have you left anything out?

3. Carrying out the plan

Write down your solution. Pay attention to things done in order (sequence), things done conditionally (selection) and things done repeatedly (iteration).

Write down the basic sequence of actions necessary to solve the general problem. This may involve hiding some of the detail in order to get the overall sequence correct. Is your ordering of actions correct? Does the order rely on certain things to be true? If so, do you know these things from the problem statement? Or have you made any assumptions? If you have made assumptions then how will you verify that they are correct?

If you cannot see a way to solving the whole problem can you see any parts of the problem that you can solve? If the problem is too complicated, try removing some of the conditions/constraints and seeing if that gives you a way in.

Go back to your sequence of actions. Should all actions be carried out in *every* circumstance? Should some actions (or groups/blocks of actions) only be carried out when certain conditions are met?

Go back to your sequence of actions. Is carrying out each action once only sufficient to give the desired outcome? If not, do you have actions (or groups/ blocks of actions) that must therefore be *repeated*?

Sleep on it again.

Go back once more. Do any of your actions/blocks of actions belong *inside* others? For example, do you have a block of actions that must be repeated, but only when some condition is met?

4. Assessing the result

Examine the results obtained when using your solution.

Use your solution to meet the requirements of the problem. Did you get the right answer or the correct outcome? If not, why not? Where did your solution go wrong? If you think you did get the right answer, how can you be sure? Did any parts of the solution seem cumbersome or not very sensible? Can you make those parts simpler, quicker, or clearer?

Get someone else to use or follow your solution.

Give your solution to someone else and ask them to use it to complete the task. Were your instructions clear enough for them? Did they have to ask for help or clarification? Did they misinterpret your instructions? If so, why?

Did they get the same answer as when you did it? If not, whose answer was correct?

5. Describing what you have learned

Make a record of your achievements and the difficulties you encountered.

What did you learn from this exercise? What do you know now that you did not know before you started?

What particular difficulties did you encounter? Were there any aspects of the problem that caused you particular difficulty? If so, do you think you would know how to tackle them if you met something similar in the future?

Compare your finished solution with your first attempt. What do the differences teach you?

6. Documenting the solution

Explain your solution. Make sure that it can be understood.

Are there any aspects of your solution that are hard to understand? Is this because they are badly written, or simply because the solution is just complicated? If you were to pick up your solution in five years time do you think any bits would be hard to understand?

3 Description Languages and Representations

3.1   **Description Languages and Representations**

3.2   **Pseudo-code – A Language for Solution Description**

3.3   **Chapter Summary**

3.4   **Exercises**

3.5   **Projects**

Learning Objectives

- Understand the different languages & representations that can be used to visualize, understand, and solve problems
- Analyze a variety of real-world problems and choose appropriate ways of representing their principal parts
- Write solutions to problems in a semi-formal structured English (pseudo-code)

This chapter begins with some of the notations and languages you can use for representing problems in Section 3.1 and concludes with Section 3.2 introducing a semi-formal language (known as *pseudo-code*) that you will use for writing down your problem solutions.

3.1 Description Languages and Representations

The strategy introduced in the last chapter advises restating the problem to gain understanding. This section looks at some common forms of representation that you can use to describe problems and design solutions.

Natural Language

Natural language is just that, natural. It is our main form of communication and it comes so naturally to most of us that we use words to describe and explain most things. Actually, that is not quite true. While we may think we predominantly use words, psychologists tell us that non-verbal communication makes up a very large part of human communication. Much of the information content of our conversations and other interactions comes from the way we stress and inflect words and the ways we change our expression and move parts of our body.

Errors of the Third Kind

We know that natural language can also be imprecise and ambiguous. Computers are neither of these things and to program them we need to be very clear in our thinking and our expression. Furthermore, in order to write good solutions our understanding of the problem needs to be clear and precise otherwise we might very well solve the wrong problem. When I was a student I was taught about *errors of the third kind*. An error of the third kind is, for example, a computer program that is extremely well written, easily maintained, efficient, quick, and accurate, but which does not do what the customer asked for. It does not matter how good your coding skills are if you do not first get a clear and correct understanding of the problem you are trying to solve. As Samuel Johnson (1709–84) wrote: *"A cucumber should be well sliced, and dressed with pepper and vinegar, and then thrown out, as good for nothing."* If you hate cucumber, preparing one for your salad is an error of the third kind.

Diagrams, Pictures, and Visual Thinking

While natural language is invaluable often we need to use other forms of representation that will give us clearer insights. St Francis of Assisi (1181–1226) told the Friars Minor to *"preach the gospel and, if necessary, use words."* We must be prepared to use other ways of describing problems.

Consider the following problem. I have a canvas bag in which there are five red jelly beans and a single blue jelly bean. If I put my hand into the bag, *without looking in*, what is the likelihood that I will pull out a red bean? And what is the likelihood that I will get the blue one? How do you visualize this problem? Do you keep a mental list that there are five red beans and a single blue bean? Perhaps you do because this is quite a simple problem (there are six beans in all, one of which is blue). Therefore, I have a one in six chance of getting the blue one, and five chances in six of getting a red one. For very small or simple problems words can be quite sufficient to give us a good enough grasp. But try solving this example that I have adapted from one used by James Adams in *Conceptual Blockbusting* (Adams, 2001, p. 4):

> One morning at eight o'clock you set off in your car to visit a friend who lives some distance away. You encounter the odd traffic delay and your driving speed varies as the speed limits on the different stretches of road change. It is a long drive so you stop twice to refresh yourself and to eat and drink something. You arrive at 6.00 p.m. and decide to stay overnight. The next morning you set off again at 8.00 a.m. You take the same route back, but encounter heavy traffic in different places. Because one traffic jam was so large you only stop once for refreshments. Still, you arrive back home at six o'clock. Question: Is there a point on the road that you pass at exactly the same time of day on the outward and return journeys?

How did you get on with that? What was your answer? Perhaps your intuition told you that there is no such point because of all the variations in speed? If so, your intuition is quite wrong for there is a point you pass at the same time of day on the way out and the way back. But how do you show that? If you tried to use natural language (verbal reasoning) then you have probably still not solved the problem. I solved the problem by drawing a picture:

FIGURE 3.1   **Journey to a friend**

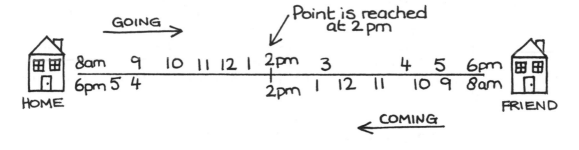

My picture is a simplified graph plotting distance travelled against time. The row of numbers above the line is the times of the outward journey marked out as hours. The gaps between the times vary to represent the changing speeds. The lower line is the return journey. This rough sketch shows that these two journeys cross the same point at around 2 p.m. This worked for me because I often reach for a pen and paper to draw a problem. Figure 3.2 shows a slightly different way of looking at the problem. This time the friend's house is at the top, home at the bottom. Time is marked along the *x* axis and the distance travelled as the two lines. Fast progress is a steep line; stopping for a rest makes the line flat. Again we can see the two routes crossing at around 2 p.m.

FIGURE 3.2   **Another visualization of my journey to a friend**

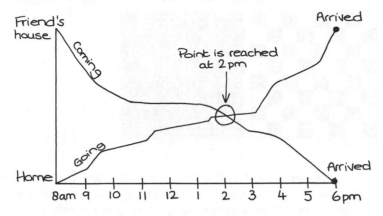

For those who can think visually the solution is even simpler if a quick change is made in the way the puzzle is phrased. Instead of thinking of two journeys on two different days and looking for a point, just imagine you and your friend each setting out from your homes at eight in the morning. Will you meet along the road? Of course you will, so the problem is solved and there is no need for a diagram or graphs and rulers. Notice what was done with the visual reasoning? We did not solve the puzzle exactly as written – instead we used the advice in Step 2 of our problem solving strategy and solved a simplified or related problem. In my case I drew a diagram, but the mental visualization works even better. The point is that sometimes a picture says much more than even two thousand words if the two thousand words do not help you get to the answer.

Huh?

I am confused: you seem to be saying that we do not need to use diagrams at all.

No. I am saying that there is generally more than one way to solve a problem. Some ways of thinking about a problem lead more easily to a solution than others, but not everybody is always able to use every way of thinking about a problem. I often use pictures to help me understand problems, hence my first solution to the problem involved a sketch, but the second solution shows that reframing the problem can also help sometimes. The lesson is to use whatever technique helps you the most, and often you will need to try more than one technique.

Chessboard and Dominoes

Try to solve this old puzzle:[1] Take a chessboard and 32 dominoes. Each domino fits over two (non-diagonally) adjacent squares on the chessboard. It is easy to cover the chessboard with the dominoes (Figure 3.3). Now cut two opposite corners from the chessboard, leaving 62 squares and then remove one domino. Can you still cover the chessboard?

---

[1] Thanks to my colleague Paul Brna for introducing me to this puzzle.

FIGURE 3.3   **Covering the chessboard with 32 dominoes**

What was your answer? If you tried a mental image because that technique worked so well for the last problem then you may have decided the answer is *yes*, you can cover the remaining squares. Alas, you cannot! There are some pieces of evidence that serve to misdirect the unwary. We began with 64 squares on the board, and 32 dominoes each of which covers two squares. The number of squares is twice the number of dominoes. So, if we remove two squares and one domino we still have twice the number of squares as dominoes, so it seems that we can still cover the board. The mistake here is that we have overlooked some of the details. The problem solving strategy advises us to look for any bits left over after we have devised a plan of attack. Our solution only took into account the number of squares, the number of dominoes, and the ratio of the two. We have formed an abstract, or less-detailed, view of the problem. ABSTRACTION can be a very useful tool; indeed, the strategy advises solving a simpler problem if the original proves too challenging at first. But we must not forget to revisit the problem to see if the abstraction, or simplification, has had an adverse affect. This can be a feature of abstraction – sometimes we must use abstraction to remove detail but with it goes a consequent loss of information that we must be aware of if we want to avoid making more incorrect ASSUMPTIONS.

So what details have we overlooked? Chessboards have 32 white and 32 black squares arranged alternately. A domino, therefore, covers one white and one black square. If you look at a chessboard you will observe that one pair of corner squares is black, the other pair white. So, if you remove two corners you have removed two squares of the same colour. This means that we cannot cover the board any more, as Figure 3.4 shows.

FIGURE 3.4   **31 dominoes cannot cover a chessboard with two corners removed**

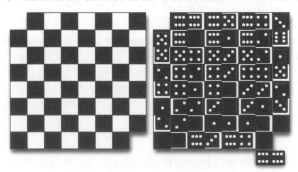

If you are puzzled, try restating the problem. Instead of a chessboard, let's imagine we have 32 men and 32 women who want to get married. Instead of dominoes we now have 32 marriage certificates which can only be used to marry one man to one woman. All the marriage certificates can be used because we have 32 eligible couples. Now, let's remove two men (white squares). Now can we use up all the marriage certificates? No, because we have 30 men and 32 women.

You must be careful to make sure you either make use of all the information in the problem, or, if you leave some out, that it does not affect the solution. By all means simplify, but do not forget to check for bits leftover once you have put it all together again. Part of the difficulty with this puzzle is that you start out forming a mental image – you visualize a chessboard – but then some numbers are given and that can trap you into thinking of the problem purely arithmetically. If you had carried on with the mental image of the chessboard and tried laying out the dominoes in your mind's eye you might have got the answer. Restating the problem made for an easier solution (and no mental gymnastics holding all those dominoes in place in your mind). Of course, you could have drawn out a chessboard, cut out some paper dominoes and experimented, but this would take longer.

Ant and Sugar

You might be thinking that everything can be understood with a diagram, but that is not so; if your reasoning is faulty your picture will not help you. Here is an example of where drawing a perfectly good diagram led me astray. Try it yourself:

> There is a large square room whose walls are 24 feet long. The ceiling is eight feet high. On the floor in a corner is a bowl of sugar. In the opposite corner by the ceiling is an ant. What is the shortest path the ant can take to get to the sugar? Adapted from an example given in Adams (2001).

Where to start with this one? Does restating the problem verbally help? I do not think so as this appears to be an arithmetic problem. It helps to pick a description language that is suited to the characteristics of the problem. Start by drawing a diagram.

FIGURE 3.5   **Diagram of room with positions of ant and sugar marked**

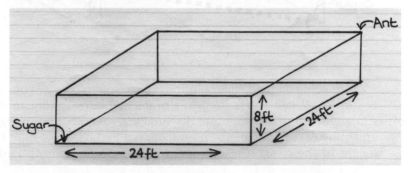

Figure 3.5 shows a three-dimensional sketch of the room together with the positions of the ant and the sugar. I have added the room's dimensions because this information is given in the problem statement. From the diagram can you see the shortest walking route to the sugar? The problem seems easy to visualize but there is still room for error.

Think about it carefully and then trace the shortest walking route from the ant to the sugar.

How did you do? Below are two candidate answers to the problem for you to consider. One of them is correct.

FIGURE 3.6   **Candidate solution #1**

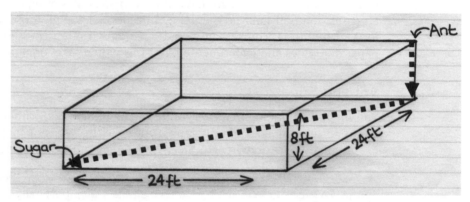

FIGURE 3.7   **Candidate solution #2**

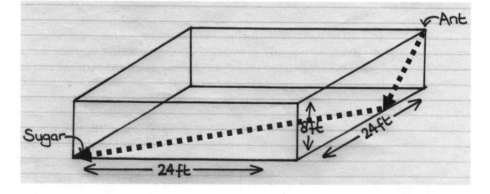

Did seeing both possible solutions cause you to change your mind? Which one is correct? When I first tried this problem I gave candidate #1 as my answer: straight down to the floor and diagonally across the floor: it was nice and simple and quite easy to calculate. The walk down to the floor is eight feet, for that is the height of the room. The diagonal can be calculated using Pythagoras' theorem

(the square on the hypotenuse of a right-angled triangle equals the sum of the squares of the two opposite sides). We know the lengths of the two opposite sides as they are the length and width of the room (twenty-four feet each). The diagonal is the hypotenuse. Let us call the diagonal d, the length l, and the width w giving:

$$d = \sqrt{l^2 + w^2}$$

which evaluates to:

$$d = \sqrt{576 + 576} = 33.941\,ft$$

? Think Spot

Does this answer look right? I must admit, this answer puzzled me as Pythagorean-type problems are usually presented in books so that you end up with a 3–4–5 triangle (i.e. the hypotenuse = 5, and the two other sides 3 and 4, as $3^2 + 4^2 = 5^2$). The solution I arrived at with decimal places felt wrong. The reason my answer seemed strange is because my shortest path was wrong – the second candidate is the correct one (Figure 3.7). This path requires the ant to walk diagonally down the wall and then across the floor to the corner. That I did not get this answer is because my diagram was not the best one for the problem. My difficulty was that I tend to see things literally. The problem talked of a room, so I drew a three-dimensional model of the room. From that I made an incorrect assumption about the quickest route and hence calculated the wrong answer. Like the earlier journey problem, this puzzle is much more easily understood if it is restated slightly. The journey-to-a-friend answer was obvious when we changed the scenario slightly to simplify the problem; we kept the essential details the same but simply moved the two opposite journeys to the same day. The ant's quickest path is much easier to see if we fold the room out flat and draw it in two dimensions:

FIGURE 3.8   Plan view of room

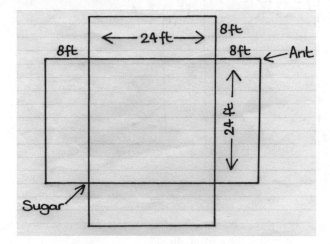

Try marking the shortest path from the ant to the sugar on this new representation of the problem. The answer is given in Figure 3.9 but think carefully and check your answer before you look.

Did you get the right answer? Calculating the length of the path is now very simple, again requiring Pythagoras' theorem. The base of the triangle is 32 ft (24 ft + 8 ft) and the height is 24 ft. Looking for the 3–4–5 pattern we can see that 32 ft is 4 × 8 ft and the height is 3 × 8 ft. Therefore, the hypotenuse (the length of the path) must be 5 × 8 ft = 40 ft.[2]

Of course, reducing the room to two dimensions takes away some of the detail and the dotted line indicating the shortest path could be interpreted two ways. It could be the line along the wall and the floor that the ant takes which is what we have used it for. But if you did not know anything of the problem and looked at the diagram from cold, you might just as well visualize the path as the straight line through the air from the top corner to the opposite bottom corner. It all depends on the context, and everyone using the diagram needs to be aware of just what the context is and what everything means. If you cannot see this interpretation then think about it some more. It may help to make (or imagine) a cardboard model of the room with a piece of elastic stretched between the two corners. Unfold the model of the room until it is flat (as in the diagram above). What does the elastic do? If you coat the elastic with ink and then unfold the model, what mark does the elastic leave on the card? You should find that it leaves a line that maps exactly onto the dotted line shown in Figure 3.9. If you fold the model back up into a box you will see that the ink trail now looks just like the path shown in Figure 3.7. Simplifying the model, or taking a more *abstract* view means the two different paths now look identical. That is ABSTRACTION again and you need to be careful.

FIGURE 3.9   **Plan view with path marked**

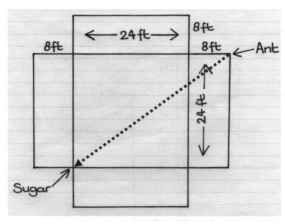

_____

[2] If you want to do this the long way, then $path^2 = 32^2 + 24^2 = 1024 + 576 = 1600$. Now take the square root of 1600 to give the answer: 40.

How many problems is the ant-and-sugar puzzle composed of? It decomposed into two subproblems: the first was to identify the shortest path and the second was to calculate the length of that path. Whether the first or second subproblem is more difficult to solve depends on the way your mind works and your knowledge of Pythagoras. I had trouble visualizing the path but found the application of Pythagoras' theorem simple. Therefore I made an error of the third kind. That is, I correctly solved the wrong problem, and so came up with a correctly-calculated but wrong answer. Maybe you could identify the path easily but had forgotten (or had never learned) Pythagoras' theorem. Without that knowledge it is much more difficult to calculate the length of the path. The advantage of this position is that you have correctly *solved* the problem of finding the path. All that remains is discovering how the answer can be *calculated* and this can be achieved by looking in a geometry text book or asking someone who is more knowledgeable in mathematics than you.

Errors of the third kind ▶

What does this problem have to do with programming? Suppose that you have been employed by a thrifty electrician who likes to use as little cable as possible when wiring rooms. He often needs to run a cable from the bottom corner of a room up to the opposite top corner. The cable can go underneath the floorboards and the electrician will chase a conduit into the plaster to take the cable up the wall. He wants you to write a program for his hand-held computer that will allow him to enter the height, length, and width of any room and which will calculate the shortest length of cable needed. We have already solved the problem of calculating the answer, so all that remains is to turn that solution into a repeatable routine (a recipe) that can, in turn, be translated into programming language code. That is the subject of the next two chapters, so we will leave the ant to get on with finding the sugar.

? **Think Spot**

Mathematics

Unfortunately, many students today are afraid of mathematics. This is increasingly common among computer science students which is a shame because an appreciation of some basic and discrete mathematics (which includes theory and logic) would make the underlying principles of computer programming much more transparent. However, it is a fact that apart from courses on which it is a central part of the curriculum, mathematics is largely ignored. You will have observed that some of the problems in this chapter have had arithmetic at their core. Of course, you do not need to be a mathematician to be able to do basic arithmetic and algebra. Applying Pythagoras' theorem does not make you a mathematician, simply someone who can do a bit of algebra. The level of mathematical skill required for the problems in this book is less than that needed for the mathematics that is taught to sixteen-year-olds in schools, so do not worry. This section is not going to deal with serious mathematics. Rather, I just want you to be aware that algebra (and the occasional bit of geometry) can give you a clearer understanding of certain problems.

Here is a puzzle of the kind found in intelligence tests: The hard drive in Nick's computer has twice the capacity of Alf's. Between them their computers have 240 gigabytes of hard-drive storage. What is the capacity of each hard drive?

Verbal reasoning is not going to help much here, but an algebraic representation is quite useful. Let x stand for Nick's hard drive and y for Alf's. We can state the following:

(1) $x + y = 240$

(2) $x = 2y$

That is, in (1) we know that the size of both drives together is 240 GB and in (2) that drive x is twice the size of drive y. As x is the same value as $2y$, then we can substitute this term for x in the first equation to give:

(3) $2y + y = 240$, or $3y = 240$

If we divide both sides by 3 we get

(4) $y = \dfrac{240}{3} = 80$

Therefore, Alf's hard drive is 80 GB. Nick's is twice the size, so it must be 160 GB (80 + 160 = 240). Problem solved. The trick was to realize that the language the problem was written in was not the best language for working toward further understanding. Do not be afraid to turn to algebra as it is a very good description tool for certain problems.

Why won't verbal reasoning be any use here?

I said it would not help much because it does not provide a manageable way to describe the problems in terms that make it easy to solve. If you are not convinced, try using verbal reasoning to represent the following problem in your head:

If my computer is worth two-thirds of the value of my computer plus two-thirds of the value of my camera plus two-thirds of the value of my radio plus two-thirds of the value of my coffee machine, and my camera is worth two-thirds of the camera plus two-thirds of the radio plus two-thirds of the coffee machine, and my radio is worth two-thirds of the radio plus two-thirds of the coffee machine, how many coffee machines is my computer worth?

Physical Models

Physical models can be very useful and are used by many professionals in their problem solving. Architects build physical models of buildings. Engineers make models and working prototypes to show how their machines will work. Physical models give you a view that natural language cannot. They give you a clear idea of the boundaries of the thing to be built. Physical models provide an all-round three-dimensional view which blueprints cannot. Blueprints, on the other hand, can be rolled up and carried easily as well as show precise and detailed measurements. Computer programs are not physical – they are intangible webs woven from logic, so how can a physical model help with writing programs? Consider the ant-and-sugar problem. I suggested visualizing a physical model of the room with a bit of elastic stretched between the corners.

▶ To write this program you will need a matchbox, a rubber band, a small knife, and some ink . . .

Now I want you to actually make the model. You do not need to get the dimensions to scale; the inside of a matchbox will suffice. Make a small hole in a bottom corner and a small notch in the opposite upper corner. Take a rubber band and cut it so that it forms a single thread. Make a knot near one end and thread it through the hole so that the knot rests against the outside of the box. Pull the band reasonably tight, put it through the notch in the upper corner and make another knot so that you now have the band forming the diagonal between the two corners. Coat the band with some ink and, holding the upper corner end of the band firmly, fold out the end of the matchbox flat so that the rubber band rests taught against the base of the box (much like Figure 3.9). Now fold the end of the box back up again. If all has gone well you should now have a trail of ink marking out the shortest walking route between the two corners (like Figure 3.7).

This physical model gives a very clear visualization of the problem. Depending on how you manipulate the model you can have both the three-dimensional and two-dimensional views of Figure 3.7 and Figure 3.9. The model should put to rest any confusion between the ant's route and that taken by a fly.

If a physical model helps you to visualize or understand a problem better, then use it. I have used physical models in lectures to illustrate basic programming concepts; sometimes acting out the steps a computer program follows can make it much easier to understand what it is doing. Not understanding how programs actually execute inside the computer is a common cause of frustration among novices who have an incorrect mental model of the program. Because they think the program is operating differently from the way they understand means they cannot discover why it does not produce the answers they want.

3.2 Pseudo-code – A Language for Solution Description

Once the problem has been described and understood we must solve it and then write down our solution. Often the solution is best phrased in a different language from the one used to describe it. For example, you may remember from school the solution for calculating the two roots of a quadratic equation as "minus *b* plus or minus the square root of *b* squared minus four *ac* over two *a*." Is that only "*b* squared minus four *ac* divided by two *a*" or is everything divided by *2a*? The algebraic description makes things clear:

$$\frac{-b \pm \sqrt{b^2 - 4ac}}{2a}$$

Everything is divided by 2*a*. If you can remember your algebra you will be able, for different values of *a*, *b*, and *c*, to calculate the positive and negative roots using the above formula. However, while algebra may be the best language for describing some algebraic problems, text for some problems, and pictures for other types of problem, the computer will understand none of them. These different forms of representation are purely to help us with understanding and solving problems. To tell a computer how to calculate the answers we must tell it the solution in the way *it* understands, hence the need for programming language systems. Because this book focuses on problem solving and solution description it does not deal with a specific programming language. However, that does not mean we can ignore the problem of translating our solution descriptions (be they mathematical, visual, physical, or textual) into the formal notation of a programming language. We still need a formalized and structured way of writing down our solutions.

James Adams (2001) observed that solving problems is a habit, that is, we do it every day, most of the day. The difficulty with programming is that we have to articulate our solutions in a precise and unambiguous way – and this we are not used to doing. You may be quite good at solving problems, but are you good at explaining your solutions to others?

Try explaining to someone how to get to your house or the post office from wherever you are right now. Did you do well? Did they look confused? How do you capture and set out all the rules of your decision making? How many of your rules are ambiguous or incompletely stated?

Much of our problem solving is unconscious or subconscious. Adams continues: *"the natural response to a problem seems to be to try to get rid of it by finding an answer – often taking the first answer that occurs and pursuing it because of one's reluctance to spend the time and mental effort needed to conjure up a richer storehouse of alternatives from which to choose"* (Adams, 2001 p. 9).

While you could probably achieve a measure of success simply by writing your instructions in natural language, this is not the way we shall go. We know how natural language can be ambiguous; indeed, many lawyers make a very good living trying to ensure that contracts and legal codes are precise and free from ambiguity. The richness of language also means that we use many different words and expressions to convey just one idea. For example, say I am training my child to do household chores, and I want her to start emptying the kitchen bin. I could say "empty the bin when it is full." Or, I could say "if the bin is full then empty it." Or even, "should the bin run out of room then you must empty it." Part of being a good programmer is learning to think precisely, to say exactly what you mean and to mean exactly what you say. We must develop this skill because the computer has no ability to question our instructions. It cannot decide that an instruction is ambiguous and ask "are you sure you meant that?" It will follow your instructions *exactly* even if your instructions are wrong.

To help develop skills of clear and precise expression we will use something called *pseudo-code* (also called structured English or even Program Design Language) for writing down the solutions to problems. It is called pseudo-code because it is not real programming language code but something that looks a bit like it. Pseudo-code is a halfway house between loose natural language and the logically precise programming languages. It is a mixture of natural language words and expressions and formal keywords and constructs that have specific meanings. Pseudo-code is a description language that many programmers use to express their ideas in a structured way but without the complexities of a real programming language. Here is an example of a pseudo-code description of the process of getting up in the morning:

| Task number |
| Task, or action |

1. Switch off alarm;
2. Get out of bed;
3. Shower/wash face, brush teeth, etc.;
4. Get dressed;

| Semicolon denotes end of actions |

What does writing some instructions in this way achieve? By using the semi-colon as a separator we can easily see that there are four distinct actions. By numbering and putting each action on a separate line the sequence of actions is also very clear.[3] The idea of sequence is very important in programming as things must be done in the right order to get the right results. Sometimes the sequence of tasks does not matter. For example, it is not vital that we switch off the alarm before getting out of bed and we could just as easily swap the ordering of the first two actions. Or can we? What if the alarm clock is on the other side of the room from our bed and we cannot reach it without getting up? In this case, it is very important in which order we write the instructions as they could not be followed otherwise. Knowing the correct sequence of actions requires us not just to understand the problem of getting up in the morning, but also to know something of the context in which this problem is situated. James Adams notes that it can be *"difficult to see a problem from the viewpoint of all the interests and parties involved,"* but that *"consideration of such view-points . . . leads to a 'better' solution to the problem"* (Adams, 2001 p. 33). To write a correct set of instructions we have to know something of the relationships between the principal parts of the problem – we must know, for instance, where the alarm is in relation to the bed.

Problem frames ▶

Looking at the problem to understand its boundaries and its context is called *framing.* When you buy a picture to hang on your wall you need a frame to hold it. The frame has to be of the correct size and of an appropriate material and colour. When we frame a problem we are describing, classifying, and relating it to other problems we have already met. Knowing if it is similar to a problem we have met before will bring to mind some relevant questions to ask and some techniques to help us solve it. We saw examples of this earlier when we considered description languages. Some problems were more easily visualized by drawing a diagram than by attempting to reason them out verbally.[4]

---

[3] As you become proficient in its use you will find you do not always need to number your pseudo-code statements. However, for the purposes of instruction I have used numbers in this book as they make it much easier to talk about individual statements. Feel free to use or not use statement numbering as you wish in your own work.

[4] Michael Jackson wrote a book on the subject of framing problems (Jackson, 2001) which you are advised to read once you have completed your programming courses.

Huh?

There are a million other things we could consider too, such as the size of the room, whether the alarm has a remote control or not and so on. How do I know when to stop?

This is not an easy question to answer. The short answer is that you will learn with experience how much detail is needed, and that you know you have not been thorough enough if your solution doesn't work. A more detailed answer involves thinking about ABSTRACTION (see earlier) and ASSUMPTIONS.

Returning to getting up in the morning, we can see other orderings are more obvious: We need to get out of bed before we can wash or shower, and it is clearly not possible to wash or shower after we have got dressed. Or is it? Certainly, taking a shower fully clothed would be silly, but if I only want to wash my face then I can do that dressed or undressed. Often, by examining the orderings of sequences we recognize that what seemed like an obvious and immutable sequence of actions is much more complex than we had first thought. In the above example, we can resolve the question of the ordering of the four actions by including some conditions. For instance, we could ask whether the clock is reachable from the bed and if it is, switch off the alarm then get out of bed, otherwise get out of bed and then switch off the alarm. By phrasing the instructions in this way our solution is more general and applies to many more arrangements of bedroom furniture. (We will deal with the issue of conditional statements in Chapter 4.)

You may be thinking that this is becoming very pedantic now, after all, what does programming have to do with whether the alarm clock is on the other side of the room? When we specified turning off the alarm before getting out of bed we made an ASSUMPTION. When programmers start making assumptions about the way things are or the way things should be then there is a chance that their programs will not perform as the customer expected. If this means your word processor occasionally inserts a spurious character or two into your documents (likê thìs) you may not be too worried. But consider something more serious. The European Space Agency's Ariane 5 rocket exploded 39 seconds into its maiden flight due to an ASSUMPTION made by the developers of its guidance software.

? **Think Spot**

So as not to bombard you with too many details too soon, we will develop our pseudo-code as we progress through the book. You can find the complete details of the pseudo-code notation in Appendix A. There is no accepted standard for pseudo-code (sometimes also called *program design language*), indeed, there are many different styles. What tends to happen is that programmers use the constructs of their chosen programming language in their pseudo-code. This makes the process of translating from pseudo-code to programming language more straightforward. Because this book does not focus on a single language, I have tried to use as general a notation as possible. You will find, therefore, that the words of the pseudo-code do not necessarily match up with the words used by your programming language.

3.3 **Chapter Summary**

In this chapter we looked at tools for describing problems, namely words, diagrams and pictures, mathematics, and physical models. We started to use a semi-formal language notation (pseudo-code) for expressing solutions to problems. This pseudo-code will form the basis of our algorithm designs and will, once its various features have been introduced over the course of the book, provide a suitable notation that can be translated into real programming languages for implementation on a computer.

3.4 Exercises

For the following exercises use the *HTTLAP* strategy and apply any visual thinking, diagrams, or algebra techniques that you find helpful. Solutions to a selection of the exercises can be found in Appendix C.

1. Nick's computer has three times the memory of Lynne's and Alf's computers put together. Shadi's PC has twice as much memory as Chris's. Nick's computer has one-and-a-half times the memory of Shadi's. Between them, Alf and Shadi's computers have as much memory as Lynne's plus twice the memory of Chris's. Shadi, Chris, Nick, Alf, and Lynne's PCs have 2,800 megabytes of memory between them. How much memory does each computer have?

2. The fly-sugar problem. This exercise is a variation of the ant-sugar problem. A room measures 3.2 m long, 2.4 m wide and 3 m high. A fly sits in one of the upper corners looking at a bowl of sugar in the lower corner diagonally opposite. Assuming the fly can, indeed, fly, calculate the shortest route to the sugar. This is easiest if you use a combination of algebra and diagrams as it is a problem in geometry.

3. Chessboards have alternate black and white squares, and the square in the top left corner is always white. Imagine you are making a chessboard but for some peculiar reason you have decided to paint each square in a random order. Without continually counting "white, black, white, black . . ." from the top left corner each time or looking at pictures of a chessboard each time, consider how else you could determine whether any given square should be black or white.[5]

4. A farmer keeps sheep and chickens. In the farmyard there are 68 animals with a total of 270 legs. Assuming every chicken has exactly 2 legs and each sheep exactly 4 legs, how many chickens and sheep are there in the farmyard? The farmer changes the number of sheep and chickens such that there are now 75 animals but still 270 legs. How many of each animal does the farmer own now?

5. When you pay cash for something, good cashiers give you your change using the fewest coins possible. Using the *HTTLAP* strategy, write an algorithm that works out the ideal change to give for any amount between 1 and 99 pence/cents. If you are working with euros or British pounds then the coins available to you are 1, 2, 5, 10, 20, and 50 (cents and pence). If working with U.S. dollars, then the available coins are 1, 5, 10, and 25 (I am ignoring the rare and unpopular half-dollar and one-dollar coins). Here are some examples:

   ■ To give 67 pence in change requires 1 × 50p + 1 × 10p + 1 × 5p + 1 × 2p.

   ■ To give 43 euro cents in change requires 2 × 20c + 1 × 2c + 1 × 1c.

   ■ To give 63 U.S. cents in change requires 2 × 25¢ + 1 × 10¢ + 3 × 1¢.

---

[5] Hint: If you number the rows and columns such that the top row is R1 (Row 1) and the leftmost column is C1 (Column 1), what do you notice about the row and column values of any white square?

If you want to use a different currency simply substitute your chosen coins.[6]

The following exercises all appeared in Chapter 2. For each, rewrite your solution using the *HTTLAP* pseudo-code notation.

6. Getting dressed in the morning (that is, just the tasks associated with getting dressed; do not include getting up, washing, etc.).

7. Using an electric filter machine (also called a percolator) make a pot of coffee and pour a cup.

8. Filling a car with fuel.

9. Making a cheese and onion omelette.

10. Travelling from home to work/college.

11. Completing a piece of homework/college assignment.

12. A wedding ceremony. Note, this is very culturally dependent, so my solution may not resemble yours at all!

13. Choosing what to study at a university.

14. Hanging a picture on the wall.

3.5 Projects

StockSnackz Vending Machine

Take your existing solution from Chapter 2 and write it using pseudo-code. Does drawing a diagram of the vending machine and its principal components help?

Stocksfield Fire Service

Take your existing solution from Chapter 2 and write it using pseudo-code.

Puzzle World: Roman Numerals and Chronograms

Take your existing solution from Chapter 2 and write it using pseudo-code.

Pangrams: Holoalphabetic Sentences

Take your existing solution from Chapter 2 and write it using pseudo-code.

Online Bookstore: ISBNs

Take your existing solution from Chapter 2 and write it using pseudo-code.

---

[6] Hint: To solve this problem you will need to think about the remainders, or left over, after division has taken place.

4 Problems of Choices and Repeated Actions

Devising and writing a program is a problem-solving process. To develop a
software system, you must understand the problem, work out a solution
strategy, and then translate it into a program.

I. Somerville (2001)

4.1 **Making Coffee**

4.2 **Making Choices**

4.3 **Making It Again: Repeated Actions**

4.4 **Chapter Summary**

4.5 **Exercises**

4.6 **Projects**

Learning Objectives

- Recognize the role of sequence, choice (selection), and repetition (iteration) in solving problems
- Apply the problem solving strategy to real-world problems involving alternative courses of action and repeated courses of action
- Understand the importance of the role assumptions and abstraction play in problem solving
- Understand the importance of reflecting upon what has been learned during a problem solving activity and how proper documentation is necessary

In this chapter we will start applying our strategy to some problems that occur in the real world. Chapter 3 ended with some exercises for you to try. If you have not tried most of them, then please go back and do so before continuing with this chapter. You will benefit much more from this chapter once you have attempted to solve those initial problems. If you did attempt the exercises, did you come up with one solution for each of them, or did you come up with a few different solutions, all of which seemed to be valid? Why did you get more than one answer? If you did not, please go back and think over the exercises to see if your solution would cover all possible situations in which you might need to solve those problems.

You will learn in this chapter about different types of problem that we encounter in programming tasks. You will learn the three basic high-level control abstractions – *sequence* (ordered sequences of actions), *iteration* (repeated actions), and *selection* (alternative courses of action) – which are the building blocks of algorithmic solutions. You will learn also the importance of evaluating your solutions as you go to make sure they are correct.

4.1 **Making Coffee**

Using Exercise 7 from Chapter 3 as a starting point we will now explore real-world problems in more detail. Exercise 7 was about making coffee. Perhaps you first came up with a solution like this:

Solution 4.1 Make coffee:

1. Put water and coffee in machine ;
2. Turn on machine ;
3. Pour coffee into mug ;

? Think Spot

On the surface this solution seems fine. Can you find any problems with it? Did you use the *HTTLAP* strategy (Table 2.2)? Perhaps you thought it was too simple a problem to waste your time using the strategy? Below is an example of applying the *HTTLAP* strategy to this problem. We will write down the process in a question-and-answer format taking the questions from the strategy. Questions taken directly from the *HTTLAP* strategy in Table 2.2 are shown in **bold type**. Questions that were triggered in my mind as a result are shown in *italics*. First, take a look at Figure 4.1 which shows a simple coffee machine.

FIGURE 4.1   **My coffee machine**

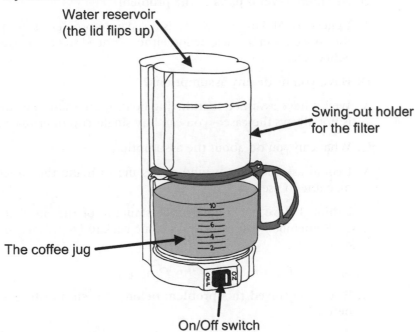

Water reservoir
(the lid flips up)

Swing-out holder
for the filter

The coffee jug

On/Off switch

Understanding the Problem

Q. **What are you being asked to do?**

A. I need to make a pot of coffee and pour a cup.

Q. What is required?

A. A cup of coffee.

Q. Is that all that is required?

A. I think that before I can get a cup of coffee I need the machine's jug to have enough coffee to pour into the cup.

Q. What is the unknown?

A. How much coffee to make. I need to pour a cup, but also I have to make a pot. How much is a pot? Does it mean a whole pot, or just enough coffee to fill one cup?

Q. Can the problem be better expressed by drawing a diagram or a picture?

A. I do not know. Looking at Figure 4.1, I can see the jug probably holds more coffee than the cup.

Q. What are the principal parts of the problem?

A. 1) Make a pot of coffee. 2) Pour a cup. Or, looking at it another way: 1) The filter machine, 2) the cup, 3) the coffee, 4) some water, 5) the cup of coffee – is there just coffee in it, or milk and sugar as well?

Q. Are there several parts to the problem?

A. I guess so. Making the coffee is a separate problem from pouring it. Making the coffee is not a single action either – I need to get the water, measure some coffee, etc.

Q. Have you made any assumptions?

A. Well, I have assumed that the jug holds more than one cupful of coffee. That is not always the case – you can buy single-cup filter machines.

Q. What can you do about the assumptions?

A. I could ask the person who wants me to make the coffee what size coffee machine to use.

I think I have got a good understanding of the problem and the issues it raises. Remember, you can always come back to Step 1 later on, so let's continue to Step 2.

Devising a Plan to Solve the Problem

Q. Have you solved this problem before/is it similar to one you have solved before?

A. In the context of this book, the answer must be *no*.

Q. Are some parts of the problem more easily solved than others?

A. Yes. Pouring the coffee is easy. Adding the water and the coffee grounds requires some thought as to *how much* to add. After pouring the coffee I do not know if anything else is needed (e.g., milk and sugar).

Q. Does restating the problem help? Try restating it in a different language.

A. I do not think that applies here. It is not a weird logical problem, or one that requires a puzzle to be solved. The picture of the coffee machine does clarify the main parts of the problem.

Q. Did you make use of all the information in the problem statement?

A. Yes, I think so. In fact, the statement seems to be incomplete as I do not know how much coffee to make or whether milk and sugar are needed.

Q. Can you satisfy all the conditions of the problem?

A. If I make some assumptions, yes. Without any further information, I have to define what is meant by "pot of coffee" (how much is in a pot) and what constitutes pouring a cup – is it *just* pouring out the coffee, or is it also adding milk or sugar?

Q. Have you left anything out?

A. No, I do not think so; I seem to have gleaned all the information I can from the statement.
Let's now move on to Step 3.

Carrying Out the Plan

According to *HTTLAP* here, we have to "write down the basic sequence of actions necessary to solve the general problem." We should do this using the pseudo-code notation introduced in the last chapter. So, now consider the solution I came up with:

Solution 4.2 Make coffee:

```
1.   Put water in coffee machine ;
2.   Open the coffee holder ;
3.   Put filter paper in machine ;    ←   An underlined action is
4.   Measure coffee for one cup ;         based on an assumption
5.   Put coffee into filter paper ;       that needs resolving
6.   Shut the coffee holder ;
7.   Turn on machine ;
8.   Wait for coffee to filter through ;
9.   Pour coffee into mug ;
10.  Turn off machine ;
```

In Step 3 of *HTTLAP* we are asked:

> *Is your ordering of actions correct? Does the order rely on certain things to be true? If so, do you know these things from the problem statement? Or have you made any assumptions? If you have made assumptions then how will you verify that they are correct?*

We shall address these questions now. Why did I have 10 steps in my sequence? Because the principal actions of making the coffee and pouring it out are insufficient to explain how to solve the problem – a sequence of actions is needed to make the pot of coffee itself. Why separate putting in the water and the coffee into two actions? Because they *are* separate actions. That covers the first step, but what of the others? Recall *HTTLAP* says not just to write down a sequence of actions but also to examine the solution carefully to look for hidden assumptions and other action orderings that would work too.

In working for understanding and planning the attack (Steps 1 and 2), we observed that while we know we need to pour one cup, a question remained over how much coffee to make. There is insufficient information, so I have made an ASSUMPTION that I should only make enough coffee for one cup. Is this assumption valid? Possibly, but I cannot be sure; in this instance I would try to get more information. I should ask the person who wants me to make the coffee how much coffee they want. They might have themselves assumed that I will make a whole pot and that after they have finished the cup I have poured, they intend to go and pour themselves another. For now I have simply made the assumption that only one cup is required, so Task #4 specifies how much coffee to put in the machine. Notice I have underlined this action as a note to myself that there is an assumption here that needs resolving.

Actually, there is at least one more assumption associated with this task. Try to identify it before continuing.

In fact, I have assumed that already I have coffee in a suitable form for putting in the machine. A filter machine uses ground coffee. What if we do not have ground coffee but only some whole roasted beans? In that case I would need to grind up enough beans for one cup of coffee first. Is this being pedantic? Yes, but it illustrates the point that what might seem like an obvious answer often masks a number of assumptions that may or may not be correct.

What assumption underlies Task #3? Some coffee machines have built-in filters that are taken out and washed. Others need a paper filter. I have assumed that this machine takes paper filters (see Task #5).

By now you may have found another assumption that I appear to have missed. Task #1 talks of putting in water, but how much? This is linked to Task #4, and we see that my solution has an assumption that I have not accounted for yet which I should correct. I do not think there are any other assumptions buried in this solution so we can look at the other tasks.[1] Task #6 has to be done if the machine is to work properly – my coffee machine needs the coffee holder to be shut otherwise the water will go straight into the pot bypassing the coffee altogether. Task #7 should be obvious – turning on my machine starts the water-pumping mechanism. Did you have something like Task #8 in your solution? It is quite an important task. Task #9 was in the problem specification. Task #10 wasn't, but as I assumed I only needed to make enough coffee for one cup then

---

[1] If you have really got your eye on the ball then you may have come up with an additional assumption – is the coffee machine plugged in and the electricity outlet switched on? If so, pat yourself on the head and carry on. If not, do not worry because I forgot it too – someone with more common sense than me pointed it out.

it makes sense to turn the machine off – I do not want the hot plate keeping an empty jug warm. Notice how my earlier assumption percolates through the whole solution (pun intended)?

If I were going to make more than one cup of coffee, when should the machine be switched off, for it certainly needs turning off at some point? I could try something like this:

```
10. When jug empty turn off machine ;
```

Both Task #8 and the rephrased Task #10 imply that a decision must be made.

4.2 **Making Choices**

Step 3 in *HTTLAP* asks whether all actions should be carried out in every circumstance, or should some actions/groups of actions be carried out only when certain conditions are met? It is very common for solutions to problems to include some decision making. Consider the extended coffee-making problem:

> *Using an electric filter machine (also called a percolator) make a pot of coffee and pour a cup for a guest. Add sugar and cream/milk as required.*

Now the problem contains some instructions that require some decisions to be made, that is, whether to add sugar and milk to the coffee.

Using Solution 4.2 above as a starting point, write out a new solution to include this extra requirement.

What has changed from the original problem? What is meant by the new requirement to "add sugar and cream/milk as necessary"? We need to return to Steps 1 and 2 of *HTTLAP* and make sure we understand the problem well before trying to solve it.

Q. What are you being asked to do?

A. In addition to what is already known about the problem I need also to add milk and sugar as necessary.

Q. What is required?

A. Possibly some milk and possibly some sugar.

Q. What is the unknown?

A. Whether to add the milk and sugar and, if so, how much to add.

Q. Can the problem be better expressed by drawing a diagram or a picture?

A. No.

Q. What are the principal parts of the problem?

A. 1) the milk, 2) the sugar, 3) the lightening and sweetening requirements of the drinker.

Q. **Are there several parts to the problem?**

A. Yes, adding the milk is a separate decision from adding the sugar. Before either can be added we need to find out whether it is wanted.

Q. **Have you made any assumptions?**

A. Not yet.

 I am confident I have a good understanding of the problem and what is required. The questions in Step 2 do not seem to add anything to my understanding of this problem: I have made use of all the information and I have not made any assumptions (that I am aware of) so we can consider the following solution as a starting point:

Solution 4.3 Make coffee:

```
1.  Put water in coffee machine ;
2.  Open the coffee holder ;
3.  Put filter paper in machine ;
4.  Measure coffee for one cup ;
5.  Put coffee into filter paper ;
6.  Shut the coffee holder ;
7.  Turn on machine ;
8.  Wait for coffee to filter through ;
9.  Add sugar ;
10. Add milk/cream ;
11. Pour coffee into mug ;
12. Stir coffee ;
13. Turn off machine ;
```

(Note, the underlined tasks are based on the assumptions made earlier in Solution 4.2.) Notice I have added a task to stir the coffee – this ensures an even distribution of the milk and sugar throughout the drink.[2] Is the solution correct? It works for someone who takes white coffee with sugar, but not if your guest wants their coffee a different way. At the point of making the coffee we make a decision and we must put that decision making into the solution description. This can be done by extending the pseudo-code to include a special *construct* that expresses *conditional actions*, that is, actions or tasks that are performed only when a specified condition is met. Solution 4.4 below uses the new construct "IF":

IF – a selection ▶
construct

Solution 4.4 Make coffee

```
1.  Put water in coffee machine ;
2.  Open the coffee holder ;
3.  Put filter paper in machine ;
```

---

[2] If you are wondering why I have added the milk and sugar to the cup before pouring the coffee, well that is my coffee-making tip to you: the sugar dissolves almost immediately if it is put into the cup before the coffee. This means minimal stirring is needed and it avoids the coffee drinker's plague of finding that the last swig of coffee contains a mouth-puckering avalanche of undissolved sugar. I do not take sugar anymore, but I remember what it was like. My guests always compliment me on my coffee.

```
4.  Measure coffee for one cup ;
5.  Put coffee into filter paper ;
6.  Shut the coffee holder ;
7.  Turn on machine ;
8.  Wait for coffee to filter through ;
9.  IF (sugar required)
        9.1.  Add sugar ;
    ENDIF
10. IF (white coffee required)
        10.1. Add milk/cream ;
    ENDIF
11. Pour coffee into mug ;
12. Stir coffee ;
13. Turn off machine ;
```

Huh?

In your first solution you didn't deal with people who don't want milk or sugar, but my solution did try to consider this. Was I wrong to deal with it this early? Do you always need so many versions of a solution? Don't you sometimes get the right answer straight off?

It was certainly not wrong to think about milk and sugar from the outset, and of course, you do sometimes get the full solution first time round. However, when starting out I think it is helpful to spend a lot of time working on the separate components of a problem. In this case we dealt with the overall structure and then considered the finer points such as milk and sugar requirements. Also, I want to introduce the pseudo-code for dealing with choice and repetition in a timely manner.

The flowchart in Figure 4.2 shows diagrammatically how the IF construct works. Flowcharts can be helpful for explaining certain programming concepts and they are considered in more detail in Chapter 8.

FIGURE 4.2   **Control flow diagram for the IF construct**

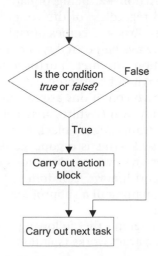

Actions, or tasks, are shown as rectangles. The arrows show what task comes next. Decision points are shown by diamonds. The pseudo-code word "IF" asks a question, the answer to which can be either *true* or *false*. (The statements "it is true that sugar is required" and "it is not true/it is false that sugar is required" should make the meaning of *true* and *false* clear.) If the answer is true then the task following the IF is carried out otherwise it is not. Parentheses in the pseudo-code () enclose the question which is called the *condition*. The action or sequence of actions to be obeyed (known as the action *block*) when the condition is satisfied (i.e., *true*) is written below the IF, indented by three spaces, and terminated by the keyword ENDIF. The indentation shows actions that are subordinate to others; in other words, one action belongs to, or is contained within, another. We will return to this idea later. The ENDIF shows clearly what actions belong to the IF, that is, what actions are carried out only when the condition is met. Consider Cases 1 and 2 below:

Case 1

```
IF (condition)
   Action 1 ;
   Action 2 ;
ENDIF
```

Case 2

```
IF (condition)
   Action 1 ;
ENDIF
Action 2 ;
```

The placement of ENDIF tells us that in Case 1 both Action #1 and Action #2 are carried out when the condition is met. In Case 2, only Action #1 is obeyed when the condition is met, while Action #2, being outside the action block, comes after the IF and so is obeyed regardless of the condition. Look back at Solution 4.4. Do you see that because Task #11 comes outside the action blocks of the two IFs that the coffee will always be poured while milk and sugar will only be added if the relevant conditions are met? Furthermore, each time we carry out this solution the outcome could be different. If the first guest wants black unsweetened coffee then the two conditions are not met and no milk or sugar is added. The next person may want white unsweetened coffee – no problem. Likewise, the person who wants sugary black or sugary white coffee can also be accommodated. It looks like this is a good general solution. The tasks are written in such a way that whatever combinations of milk and sugar requirements arise we have an algorithm we can follow that will give the desired result. Well, nearly. There remains still a subproblem: what if our guest wants two spoonfuls of sugar? D'oh!

Before continuing you should attempt the following exercises that will ensure you understand how the IF construct works (solutions in Appendix C).

Before you leave home in the morning you check to see whether it is raining; if it is you take an umbrella with you. Write an `IF...ENDIF` construct that shows this decision-making process.

Write an `IF...ENDIF` construct that adds a 10% tip to a restaurant bill and compliments the chef if the service was of a high standard. After the `ENDIF` add a statement to pay the bill. Convince yourself that the tip is only added when good service is received.

4.3 Making It Again: Repeated Actions

While Solution 4.4 is good it does not allow for situations where more than one spoonful of sugar is required. How could we solve the problem of adding enough sugar? We could first ask our guest if sugar is required and then add a spoonful. Then we could ask if more is required and add another spoonful. For a guest who wants two sugars, the action sequence would look like this:

Solution 4.5 More than one sugar:

```
IF (sugar required)
    Add spoonful of sugar ;
ENDIF
IF (more sugar required)
    Add spoonful of sugar ;
ENDIF
```

The trouble here is that the solution works only if we decide to ration guests to two spoonfuls each. Of course, we could add another `IF` to allow for three spoonfuls, but it is not a very elegant solution as it requires us to ask our guest three times if he wants sugar even if the answer to the first question was *no*. Even then it does not cater for those who want four or even more sugars. The good thing about Solution 4.4 was that it worked for all the combinations of milk and single spoonful of sugar. We would like to achieve the same general-purpose type of solution for the question of how many sugars to add. Looking at Solution 4.5 do you notice anything special? What about the fact that the action "Add spoonful of sugar" has been repeated? Think about how you would go about this for real. You probably would not ask your guest if sugar is required and then keep on asking and adding more until they say no. Rather, you would ask how many sugars are wanted and then repeatedly add a spoonful until the request is satisfied; if no sugar is required we simply add no sugar.[3] To express actions that are repeated we add the `WHILE` construct to the pseudo-code.

Think Spot

WHILE – an iteration construct ▶

---

[3] In programming terms we might say that we carry out the action "Add a spoonful of sugar" zero times. That may sound weird (doing something zero times) but it is an important concept and one which will be revisited in Chapter 6.

FIGURE 4.3 **Layout of the** WHILE **construct**

```
WHILE (condition is true)
    Action 1 ;
ENDWHILE
```

Or with multiple actions:

```
WHILE (condition is true)
    Action 1 ;
    Action 2 ;
    . . .
    Action n ;
ENDWHILE
```

Is condition true or false? — False

True

Carry out action block

Next task

The first example in Figure 4.3 shows a WHILE construct whose action block contains a single task. The second example has an action block with multiple tasks. The layout should be fairly clear as it resembles the IF construct. Recall that the IF means "if the specified condition is true (satisfied) then carry out the tasks in the subsequent action block." In contrast, the WHILE says "while the specified condition is true carry out the tasks in the action block." The difference is that the action block is repeatedly obeyed while, or as long as, the condition is true (this is known as a *loop* because we keep *looping* around the action block). Thinking of our coffee problem we could say "while (or, as long as) sugar is still required, perform the task of adding a spoonful of sugar." Of course, we must make sure there is some way for the condition to eventually become false otherwise we will be stuck forever repeatedly carrying out the tasks in the action block.

Write a **WHILE** loop to handle adding sugar to the coffee (use the notation from Figure 4.3). Remember to close the action block with an **ENDWHILE**

Here is my solution based on what we have learned so far. I have included the tasks that come before and after the sugar-adding to provide context:

Solution 4.6 More sugar required using WHILE

```
8.  Wait for coffee to filter through ;
9.  WHILE (sugar required)
        9.1  Add spoonful of sugar ;
    ENDWHILE
10. IF (white coffee required)
        10.1 Add milk/cream ;
    ENDIF
11. Pour coffee into mug ;
```

? **Think Spot**

On the surface Solution 4.6 seems to do the trick: there is a mechanism for dealing with the repeated action "Add spoonful of sugar" and milk is only added once if required. But consider what this means for a moment. Taking the milk question first, how do you get the information necessary to decide whether the condition "white coffee required" has been satisfied? You would ask your guest whether they want milk. Look at Task #10 which we can treat as asking a question, the answer to which tells us whether to carry out the conditional task "Add milk/cream." We ask the question once (Task #10) and then, depending on the answer, either carry out Task #10.1 or not. Now look at the WHILE construct which repeatedly adds spoonfuls of sugar. Like the IF, the WHILE needs to ask a question in order to decide whether to carry out the tasks in the action block. If the answer to the question is *true* then the action block is carried out. After obeying the tasks in the action block the construct *loops* back to ask the question again (as you can see from the flowchart in Figure 4.3). This cycle repeats until the condition in the question becomes false at which point we step through to the next task following the WHILE (Task #10 in the case of Solution 4.6).

The question is, each time we come back to the WHILE's condition how do we decide whether enough sugar has been added yet? If we treat the WHILE the way we treated the IF we could simply ask our guest if they want any sugar. If so, we add a spoonful and then loop back and ask the question again. However, this is inelegant as you would not really keep going back to interrogate your guest after every spoonful of sugar. Rather, you would ask the guest first how many sugars are required. Armed with the answer we can go the kitchen to get on with the task without needing to trouble the guest further. If we have a particularly poor memory we could write down the number of sugars required on a piece of paper. Then, when we come to Task #9 a simple bit of arithmetic tells us whether sugar is needed. Supposing our guest asked for one sugar, let's see how to carry out Task #9. The coffee has filtered through (Task #8) and so we arrive at the WHILE loop with the condition (sugar required). Our guest asked for one spoonful and we have not added any yet, so the condition is *true* – sugar is required. We add a spoonful of sugar (Task #9.1) and then loop back to the WHILE. The condition is now *false* (the guest wanted one spoonful and that is what we have put in) so we proceed to Task #10. If two sugars were wanted, then we would loop round twice before the condition becomes false. What if our guest did not want any sugar at all? The first time we reach the WHILE its condition is already false because number of spoonfuls required and the number of spoonfuls we have put into the coffee are already equal (both zero). You should be able to see that what we are doing is keeping a count in our heads of the number of spoonfuls of sugar added to the coffee. When that number reaches the required value then no more sugar is required. We can represent this process explicitly in pseudo-code thus:

```
Find out how many sugars required ;
WHILE (sugars added not equal to number required)
    Add spoonful of sugar ;
    Add 1 to number of sugars added ;
ENDWHILE
```

We will return to keeping track of numbers in the next chapter when we deal with working storage.

In the above **WHILE** loop, why is there a statement to add 1 to the number of sugars added?

To recap, here is the full solution to the coffee-making problem so far:

Solution 4.7 Coffee making

```
 1.  Put water in coffee machine ;
 2.  Open coffee holder ;
 3.  Put filter paper in machine ;
 4.  Measure coffee for one cup ;
 5.  Put coffee into filter paper ;
 6.  Shut the coffee holder ;
 7.  Turn on machine ;
 8.  Wait for coffee to filter through ;
 9.  Find out how many sugars required ;
10.  WHILE (sugars added not equal to number required)
         10.1   Add spoonful of sugar ;
         10.2   Add 1 to number of sugars added ;
     ENDWHILE
11.  IF (white coffee required)
         11.1   Add milk/cream ;
     ENDIF
12.  Pour coffee into mug ;
13.  Stir coffee ;
14.  Turn off machine ;
```

How does it look? Does it work? The last part of *HTTLAP* Step 3 says:

> *Go back to your sequence of actions. Should all actions be carried out in every circumstance? Should some actions (or groups/blocks of actions) only be carried out when certain conditions are met?*
>
> *Go back to your sequence of actions. Is carrying out each action once only sufficient to give the desired outcome? If not, do you have actions (or groups/blocks of actions) that must therefore be repeated?*
>
> *Go back once more. Do any of your actions/blocks of actions belong inside others? For example, do you have a block of actions that must be repeated, but only when some condition is met?*

Taking the first question we have seen that not all the actions should be carried out in every circumstance, hence the IF construct to deal with adding milk and the WHILE construct to cope with adding sugars: milk and sugar must only be added when they are wanted by the drinker.

The second question helps to refine the solution by differentiating between the cases where we need an IF construct and a WHILE construct. To carry out an action (or group of actions) once when a certain condition is met, we use the IF construct (as we did when adding milk). Adding the milk once is sufficient to satisfy the whitening requirements of coffee-making,[4] but adding sugar once may not be enough. We see that we have an action (add spoonful of sugar) that must be repeated while (as long as) a certain condition remains true (sugar required), hence the use of the WHILE construct.

The third question tries to ensure that we have put every action in the right place. Updating the count of the number of sugars added (see Task #10.2 in Solution 4.7 above) belongs inside the loop as it needs to be done each time a spoonful of sugar is added. Having carried out the plan, that is, written down a solution to the problem, we can progress to Step 4 of *HTTLAP*.

Assess the Result

In Step 4 of *HTTLAP* we examine the results obtained using our solution. There are two principal reasons for this. First, we need to make sure the solution produces the correct results. Secondly, we should make sure that it produced the results in a sensible and efficient manner. The solution should be clear to follow, as easy to carry out as possible, and not be unwieldy. An example of an unwieldy solution would be the sugar-adding routine in Solution 4.5. Examination of Solution 4.5 revealed a repeated action that was better expressed using a WHILE loop. We then examined the WHILE and discussed how its condition is tested. In this case, the condition was "sugar required," meaning we keep on adding sugar while more is needed. The question arose as to how to get the information to test the condition. It did not seem sensible to keep on asking our guest how many sugars he wanted, so we solved that problem by asking once (Task #9, Solution 4.7) and then comparing that value with the number of spoonfuls added so far. The next task is to add the milk. How do we

Think Spot

know whether to add milk? We ask our guest. Think about this for a moment. Remember, we are supposed to test these solutions and see if any parts can be made simpler, quicker, or clearer. Is there any opportunity for that here? Ideally you should get someone else to take the solution away and follow its instructions. Let's trace through Solution 4.7 as if we were doing it for real. The first eight actions are:

1. Put water in coffee machine ;
2. Open coffee holder ;
3. <u>Put filter paper in machine ;</u>
4. <u>Measure coffee for one cup ;</u>
5. Put coffee into filter paper ;
6. Shut the coffee holder ;
7. Turn on machine ;
8. Wait for coffee to filter through ;

These tasks deal with setting up the machine, putting in the water and coffee, and getting it going. They seem reasonable and it is hard to see how changing the order of any of the tasks would lead to a better solution.

---

[4] Alright, so I am assuming that everybody who takes milk takes the same amount. Experience tells me that this is clearly not the case. Some people just want a spot of milk while others go as far as wanting half coffee, half milk. If you think about it, this is a very interesting problem in its own right.

Convince yourself of this by writing down a few different orderings of the eight actions above. Are any tasks dependent on other tasks happening first?

Task #9 from Solution 4.7 says:

```
9.  Find out how many sugars required ;
```

This task requires some interaction with our guest, and armed with the answer we can then proceed to Task #10:

```
10.  WHILE (sugars added not equal to number required)
        10.1   Add spoonful of sugar ;
        10.2   Add 1 to number of sugars added ;
     ENDWHILE
```

Assume that our guest asked for two spoonfuls of sugar. The condition asks whether the number of sugars added is equal to the number required. If not then we carry out the tasks in the WHILE's action block. Table 4.1 below gives a trace of the sugar-adding loop. Each row represents one execution of the WHILE. The first column shows the number of sugars asked for by the guest. Column 2 shows how many sugars have been added **at the point of testing the condition**, that is, before the action block is obeyed. The third column shows the state of the condition given the values in Columns 1 and 2. The final column shows what tasks we carry out as a result of the value of the condition in Column 3.

Table 4.1 **Tracing through the** WHILE

Sugars Required	Sugars Added	Condition True/False	Actions Taken
2	0	True	#10.1 – Add spoonful of sugar #10.2 – Add 1 to number of sugars added (now 1)
2	1	True	#10.1 – Add spoonful of sugar #10.2 – Add 1 to number of sugars added (now 2)
2	2	False	Leave the **WHILE** and proceed to task #11

The first time Task #10 is encountered we see that two sugars are required and we have not yet added any. The condition is true (the number of sugars required is **not** equal to the number of spoonfuls added so far) and we proceed to Task #10.1 (adding a sugar) and Task #10.2 (increasing the count of the number of sugars added so far, i.e., one).[5] We loop back to the top of the WHILE and test

---

[5] We have assumed that the value of the number of sugars added begins at zero. This is not a reasonable assumption for some programming languages – see the reflection on INITIALIZATION OF VARIABLES. Do not worry about it yet, though – we have got coffee to make.

the condition again. This time we have added one sugar, but that is not equal to the number required; the condition is true and we carry out Tasks #10.1 and #10.2 again. Once more we go back to the top of the WHILE. Now the number of sugars added and the number required are the same (both two) so the condition is now false and we end the WHILE and proceed to Task #11.

```
11. IF (white coffee required)
        11.1  Add milk/cream ;
     ENDIF
```

Task #11 is about adding milk (or cream) to the coffee.[6] How do we test the condition? We ask our guest. If he says *yes* we add the milk, otherwise we do not. Either way we then proceed to:

12. Pour coffee into mug ;

13. Stir coffee ;

14. <u>Turn off machine ;</u>

These tasks are fairly clear. Look at Task #11. Recall that we are inspecting the solution to see if it is cumbersome or could be made simpler, quicker, or clearer. Think about the way we interact with our guest. First we get the machine going (Tasks #1–#8). Next, we ask whether sugar is required. Armed with that knowledge we go to the kitchen and add any sugar. Then we go back and ask whether milk is required and then return to the kitchen again to add any milk and then pour the coffee. This is cumbersome. Perhaps it would be better if we added another information gathering task so that we can get the milk and sugar requirements in one go? This would give the task sequence in Solution 4.8 below. The new task is #10 "Find out whether milk required." For the person making the coffee this seems like a more sensible arrangement of the tasks. It is better because gathering the information requires effort – in this case it means travelling from the kitchen to the living room. By putting Tasks #9 and #10 next to each other we have minimized the effort.

Huh?

As Action #11.1 comes after Action #11, won't it always be carried out regardless of whether milk is wanted? I thought actions that followed each other sequentially were executed sequentially.

This is a common misunderstanding. It is true that #11.1 follows #11, but the key is in the use of the IF construct. Recall that the actions between the IF and ENDIF keywords are only executed when the condition next to the IF keyword is true. If the condition is not true, i.e., no milk is wanted, then Action #11.1 will not be obeyed. Of course, if the action block had more than one statement (e.g., #11.2 and #11.3 as well) then these would be executed in the order written when the condition is true.

---

[6] I am aware that I have left in an unresolved choice until now; that is, the choice between milk and cream. Actually, I do not mean there to be a choice: if you are in Europe then you would likely be offered milk, whereas in the United States it is typically called cream. For the purposes of this example let's say they are the same thing.

Solution 4.8 The final coffee making routine?

```
1.   Put water in coffee machine ;
2.   Open coffee holder ;
3.   Put filter paper in machine ;
4.   Measure coffee for one cup ;
5.   Put coffee into filter paper ;
6.   Shut the coffee holder ;
7.   Turn on machine ;
8.   Wait for coffee to filter through ;
9.   Find out how many sugars required ;
10.  Find out whether milk required ;
11.  WHILE (sugars added not equal to number required)
         11.1  Add spoonful of sugar ;
         11.2  Add 1 to number of sugars added ;
     ENDWHILE
12.  IF (white coffee required)
         12.1  Add milk/cream ;
     ENDIF
13.  Pour coffee into mug ;
14.  Stir coffee ;
15.  Turn off machine ;
```

Ideally, you should give your coffee-making solution to someone else to work through. Make sure you explain to them how to obey the **IF** and **WHILE** constructs.

Think Spot

There is always a danger when evaluating your own work that you will miss an error. You have probably experienced this when completing written work. You can read a page of your own work over and over and never spot a glaring mistake; only when someone else proofreads it for you does the error get noticed. If you gave your solution to someone else, did they get the same result as you? If not, do you know why? Was it because you (or your friend) did not follow the instructions correctly, or is there an error in the instructions?

If your friend interpreted an instruction differently from the way you intended, it can be useful to get a third person to give their opinion. If they both see it differently from you then perhaps your understanding of how to phrase things is the problem. This is an important programming issue because all software defects are the result of a difference between the programmer's intentions and the way they are expressed in the programming language code. Remember, the computer is incapable of misinterpreting your program; it is your understanding of what you have written that is wrong. There is no such thing as COMPUTER ERROR, only programming error. Computers only produce wrong results because their programs are in error. The only real computer error is if the electronic components break down, the hard drive crashes, etc. The rest are all defects introduced by programmers. If the solution worked, and we cannot find any way to improve we can proceed to Step 5 of *HTTLAP*.

► **There is no such thing as computer error, only programmer error**

Describing What We Have Learned

In Step 5 we make a record of our achievements and list any difficulties we encountered. Here is my dialogue with *HTTLAP*:

Q. What did you learn from this exercise?

A. What seemed like a really straightforward task (describing the process of making coffee) turned out to have some unexpected twists. Also, I became aware of how many assumptions I made: there are aspects to the problem that cannot be addressed without further dialogue with the problem owner.

Q. What do you know now that you did not before you started?

A. There are lots of ways of arranging task orders. Some of them led to the same result but were harder to carry out (e.g., the difference between asking the milk and sugar requirements in the same place (Solution 4.8) and separating the two tasks (Solution 4.7). It is important to consider how straightforward the instructions are to carry out.

Q. What particular difficulties did you encounter? Were there any aspects of the problem that caused you particular difficulty? If so, do you think you would know how to tackle them if you met something similar in the future?

A. I think the trickiest bit was dealing with the milk and sugar requirements. Knowing how to handle repeated actions and conditional actions is useful and I think I will be able to use this idea again. The adding sugars loop could be applied to activities like making tea or even in cooking meals; recipes call for quantities of ingredients to be added. It could even apply to feeding a parking meter: you have to keep putting coins in until there is enough money to cover your parking period.

The last piece of advice in Step 5 of *HTTLAP* is to compare the finished solution with your first attempt and say what the differences teach you. Here is the first solution that we wrote down after following the first three steps of *HTTLAP*:

```
1.   Put water in coffee machine ;
2.   Open the coffee holder ;
3.   Put filter paper in machine ;
4.   Measure coffee for one cup ;
5.   Put coffee into filter paper ;
6.   Shut the coffee holder ;
7.   Turn on machine ;
8.   Wait for coffee to filter through ;
9.   Pour coffee into mug ;
10.  Turn off machine ;
```

And here's the final solution:

1. Put water in coffee machine ;
2. Open coffee holder ;
3. <u>Put filter paper in machine ;</u>
4. <u>Measure coffee for one cup ;</u>
5. Put coffee into filter paper ;
6. Shut the coffee holder ;
7. Turn on machine ;
8. Wait for coffee to filter through ;
9. Find out how many sugars required ;
10. Find out whether milk required ;
11. WHILE (sugars added not equal to number required)

      11.1 Add spoonful of sugar ;

      11.2 Add 1 to number of sugars added ;

   ENDWHILE
12. IF (white coffee required)

      12.1 Add milk/cream ;

   ENDIF
13. Pour coffee into mug ;
14. Stir coffee ;
15. <u>Turn off machine ;</u>

? Think Spot

What are the differences? The first eight tasks are the same at which point the two solutions diverge (apart from pouring the coffee and turning off the machine). The milk and sugar requirement was not part of the original algorithm and was introduced later on. Even so, compare the original solution involving the new requirement (Solution 4.3) with the final one. Solution 4.3 only had two simple milk and sugar actions (#9 and #10): add sugar and add milk/cream. Thinking about these two tasks revealed two subproblems, one involving a simple choice (whether to add milk or not) and the other involving a repeated action. It became clear that trying to describe exactly what to do in order to add milk and the right amount of sugar is more complicated that it first appeared. Perhaps the instructions are a little more detailed than we would normally make them for a person: saying something like "add as many sugars as the guest wants" should be sufficient. But if you wanted to learn to manage staff in a coffee shop you would not be reading this book. Remember, a computer does not possess intelligence and needs every task to be spelled out in minute detail. This detailed description of making coffee is half the way between instructing a person who can think for himself and use prior knowledge and experience to interpret instructions, and writing a program for a machine that has the intelligence of a piece of rock. And just like a rock, a computer will not be affected in the slightest by you shouting at it just because it is not doing what you want it to.

This technique of comparing the initial draft solution with the finished one is one I have used when teaching novice programmers. It can be particularly instructive to see just how different the finished product can be from the first attempt. It works best when you say *why* the differences are there rather than just identifying them. If you can explain why you have included certain aspects in your solution then it is more likely that you understand it. Often, the first attempt at a solution is made before good understanding of the underlying problem has been gained. This is why the *HTTLAP* strategy is so important because it forces you to address your understanding. It is the half-baked first solution with which many novices proceed that causes so much bewilderment. The reflection and dialogue in Steps 1–3 should reduce confusion and lead to better solutions. It is alright to produce a poor first solution as long as you treat it as the starting point of an iterative process of seeking understanding. By getting into the discipline now of critically evaluating your solutions **before** you try implementing them on a computer you will save yourself much confusion later on. Turning a solution into programming language code is challenging enough without being saddled with a poor solution as well.

Documenting the Solution

The final step in *HTTLAP* is to write the documentation. Actually, you should be documenting as you go along. If you leave all the documentation until the end then it is unlikely you will complete it or even do it at all. In fact, we have completed some of the documentation already. Look back at the dialogues with the *HTTLAP* questions. The answers to those questions help to explain why the solution is designed the way it is. Furthermore, a well set out solution is itself part of the documentation. That is, an easy to understand instruction is self-documenting. For all but the simplest of problems and solutions, it is unlikely that you can avoid writing at least some extra documentation. Many computer programs last for years undergoing continual amendment and improvement  (known as SOFTWARE MAINTENANCE). Is it likely that an undocumented solution will be easy to understand in, say, five years time after the memory of its construction has faded? Now that we have what we think is a working solution, we must go through it and ensure that it is as clearly explained as possible. *HTTLAP* has one more set of questions to help achieve this.

Q. Are there any aspects of your solution that are hard to understand?

A. That is a hard question to answer. The IF and WHILE could be hard for someone who is not familiar with the idea of expressing choices that way. Let's agree that we do not need to worry about explaining how IFs and WHILEs work in principle as we can explain the pseudo-code language to our friend before we give him any solutions to try out. Putting aside the details of how the constructs work, are there any other aspects of the solution that are hard to understand? One way to approach this question is to think about parts of the solution that were hard to produce. If deriving the solution was not obvious to you, then its expression may not be easy to understand for someone who has not invested the same time as you in working through the intricacies of the problem. For example, take the two questions we ask our guest in Tasks #9 and #10 (Solution 4.8). Why are they there, and why are they in the place they are? Why is Task #10 not closer to the IF that uses its answer? Because it is less cumbersome to get the answers to both questions in one go rather than run back and forth between the guest and the kitchen. We could document our solution with a comment to that effect.

Q. **If they are hard to understand, is it because they are badly written, or simply because the solution is just complicated? If you were to pick up your solution in five years time do you think any bits would be hard to understand?**

A. The thing about documentation is that it is not for the benefit of our friend who is to carry out the instructions. The computer that executes a program does not read the manual. The documentation is for the benefit of the person who will have to maintain the solution later on in order to correct any defects or add extra bits to cope with new requirements (such as the request to add milk and sugar). You do not want this person to have to work through the entire problem-solving process again just to understand your solution. The documentation should help that person to understand what your solution does and why it is structured the way it is. That will make it much easier for them to change it. And here's the clincher: that person could be you.

How, then, should we document solutions? It is common practice to write two kinds of documentation. The first kind is text that describes the solution, making mention of the information that is needed to be able to carry out the task, and what is produced at the end. The second type is commentary documentation, short explanations placed within the solution to amplify or clarify particular aspects. Solution 4.9 below shows Solution 4.8 with added documentation.

The first part of Solution 4.9 is the general textual documentation. It is not very long or detailed as this is a fairly simple problem. Interspersed throughout the solution you will notice lines beginning with "//." These are commentary lines and have the "//" to distinguish them from the actual tasks. Thus "// Set up coffee machine" is a comment to tell the reader that the tasks following it are to do with setting up the machine. With these comments we have broken the solution tasks into smaller groups each of which deals with a discrete part of the coffee-making problem.

Looking at the documentation, especially the comments that separate sections of the pseudo-code, can you take an abstract view of the algorithm and restate it as a small number of higher-level parts? Hint: for example, what do Tasks #13 and #14 have in common?

Solution 4.9 Documented coffee-making solution

Instructions for making coffee

```
These instructions will allow you to make a cup of coffee for a guest
using a filter machine. To complete the task you will need to find
out the sugar and milk requirements of your guest.
```

```
// *******************************************
// Instructions for making coffee
// Written by Paul Vickers, June 2007
// *******************************************
```

```
// Set up coffee machine
1.   Put water in coffee machine ;
2.   Open coffee holder ;
3.   Put filter paper in machine ;
4.   Measure coffee for one cup ;
5.   Put coffee into filter paper ;
6.   Shut the coffee holder ;
7.   Turn on machine ;
8.   Wait for coffee to filter through ;
// Add sugar and milk as necessary
9.   Find out how many sugars required ;
10.  Find out whether milk required ;
11.  WHILE (sugars added not equal to number required)
         11.1  Add spoonful of sugar ;
         11.2  Add 1 to number of sugars added ;
     ENDWHILE
12.  IF (white coffee required)
         12.1  Add milk/cream ;
     ENDIF
// Pour and serve coffee
13.  Pour coffee into mug ;
14.  Stir coffee ;
// Shut the machine down
15.  Turn off machine ;
// End of instructions
```

An abstract view of the solution reveals that it comprises three principal parts:

1. Setting things up – loading the machine, turning it on, etc.
2. Dealing with a cup of coffee – adding milk and sugar, pouring and stirring the coffee.
3. Shutting things down – turning off the machine.

As you become more familiar with programming you will start to recognize this as a general pattern. In programming terms it would be phrased as:

1. Initialization
2. Processing
3. Finalization

You will commonly find yourself writing algorithms that have these three main components. It will not always be easy to neatly divide an algorithm up into such sections, but you should see elements of this pattern in much of what you do.

4.4 **Chapter Summary**

In this chapter we have taken the real-world problem of making coffee and have followed the *HTTLAP* strategy to produce a workable solution that is generally applicable to a range of coffee requirements. *HTTLAP* helped us to gain a detailed understanding of the problem and to reflect on our attempts at solving the problem. The solution is still based on a few underlying assumptions that need resolving. It is also limited in that it can only be used to make a single cup of coffee. Of course, it would not take much work to amend it so that we could first find out how many cups of coffee are required and then proceed accordingly. In fact, this is exactly what we will do in the next chapter. Strictly speaking, if we were intending to turn our solution into a computer program then there is still a little more work to do, and the condition for the WHILE needs to be refined. But we will deal with the issues behind this in Chapter 6 where we will look at forming loop conditions and will explore three different loop constructs.

4.5 **Exercises**

1. In what circumstances would you use the IF and WHILE constructs? How are they different?

2. Examine the following algorithm fragment:

   ```
   put on hat ;
   IF (weather is sunny)
      put on sunglasses ;
   ENDIF
   put on shoes ;
   ```

   What items of clothing will be put on a) when it is raining and b) when it is sunny?

3. Examine the following algorithm fragment:

   ```
   Go to shop ;
   buy milk ;
   IF (today is Saturday)
      buy weekly newspaper ;
   buy peanuts ;
   ENDIF
   buy bread ;
   ```

   What items will be purchased a) on Thursday, b) on Saturday?

4. Consider the following algorithm fragment:

   ```
   1.  Eat breakfast ;
   2.  Wash breakfast dishes ;
   3.  WHILE (not finished breakfast) ;
           3.1 Read a story in morning paper ;
           3.2 Take next bite of breakfast ;
       ENDWHILE
   ```

   How many stories in the morning paper will the person get to read?

5. In the *Stocksfield Diner* customers can choose whether or not to have their hamburgers plain or with any combination of cheese, lettuce, and tomatoes. Write three IF constructs that add as required by the customer.

6. Use the *HTTLAP* strategy to design an algorithm to represent filling a bath. The taps should be turned off altogether when the bath is full. When the bath is half full check the water temperature and if it is not warm enough adjust it by turning the cold tap down a quarter turn.

7. The Department of Horticulture at the University of Stocksfield is testing a new fertilizer. They are interested in how long the fertilizer may be kept before its effectiveness is lost. They have done some calculations that indicate the fertilizer loses 6% of its potency every month. Using HTTLAP, design an algorithm that finds how many months it takes before the fertilizer has lost more than 50% of its effective power after which is must be thrown away. The first four months of potency figures would look like this:

```
Month 1, potency 100%
Month 2, potency 94%
Month 3, potency 88.36%
Month 4, potency 83.0584%
```

The algorithm should produce summary messages for each month as above stopping after the potency has gone below 50%.

Note, you are removing 6% of the fertilizer's remaining potency each month, not its original potency. That is why after month 3 the potency is 88.36% and not 88%.

8. For the following scenarios write down a basic sequence of actions (no selections or iterations needed) and then try to partition the actions to see if the sequence fits the Initialization, Processing, and Finalization algorithm pattern:

a) Getting up and ready in the morning

b) Cooking a meal

c) Writing an essay or school report

For the problems below follow the stages of *HTTLAP* to produce a set of instructions for carrying out the task (including any necessary selections and iterations). Do not try to cut corners and, wherever possible, get a friend to try out your solutions as you would be amazed at what issues this will raise. **Do not** neglect the documentation step.

9. Mow a lawn. Start with the simplest form of the problem and then introduce some of the real issues that you would face when mowing the lawn such as, height of cut, what happens when the grass box gets full, the role of the weather, and so on.

10. You are a judge in the new hit reality TV show *Earth's Next Top Professor*, in which a number of university professors all compete in a series of weekly tasks to be crowned Earth's Top Professor and win a job teaching in the Department of Applied Studies at the world renowned University of Stocksfield. In order to decide which professor must leave the show each week you score each candidate according to four characteristics:

- Teaching ability, from 1–10
- Sense of humor, from 1–10
- Subject knowledge, from 1–10
- Good looks, from 1–10

Using the *HTTLAP* strategy design an algorithm that asks a judge for the name of one of the candidates followed by the score the judge is awarding for each of the four character- istics. There is a constraint: the total points value must not exceed 20 points. If the judge awards more than 20 points then a score of 5 is assigned to each characteristic.

Now extend your solution so that the judge is asked for scores for each of the remaining professors.

Now extend your solution so that each of the three judges on the show is asked for their scores for each of the remaining professors.

11. Make a single cheese and onion omelette to feed up to three people. The number of peo- ple will vary each time. A one-person portion needs two eggs, a pinch of salt and pepper, a small amount of milk (say 3 fl. oz/100 ml), 1/4 of a small onion, 2 oz (about 60 g) of cheese, and a pat of butter (or margarine if you prefer). The milk, eggs, onion, cheese, and butter need to be mixed prior to cooking in a large frying pan. Make sure the pan is not too hot when you add the mixture. Cook until the surface of the omelette is just start- ing to firm up. Serve and garnish with parsley and grated parmesan cheese if desired.

12. Decorate your bedroom with new wallpaper.

A Harder Exercise for the More Ambitious

13. What difficulties would you have if the requirements of Exercise 5 were changed so that a customer **cannot** have a plain hamburger but has a choice of **either** cheese **or** lettuce and tomatoes – that is, hamburger with cheese **or** hamburger with lettuce **and** tomatoes? What facility does the IF construct seem to be lacking?

4.6 Projects

StockSnackz Vending Machine

We dealt with our vending machine dispensing snacks throughout the day by a single highly abstract action "Dispense snacks." Now we have the constructs available to deal with optional and repeated actions we can extend the solution. Using pseudo-code notation, add any iterations and selections necessary to your solution from Chapter 3 to show many individual items being dispensed. You might want to start with the subproblem of dispensing the correct snack that cor- responds to the button that was pressed. After that, move on to solving the prob- lem of allowing this to happen repeatedly.

Stocksfield Fire Service

Using pseudo-code notation, add any selections and iterations necessary to your solution from Chapter 3 to the problem of decoding the hazchem Emergency Action Code.

Puzzle World: Roman Numerals and Chronograms

Go back to the problem of translating Roman numbers into decimal that you looked at in Chapter 3. You should be aware that just as English words can be misspelled, so can Roman numeral strings be malformed. For example, the

Roman numeral string MCMC is malformed as it contradicts the syntax of the system. Before we can translate a Roman number into decimal we must first determine whether the Roman number is valid. If it is, then we can translate it into decimal. The rules for forming valid Roman numeral strings are:[7]

1. Smaller numerals follow larger numerals (see Rule 3 below). Summing the values of the numerals gives the value of the number.
2. The numerals I, X, C, and M (1, 10, 100, 1000 – all powers of 10) may be repeated up to three times in a row. No other numerals may be repeated.
3. Sometimes, a smaller numeral may precede a larger one (as in IV). These cases form compound numerals which are evaluated by subtracting the value of the smaller numeral from the larger one. To form a compound numeral **all** the following conditions must be met:

   a) The smaller numeral must be a power of ten (1, 10, 100, 1000).
   b) The smaller numeral must be either one-fifth or one-tenth the value of the larger one.
   c) The smaller numeral must either be the first numeral in the number, or follow a numeral of at least ten times its value.
   d) If the compound numeral is followed by another numeral, that numeral must be smaller than the one that comes first in the compound numeral (i.e., you can have XCI but not IXI).

Work through the *HTTLAP* strategy to draft an outline solution to the problem of validating a Roman number.

Pangrams: Holoalphabetic Sentences

Using iteration and selection constructs (`WHILE` and `IF`) update the sequence of actions you produced in Chapter 3 for determining whether a sentence is a pangram.

Online Bookstore: ISBNs

The check digit in an ISBN is calculated by a *Modulus 11* technique using the *weights* 10 to 2. This means that each of the first nine digits is multiplied by a number in a sequence from 10 to 2. If you add these products together and then add the value of the check digit, this total sum should be divisible by 11 without leaving a remainder. If it does give a remainder then the check digit does not match the rest of the number and we know the ISBN has been copied down incorrectly. The check digit is calculated in the following manner:

Multiply the first nine digits by 10, 9, 8, 7, . . ., 2 respectively and add the results. Divide this sum by 11 and take the remainder. Finally, subtract this remainder from 11 to give the check digit. If the value is 10 the check digit

---

[7] Rules taken from Edward R. Hobbs' *Compvter Romanvs* resource at http://www.naturalmath.com/tool2.html.

becomes "X." For example, we can validate the ISBN 0-14-012499-3 as follows:

$$\text{Check digit} = \frac{(0 \times 10) + (1 \times 9) + (4 \times 8) + (0 \times 7) + (1 \times 6) + (2 \times 5) + (4 \times 4) + (9 \times 3) + (9 \times 2)}{11}$$

$$= 118 \div 11$$

$$= 10, \text{ remainder } 8$$

So, the check digit $= 11 - 8 = 3$. As this is the same as the last number in 0-14-012499-3 we know that 0-14-012499-3 is a valid ISBN.

Using *HTTLAP*, write down the basic sequence of actions necessary to calculate the check digit for any ten-digit ISBN (assume the ISBN will be in a raw format without hyphens). Once you have identified the sequence, look to see if you can identify any repeated actions which could be better expressed using an iteration.

5 Calculating and Keeping Track of Things

If you cannot describe what you are doing as a process, you do not know what you are doing.

W. Edwards Deming (1900–1993)

Panel 1: I'VE BEEN ASKED TO REDUCE HEADCOUNT.

Panel 2: TO BE FAIR ABOUT IT I CREATED A SCIENTIFIC ALGORITHM TO DECIDE WHO GOES.

Panel 3: I THOUGHT YOU WERE FIRING THE PEOPLE WITH THE HIGHEST SALARIES. OKAY, MAYBE "ALGORITHM" IS AN OVERSTATEMENT.

5.1 **Problems Involving Working Storage**

5.2 **Chapter Summary**

5.3 **Exercises**

5.4 **Projects**

Learning Objectives

- Understand the role of working storage in algorithms
- Identify the variables (data items) needed in a problem solution (algorithm)
- Estimate likely ranges of values for variables
- Apply the problem solving strategy to real-world problems involving variables and nested action blocks

We ended the last chapter with a solution to a coffee-making problem. As we delved deeper into the details of parts of the task we began to see the need to keep track of certain pieces of information. For instance, we kept a running tally of the number of sugars we had put into the coffee to ensure that the correct number was added. Keeping track of things is a key feature of algorithms and this chapter explores this further.

In Section 5.1 you will be introduced to the notion of *working storage* and how the need to write down and record values (known as *variables*) as you go is central to programming. Section 5.2 shows how these variables can be manipulated using arithmetic to solve programming problems. We then see how this knowledge enables us to talk about high-level data abstractions. As with the previous chapter, the problem solving strategy introduced in Chapter 2 is applied throughout.

5.1 **Problems Involving Working Storage**

Solution 4.6 described how to add the right number of sugars to a cup of coffee. However, as we noted there was not sufficient information in the instructions to be able to work out when the condition "sugar required" was actually met. We further realized that the way we can tell whether sufficient sugar has been added is to first find out how many are needed and then to keep a count of how many spoons we have added. This led to Solution 4.7 in which these two aspects (finding out how much sugar is wanted and keeping count) were made explicit. This may have seemed laborious and long-winded because anyone with any common sense would have understood what we meant. But that is precisely the problem: Computers do not have any common sense and cannot *understand* anything. Instead of writing your coffee-making solution for an adult, imagine you are writing it for a small child who has never done anything quite like it before. You would be quite happy to spell out in detail the steps required. Likewise, a computer needs the most precise instructions possible. In order to add the correct number of sugars we explained how to keep track of two items of information which were needed to test whether the sugar requirements of our guest had been met.

Most problems for which we write programs need the computer to do the equivalent of keeping things in its head (such as running totals). The last coffee-making problem in Chapter 4 got close to this with the repeated adding of sugar. We can see this more clearly if we think more about the coffee problem. So far we have only considered the actions and decisions necessary to make the coffee itself. We did not think about where to pour it (we took the existence of a mug for granted).

FIGURE 5.1   **Drink choices of some guests**

We began by making coffee for one person, so naturally we would fetch one cup or mug. The number of mugs is related to the number of people wanting coffee. Imagine you have some friends over for the evening and you ask them if they want a drink. You ask who's for tea, who's for coffee, who's for water, who's for a soft drink, and so on. For those taking tea or coffee you ask whether milk or sugar is required. Some people are very good at this and can keep track of everything while others write a list (Figure 5.1). Whichever way you do it you make a record of all the facts you need to be able to go into the kitchen and prepare the drinks. Having made a note of how many coffees, teas, etc. are wanted you can now get out the correct numbers of mugs, cups, and glasses without having to interrupt the task to make further enquiries.

To simplify matters, think only about the coffee drinkers. What do we need to know to complete the task? First we must find out how many want coffee, and whether they want milk or sugar. Suppose five want coffee: three black without sugar, one black with one sugar, and one white with two sugars. We have the information needed to go and make the drinks.

Suppose the next day there are eight guests and this time six people want coffee. Three want it black, three want it with milk, and nobody wants sugar.

What has changed? What aspects of the problem remain constant between the two days?

The number of coffees required has changed as have the milk and sugar requirements. Although the numbers are different, the things they represent (i.e., the number of coffees required, the number of coffees with milk, and the number with sugar) remain the same. That is, we are asking the same questions but each time getting different answers depending on the desires of our guests.

Variables ▶

What we have here are *variables*. In programming a variable is a quantity, or item of information or data, whose value changes each time the program is run, or many times during one execution of the program. A name is given to the item to identify it and then values are assigned to it. You will remember something similar in mathematics lessons in school when you were given questions such as:

In the equation $y = 2x + 3$ calculate the value of y when x has the values 4 and 5.

Both x and y are variables because the values they stand for can change. If x stands for the value 4, then y stands for the value 11 ($y = 2 \times 4 + 3 = 8 + 3 = 11$) and when x stands for the value 5 then y stands for the value 13.

Is a variable in programming the same as a variable in algebra?

It is very similar. In algebra we use letters like x and y to stand for values that can change. The difference is that we cannot assign values to variables in algebra – they are only used to stand for unknown values. You will see below that variable *assignment* is a fundamental feature of the sort of programming this book is looking at.

? **Think Spot**

What are the variables in the coffee-making problem? What are the values that you need to keep track of to solve the problem and which may change each time you make coffee? Approach the problem by following *HTTLAP*. Here is the problem to solve:

Using an electric filter machine (also called a percolator), make coffee for up to six guests. Add milk and sugar as required.

Was the problem harder to understand than the previous one? Here is my own dialogue with *HTTLAP*.

Understanding the Problem

Q. What are you being asked to do?

A. Make coffee for up to six people.

Q. What is required?

A. Between zero and six cups of coffee. Each cup may or may not need milk and/or sugar to be added.

Q. What is the unknown?

A. How much coffee to make. I need anything up to six cups (and that could be none). I do not know the capacity of the pot. Is it large enough to hold six cups of coffee? I also do not know how much milk or sugar is needed.

Q. Can the problem be better expressed by drawing a diagram or a picture?

A. Maybe. Here is a picture of the main parts of the problem.

FIGURE 5.2   **Pictorial representation of the coffee making problem**

Q. What are the principal parts of the problem?

A. 1) Make a pot of coffee. 2) Pour several cups. 3) Each cup may or may not need milk or sugar. Or, looking at it another way: 1) The filter machine, 2) the cups, 3) the coffee, 4) some water, 5) the cups of coffee – just coffee, or milk and sugar as well?

What if no coffee is wanted? Is this what you mean by zero cups being required? Why even make a pot at all? How do I *not* make coffee, the solution already seems to assume we will always need to make some?

This is an interesting point. Look back at one of the earlier coffee making solutions and see how you could adapt it to allow for this possibility. *Hint: there is some kind of condition involved.* In fact, this problem is dealt with in a few pages time – if the problem is too difficult for you at the moment you may choose to wait to see how to deal with it.

Q. Are there several parts to the problem?

A. I guess so. Making the coffee is a separate problem from pouring it. Each cup of coffee is an individual problem as I need to decide whether to add milk or sugar. Making the coffee is not a single action either – I need to get the water, measure some coffee, etc.

Q. Have you made any assumptions?

A. No, not yet. But I could assume that the pot holds enough coffee for six cups. But I guess that the problem could just as easily have asked for twelve cups of coffee, or even twenty. Is it reasonable to assume the pot will always be big enough?

Q. What can you do about the assumptions?

A. Not sure yet.

Did you think about the problem of the pot size too? Having understood the problem as best we can we shall move on to devising a plan to solve the problem in Step 2.

Devising a Plan to Solve the Problem

Q. Have you solved this problem before/is it similar to one you have solved before?

A. Yes, I know how to make coffee for one person.

Q. Are some parts of the problem more easily solved than others?

A. Yes. Pouring the coffee is easy. Adding the water and the coffee grounds requires some thought as to *how much* to add. After pouring the coffee I do not know if anything else is needed (e.g., milk and sugar). Also, I do not know whether my pot of coffee is big enough to make all the coffee required.

Q. If the problem is too hard, can you solve a simpler version of it, or a related problem?

A. Good idea. Let's keep things simple. I think it will be hard enough to try and solve the problem with the assumption that the coffee pot is large enough for the required coffee so I'll solve that problem first. Once I have done that I'll come back and have a look at the more general problem of making coffee for any number of people.

Q. Does restating the problem help? Try restating it in a different language.

A. No.

Q. Did you make use of all the information in the problem statement?

A. Yes, I think so.

Q. Can you satisfy all the conditions of the problem?

A. If I make the assumption that the pot is big enough to make all the coffee.

Q. Have you left anything out?

A. No, I do not think so; I seem to have gleaned all the information I can from the statement.

Time for Step 3:

Carrying Out the Plan

This is where we write down the basic sequence of actions necessary to complete the task. We have already solved a problem like this in Chapter 4 (Solution 4.8) so we can use that solution as the starting point for this one.

Solution 5.1 Making coffee for six people – first draft

```
1.   Put water in coffee machine ;
2.   Open coffee holder
3.   Put filter paper in machine ;
4.   Measure coffee ;
5.   Put coffee into filter paper ;
6.   Shut the coffee holder ;
7.   Turn on machine ;
8.   Wait for coffee to filter through ;
9.   Find out how many sugars required ;
10.  Find out whether milk required ;
11.  WHILE (sugars added not equal to number required)
        11.1  Add spoonful of sugar ;
        11.2  Add 1 to number of sugars added ;
     ENDWHILE
12.  IF (white coffee required)
        12.1  Add milk/cream ;
     ENDIF
13.  Pour coffee into mug ;
14.  Stir coffee ;
15.  Turn off machine ;
```

Look over Solution 5.1 above and identify in what ways the algorithm needs to be updated. You do not need to write new statements at this point, just identify the parts of the current problem that this solution does not yet address.

software ▶
reuse

It is clear that some changes are needed because this solution only deals with making one cup of coffee. You may have noticed that I have already removed the one-cup reference from Action #4. By using Solution 4.8 as the basis for this solution, what we have done is to solve a simpler version of the current problem. Actually, we have not even solved a simpler problem; we have *reused* a solution of a simpler problem. Reuse is an important idea in programming. The philosopher wrote *"there is no new thing under the sun"* (Ecclesiastes 1:9), and, with experience, you will find that you are able to reuse a great many ideas from the algorithms that you write. You will have to change some of the details but you will learn that a technique that works well for one problem will work well for other problems of the same (or similar) type.

Huh?

Isn't reusing solutions like this simply cheating?

If you were an architect, would not you reuse techniques and tricks you had learned to help with designing new buildings? If you are making use of structures and algorithms you developed previously for a different purpose then this is just an efficient use of time. If you are using algorithms created by other people then there are issues of intellectual property rights to be faced (particularly in countries where algorithms can be patented). You would do well to read a book on ethics for computing professionals which will help you understand this issue more fully.

Of course, you must make sure before you use solutions written by other people that you first have their permission to do so. All algorithms are made up of only three basic building blocks (see Chapters 6 and 8) so the skill of programming is learning the right combinations of these blocks.

In the above dialogues with *HTTLAP* where I identified the principal parts of the problem I decided that making the coffee is a separate (but related) problem from pouring a cup; that is, I have identified *sub*problems. Making the coffee is one task that comprises several actions. Pouring a cup is a separate task that requires decisions to be made and actions to be repeated.

Look at Solution 5.1 and identify these two aspects of the problem. State which group of actions deals with making the coffee and which group describes how to process a single cup.

The problem asks us to make coffee for up to six people. Step 3 of *HTTLAP* asks the question:

Q. Is carrying out each action once only sufficient to give the desired outcome? If not, do you have actions (or groups/blocks of actions) that must therefore be repeated?

As we need to make coffee for up to six people what does that say about Tasks #9 through #14? Clearly, they will need to be repeated for each cup of coffee.

Using a **WHILE** structure try writing the pseudo-code that allows Tasks #9 to #14 be applied to the problem of processing up to six cups of coffee.

Here is a possible solution:

Solution 5.2 Processing more than one cup of coffee

```
1.   WHILE (cups of coffee required)
        1.1  Find out how many sugars required ;
        1.2  Find out whether milk required ;
        1.3  WHILE (sugars added not equal to number required)
                1.3.1  Add spoonful of sugar ;
                1.3.2  Add 1 to number of sugars added ;
             ENDWHILE
        1.4  IF (white coffee required)
                1.4.1  Add milk/cream ;
             ENDIF
        1.5  Pour coffee into mug ;
        1.6  Stir coffee ;
     ENDWHILE
```

As all the tasks (#9 through #14 in Solution 5.1) needed to be carried out once each for each cup of coffee we can make them into the action block of a WHILE. To understand how this works follow it through for six cups of coffee. The first time we encounter the WHILE the condition "cups of coffee required" is true as we still need to pour six cups and we go into the action block. For this current cup of coffee we ask how many sugars are required and whether milk is wanted. Then, the next WHILE (Task #1.3) repeatedly adds spoons of sugar to the cup. Following that, if milk is required we add it. Finally we stir the coffee and go back up to the first WHILE (the outer one). The condition is still true so we carry out the action block once more. And so it goes on repeating until we have poured six cups each with its own milk and sugar requirements. After pouring the sixth cup the condition for the outer WHILE is false (no more coffee is required) so we leave the WHILE and carry on with the next

construct ▶
nesting

task in the sequence (turning off the machine). Notice how the WHILE and the IF from the original solution are now *inside* another WHILE? That is, the sequence of Actions #9 to #14 is itself repeated within an enclosing WHILE. This enclosing of structures within one another is called *nesting* and it allows us to describe solutions to complex problems.

? Think Spot

Look at Solution 5.2. Is it sufficient to solve the problem of pouring up to six cups of coffee? What about the condition belonging to the outer WHILE (Task #1)? How can we tell when it has been satisfied? Just as we had to keep count of the number of sugars added to a cup, so we need to keep count of the number of cups of coffee we have poured. Using the same technique as last time we can extend Solution 5.2 to include this aspect. The updated version is given below as Solution 5.3; new or changed tasks are shown in bold type.

Solution 5.3 Keeping count of the coffees

```
1.   Find out how many coffees required ;
2.   WHILE (cups poured not equal to cups required)
        2.1  Find out how many sugars required ;
        2.2  Find out whether milk required ;
```

```
2.3   WHILE (sugars added not equal to number required)
        2.3.1   Add spoonful of sugar ;
        2.3.2   Add 1 to number of sugars added ;
      ENDWHILE
2.4   IF (white coffee required)
        2.4.1   Add milk/cream ;
      ENDIF
2.5   Pour coffee into mug ;
2.6   Stir coffee ;
2.7   Add 1 to number of cups poured
ENDWHILE
```

We have introduced two new tasks: #1 to find out how many coffees are wanted and #2.7 to update the number poured so far. The condition on the outer WHILE loop (statement #2) has also been amended to show exactly how to decide when enough cups have been poured. Does this solution let us deal with up to six cups of coffee? If after carrying out Task #1 we find out that nobody wants coffee then we will not even enter the WHILE loop in Task #2 as its condition will immediately be false. Likewise, if Task #1 results in an answer such as 1, 2, or 6, and we follow Task #2 correctly then we will pour one, two, or six coffees, so everything looks fine. In fact, there is a problem.

Think about it now to see if you can spot it – we will deal with it fully later.

Consider the rest of the problem we have been asked to solve. Currently we have a candidate solution for the coffee-pouring part of the problem; the coffee-making aspect still needs attention. Solution 5.1 had the following sequence of actions for this part:

```
1.   Put water in coffee machine ;
2.   Open coffee holder ;
3.   Put filter paper in machine ;
4.   Measure coffee ;
5.   Put coffee into filter paper ;
6.   Shut the coffee holder ;
7.   Turn on machine ;
8.   Wait for coffee to filter through ;
```

The above sequence was written on the assumption that only one cup of coffee was required (that was the problem that was being solved in Chapter 3 from which this solution has been reused), thus Tasks #1 and #4 did not specify exactly how much water and coffee to measure. The current problem calls for us to make an arbitrary quantity of coffee – anything up to six cups. If the number of cups can change then we must be more specific about the meanings of

Tasks #1 and #4. By now you should have a good idea of how to go about solving this subproblem.

Rewrite the above sequence of actions to accommodate the requirement for a variable number of cups. If you get stuck look back at Solution 5.3 for clues as it solved a similar problem.

Here is my solution to this subproblem:

Solution 5.4 Making the pot of coffee

1. **Find out how many cups are required ;**
2. Put water for number of cups required in coffee machine ;
3. Open coffee holder ;
4. Put filter paper in machine ;
5. Measure coffee for number required ;
6. Put coffee into filter paper ;
7. Shut the coffee holder ;
8. Turn on machine ;
9. Wait for coffee to filter through

Carrying out the tasks for adding water and coffee depends on knowing how much coffee to make. Therefore, I have added a new Task #1 to find out how many coffees are needed. The renumbered Tasks #2 and #5 have been reworded to take account of this. Now we can put the two parts of the solution together. You may have noticed that both Solution 5.4 and Solution 5.3 have a Task #1 for finding out how many coffees are required. Clearly we do not need to do this twice, so we will remove the task from the cup-processing solution because Task #1 in Solution 5.4 provides the same information. Putting the two solutions together (and remembering to turn off the machine at the end) we get Solution 5.5 below. Notice that I have started putting in the documentation as this should never be left until the very end.

Solution 5.5 Complete solution for making coffee

```
// Set up coffee machine
```
1. Find out how many cups are required ;
2. Put water for number of cups required in coffee machine ;
3. Open coffee holder ;
4. Put filter paper in machine ;
5. Measure coffee for number required ;
6. Put coffee into filter paper ;
7. Shut the coffee holder ;
8. Turn on machine ;
9. Wait for coffee to filter through

```
// Process the cups of coffee
10. WHILE (cups poured not equal to cups required)
        // Add  sugar and milk as necessary
      10.1  Find out how many sugars required ;
      10.2  Find out whether milk required ;
      10.3  WHILE (sugars added not equal to number required)
              10.3.1  Add spoonful of sugar ;
              10.3.2  Add 1 to number of sugars added ;
            ENDWHILE
      10.4  IF (white coffee required)
              10.4.1  Add milk/cream ;
            ENDIF
      10.5  Pour coffee into mug ;
      10.6  Stir coffee ;
      10.7  Add 1 to number of cups poured
    ENDWHILE
11. Turn off machine ;
```

Assessing the Result

> Does this solution work, that is, does it produce the right results? Try it out by giving it to your friend to test.

In the exercise below Solution 5.3 I asked you to try and spot a residual problem with the coffee-brewing aspect of the solution. The difficulty is this: the problem statement asked us to write the actions necessary for making and pouring up to six cups of coffee, adding milk and sugar as necessary. With Solution 5.5 as it stands there is nothing to limit the number of cups we try to make. If Task #1 results in 12 requests for coffee then Tasks #2, #5, and the WHILE loop in Task #10 will accommodate this request. You may say that there is nothing wrong with that because a) the solution still lets us make six cups and b) this version is better because it is even more flexible. That is not the point. The requirement was to produce a solution for making up to six cups. If we provide something that goes against what was asked for then we are not doing our job as programmers properly.[1] This also brings us back to the assumption I made that the pot is big enough to hold six cups of coffee. What if it weren't? Or what if Solution 5.5 were applied to trying to make 30 cups of coffee? In either case we would realize something was wrong when we tried to carry out Task #2 – the water simply would not fit into the machine. The so-called "better" solution is actually worse because it will go wrong when the demands for coffee exceed the capacity of the machine.

---

[1] Such imprecise adherence to specifications is the cause of many defects in programs today. Serious and even life-threatening problems can arise as a result.

Huh?

I still don't see what is wrong with Solution 5.5 as it lets us make the number of coffees we need. You say that it places no restriction on the number of cups we could make. How is this a drawback?

There are two issues here. First, the solution does not precisely and exactly meet the stated requirements. This may sound very picky, but requirements are stated for a reason and just because they do not seem sensible to us as programmers does not mean there is not a strong justification for them. Of course, if you are responsible for gathering the program requirements as well then you can ask your client if they really want a six-cup restriction and, perhaps, you will find out that the restriction was a mistake. But in the absence of further information we must assume the requirement is correct. This leads us to the second issue: it may be that the coffee machine cannot fit more than six cups in its pot. You would notice this when you tried to overfill the machine and would likely stop pouring in water before flooding the kitchen counter. However, this implies the person following the algorithm has common sense or intelligence, neither of which is possessed by the computer we are ultimately hoping to write programs for. Not specifying both the upper and lower bounds of iterations (or other values) can lead to catastrophic failure – see the discussion on assumptions in the Reflections chapter for a real-life example.

Thus, we have another problem. How to solve it? Start with the simpler problem first: continue assuming, for the time being, that the machine is big enough to hold six cups of coffee and look at how to limit the solution so that it cannot make more than six cups. We will consider the more general problem of making an unspecified number of cups of coffee later.

Think about the different ways you could prevent Solution 5.5 from being applied to more than six cups of coffee. Any problem always has more than one solution, so spend some time now writing down some possible ways of solving this problem. Here are some hints to get you started:

- Consider rephrasing the condition in the `WHILE` (Task #10)
- Can you restrict carrying out Tasks #2 through #11 in some way?
- How about putting some conditions on Task #1?

There are several ways to solve this problem. Here is a very simple solution:

Solution 5.6 Restricting the number of cups: first attempt

```
1.   Find out how many cups are required ;
2.   IF (six or fewer cups wanted)
        2.1  Put water for cups required in coffee machine ;
        2.2  etc. etc.
     ENDIF
```

Think Spot

In other words, if asked to make six (or fewer) cups then we follow the existing coffee-making instructions, otherwise we do nothing. It solves the problem but it is rather all-or-nothing. Think about how you would do it in real life. Imagine there are ten guests in your house and you have enough coffee left in the tin to make six cups. You ask if they want coffee and eight of them respond. What do you do? You would not do it the way I have just suggested above and not let anybody have coffee; rather, you would probably give coffee to the first six who asked and tell the other two that they can have something else to drink. We could express this in pseudo-code as:

Solution 5.7 Restricting the number of cups: second attempt

```
1.  Find out how many cups are required ;
2.  IF (more than six cups wanted)
        2.1  limit cups required to six ;
    ENDIF
3.  Put water for number of cups required in coffee machine ;
4.  etc. etc.
```

What we have done is to allow the number of cups required to have any value up to and including six. If more than six people ask for coffee then we simply say that the number of cups required is six. What if the number of cups required were zero? We have already discussed this question in relation to the part of the solution that deals with pouring the individual cups. We noted that the WHILE loop that controlled that part could cope with a zero cups requirement because the action block would simply be ignored in such a case. However, what of the rest of the solution? As it stands, if nobody asks for coffee the solution still requires us to measure water for zero cups (Task #2 in Solution 5.5), put in the filter paper, measure out no coffee, shut the coffee holder, turn on the machine, wait for no coffee to filter through and then turn off the machine. Something is still not right. We need to prevent Task #2 onwards from being carried out if no coffee is wanted. The partial Solution 5.6 above, while wrong for the more-than-six-cups problem,[2] would actually work for the zero cups problem. Putting it all together should make this clearer:

Solution 5.8 A final solution to making six cups of coffee?

```
1.  Find out how many cups are required ;
2.  IF (more than zero cups wanted)
        2.1.  IF (more than six cups wanted)
                  2.1.1  limit cups required to six ;
              ENDIF

        2.2.  Put water for cups required in coffee machine ;
        2.3.  Open coffee holder ;
        2.4.  Put filter paper in machine ;
        2.5.  Measure coffee for number required ;
        2.6.  Put coffee into filter paper ;
        2.7.  Shut the coffee holder ;
        2.8.  Turn on machine ;
        2.9.  Wait for coffee to filter through ;
```

---

[2] By "wrong" I mean that if more than six cups are requested then nobody gets any coffee whereas a better solution would be to give coffee to the first six people who asked.

```
// Process the cups of coffee
2.10. WHILE (cups poured not equal to cups required)
      // Add sugar and milk as necessary
         2.10.1.  Find out how many sugars required ;
         2.10.2.  Find out whether milk required ;
         2.10.3.  WHILE (sugars added not equal to required)
                  2.10.3.1.  Add spoonful of sugar ;
                  2.10.3.2.  Add 1 to number of sugars
                             added ;
                  ENDWHILE
         2.10.4.  IF (white coffee required)
                  2.10.4.1.  Add milk/cream ;
                  ENDIF
         2.10.5.  Pour coffee into mug ;
         2.10.6.  Stir coffee ;
         2.10.7.  Add 1 to number of cups poured
      ENDWHILE
2.11. Turn off machine ;
ENDIF
```

Finding the Variables

Now we must think about the variables of the problem. I asked earlier what values you need to keep track of to solve the problem and which may change each time you make coffee.

Find the variables in the coffee-making solution above. Write down their details in the table below. Give them meaningful *identifiers* (names) as this makes the solution much easier to read and understand. For each variable you identify give a short description that clearly explains what the variable represents. Also, indicate the range of values that the variable might typically represent. There are five variables to find. To get you started I have put in the first one.

Variables for Coffee Making Problem

Identifier (variable's name)	Description	Range of Values
1. coffeesRequired	Holds the number of cups of coffee to be made	0 to 20
2. _____	_____	_____
3. _____	_____	_____
4. _____	_____	_____
5. _____	_____	_____

Think Spot

The easiest variable to find is the one that stands for the number of cups of coffee required. We can call it `coffeesRequired` because that concisely sums up the value that it stands for. What is this variable's purpose? It should store the number of cups of coffee we need to make. Typical values it might take are 3, 4, 8, 10, etc. In the context of making coffee at home it is unlikely ever to go much above 10, but it could. Let's say the range will normally be between 0 and 20. How probable is it that it would be 30, 60, or even 100? Estimating the range of values that a variable is likely to take is important in programming because when it comes to writing the solution in a programming language we will need to specify how much of the computer's memory each variable will take up. Getting this aspect wrong can cause programs to function incorrectly. In the case of the Ariane V rocket, a software malfunction had disastrous consequences (see ASSUMPTIONS). What is important at this stage is to assess the likely *magnitude* of the variable, that is, is it going to be 10 or less, 100 or less, 1000 or less, etc.?

Naming Conventions

Before we continue, consider some naming conventions for variables. In the example above I used the name `coffeesRequired` for the variable to hold the number of cups of coffee. Why not just call it "`coffees required`" rather than running all the words together without spaces? It comes back to what we will have to do when writing up the program in programming language code. The grammatical rules of programming languages generally say that identifiers (variable names) must not have any spaces in them (for reasons we do not need to explore here). How do you make variable names easily readable without spaces? A convention used some years back was to separate out the words within an identifier by using the underscore "_" character. This would give us `coffees_required`. Sometimes the initial letters of each word are capitalized (`Coffees_Required`), or just the first letter (`Coffees_required`). In recent years a different naming style has found favour in the programming community. In this style underscore characters are not used (except as the first character of some special variable types). Instead, all the words of the identifier are run together, but the initial letter of the second and all subsequent words is capitalized. All other letters remain in lower case, hence `coffeesRequired`. This seems to work quite well and people generally find it easy to read.[3] There are no hard rules, merely conventions. However, be aware that some languages (e.g., C, C++, C#, and Java) are *case sensitive* which means that capital and lower case letters are treated differently. This means that `coffeesRequired` and `CoffeesRequired` are **different** names in C, C++, C#, and Java. As long as you

---

[3] This naming convention is called *camel casing*. I'm not sure why it is called that. The best explanation I have seen is that camelCasing looks something like the humps on a camel. For recommendations on which casing styles to use for which types of program information see Microsoft's guidelines at http://msdn.microsoft.com/library/default.asp?url=/library/en-us/cpgenref/html/cpconcapitalizationstyles.asp for more details.

familiarize yourself with the rules of the programming languages you are working in then you will be alright.

I want to make two more points on style before we return to making the coffee. First, we will not use UPPER CASE LETTERS for variable names.[4] For a start, they do not look very nice and C (and C++, C#, and Java) programmers have largely adopted a convention whereby variable names are put in lower case (with initial capitals) with upper case names being reserved for other types of program information. The second point to make is that while single letter identifiers are common in algebra and mathematics, they are not generally considered good practice in programming. This is because variable names such as a, b, and c tell the reader nothing about what the variable stands for. Using identifiers like `numberOfCups` makes it much easier to remember what the variable represents and how it should be used. Some programmers use single letter variables for temporary values, but for now I would simply advise their avoidance.

Returning to the coffee problem, Table 5.1 has my version of the completed variable table:

Table 5.1 **Variable Definitions for the Coffee-making Problem**

Variables for Coffee Making Problem		
Identifier (variable's name)	Description	Range of values
1. `coffeesRequired`	Holds the number of cups of coffee to be made	0 to 20
2. `milkRequired`	Holds the milk preference for one drinker	{Yes, No}
3. `sugarRequired`	Holds the sugar requirements for one drinker	0, 1, 2, 3
4. `coffeesPoured`	Holds the number of cups poured so far	0 to 20
5. `sugarsAdded`	Holds the number of sugars added so far	0, 1, 2, 3

The four other variables I have listed are `milkRequired`, `sugarsRequired`, `coffeesPoured`, and `sugarsAdded`. `milkRequired` is to store whether or not a person wants milk/cream in their coffee. If you ask someone if they want milk/cream and disallow vague answers like "just a spot please" or "yes, lots" they will answer "yes" or "no." Therefore, there are only two possible answers, and so in the "Range of Values" column I have enclosed the two values with braces "{ }" to show that this is the full set of possible values. Contrast this with `coffeesRequired`. Although its indicated range is 0 to 20, it is possible (albeit unlikely) that it could be higher

---

[4] Except, of course, for the COBOL language in which everything is written in upper case characters.

still. Therefore, as 0 to 20 is only an indicative range and does not express the complete set of values that `coffeesRequired` could theoretically represent we have not enclosed it by braces. Also, notice that the values represented by `milkRequired` are not numeric but the yes/no answers to a question. You will see in Chapter 6 it is important in many programming languages to distinguish between different *types* of data. In this case we are noting that some variables are numeric while others (e.g., `milkRequired`) represent another kind of data that stands for the answers to yes/no or true/false-type questions.[5] The variable `sugarsRequired` stands for the number of spoons of sugar wanted by an individual drinker, so for each person its value could be different.

> Why has `milkRequired` not been used to represent the number of cups of coffee in which we need to put milk? Why has `sugarsRequired` been chosen to represent the sugar requirements for an individual drinker rather than the total number of spoons needed for all the cups put together? If you cannot see the answer think about what the alternative would be.

Think Spot

In the case of `sugarsRequired` its value would be 1 (the total number of sugars required by all those who want coffee in Figure 5.1). Now can you see the difficulty? If not, consider `milkRequired`. We cannot use this variable to represent the total milk requirements as the answer is "No" for Dave and "Yes" for Annie – what is the sum of "no" + "yes"? Granted, we could use a numeric variable instead and have `milkRequired` represent the number of cups of coffee in which milk is needed, but what is lost in following such an approach?

The reason these variables stand for the requirements of an individual coffee drinker is that it is individual cups of coffee that we deal with. You do not make a pot of coffee, add milk and sugar to the pot, and then pour the contents into several mugs. Rather, you make a pot and then *for each cup* you add milk and sugar as required. If `sugarsRequired` represented the total number of sugars required how would we know how many to put into each cup? You can see that each time we pour a cup of coffee the values of `milkRequired` and `sugarsRequired` could be different; their values *vary* over the course of making coffee for our guests.

There are two variables remaining: `coffeesPoured` and `sugarsAdded`. Recall that the problem requires us not just to know how many coffees to make and how many sugars to add, but also to keep track of how many coffees we have poured and how many spoons of sugar have been added to each cup. This information is necessary in deciding whether or not to stop pouring coffee and adding sugar. The variables `coffeesPoured` and `sugarsAdded` keep track of this information. `coffeesPoured` has the same value range as `coffeesRequired` and `sugarsAdded` has the same range as `sugarsRequired`.

---

[5] `milkRequired` represents a special type known as Boolean data, named after George Boole (1815–1864). Boole devised a system of algebra (Boolean algebra) in which elements can have one of two possible values (True and False). Operations on the elements are logical (`AND`, `OR`, `NOT`, etc.) rather than arithmetic ($+$, $-$, $\times$, $\div$, etc.).

? **Think Spot**

Now that we have identified the variables, it is worth looking back at Solution 5.8. Task #2.10.3.2 adds 1 to sugarsAdded and Task #2.10.7 adds 1 to coffeesPoured. Think about what this means. Each time you add a spoonful of sugar you add 1 to the variable sugarsAdded in order to keep track of where you are up to; after dealing with each cup of coffee you add 1 to coffeesPoured. Suppose six coffees are required. After pouring one cup and adding two sugars we go back to the WHILE in Task #2.10 and decide whether to continue. The number of cups poured does not yet equal the number required so we go back into the loop and deal with another cup of coffee. Suppose when we reach Task #2.10.1 that the next guest also asks for two sugars. The WHILE that follows (#2.10.3) adds sugars as long the number of sugars added is not equal to the number required. But the variable sugarsAdded still holds the value 2 from the last time we added sugars. In real life we would start counting afresh with each new cup, so we must do the same in the algorithm. Thus, we need a task to set sugarsAdded back to zero each time we start a new cup of coffee. Also, the variable coffeesPoured strictly needs initializing to zero before Task #2.10. See Solution 5.9 below in which I have added these two initialization instructions. Notice also that I have enclosed the variables' identifiers in boxes. The box makes it clear that a variable is being talked about. You should also notice that wherever the value that the variable stands for is mentioned I have replaced it with the variable identifier in a box. For example, in Solution 5.8 Task #1 reads "Find out how many cups are required" while in Solution 5.9 it reads "Find out how many cupsRequired."

Solution 5.9 Coffee making solution with variable initialization

1. Find out how many cupsRequired ;

2. IF (more than zero cupsRequired)
   2.1. IF (more than six cups wanted)
         2.1.1. limit cupsRequired to six ;
         ENDIF
   2.2. Put water for cups required in coffee machine ;
   2.3. Open coffee holder ;
   2.4. Put filter paper in machine ;
   2.5. Measure coffee for number required ;
   2.6. Put coffee into filter paper ;
   2.7. Shut the coffee holder ;
   2.8. Turn on machine ;
   2.9. Wait for coffee to filter through ;

   // **Prepare the cups of coffee**
   2.10. Initialize number of cupsPoured to zero ;
   2.11. WHILE (cupsPoured not equal to cupsRequired)

         // **Add sugar and milk as necessary**
         2.11.1. Initialize sugarsAdded to zero ;
         2.11.2. Find out how many sugarsRequired ;
         2.11.3. Find out whether milkRequired ;

```
            2.11.4.  WHILE (sugarsAdded not equal to
                     sugarsRequired)
                        2.11.4.1.  Add spoonful of sugar ;
                        2.11.4.2.  Add 1 to number of
                                   sugarsAdded ;
                     ENDWHILE
            2.11.5.  IF (white coffee required)
                        2.11.5.1.  Add milk/cream ;
                     ENDIF
            2.11.6.  Pour coffee into mug ;
            2.11.7.  Stir coffee ;
            2.11.8.  Add 1 to number of cupsPoured
         ENDWHILE
    2.12.  Turn off machine ;
ENDIF
```

Problems Involving Arithmetic

Now you are wired on caffeine,[6] we will leave the coffee machine alone for a while and consider a different problem that involves a little more arithmetic than counting spoons of sugar (though not much more).

Paul's Premier Parcels (PPP) is a delivery company. Each morning the parcels to be delivered for that day are lined up on a conveyor belt in the warehouse by the warehouse staff. The belt takes the parcels to the loading bay where a van waits. The loading crew weigh each parcel to see if it will fit on the van. If so, they put the parcel on the van and wait for the next parcel to arrive. As soon as a parcel arrives that would take the van over its maximum payload the van door is closed, the van sent off on its rounds and another empty van is brought up. The van is not kept waiting to see if any lighter parcels that will fit show up. This activity continues until all the parcels have been loaded onto vans. Happily, there are always enough vans for the waiting parcels. PPP wants to install a weighing machine on the conveyor belt linked to a computer so that the process of weighing parcels can be speeded up. Each van has the same maximum payload of 750 kg, and PPP only accepts parcels up to 120 kg in weight. After all the parcels have been loaded the company's managing director wants to know how many vans were needed that day and what was the heaviest payload that was sent out.

> Following the *HTTLAP* strategy, understand the problem and devise a plan to solve it.

Where do we begin with this? The thing you absolutely **do not do** yet is write down the solution; you must first make sure the problem is well understood. Starting with Step 1 "understanding the problem," work through the questions in

---

[6] Grief! We have assumed nobody has asked for decaffeinated coffee. How would you deal with that?

the *HTTLAP* strategy to make sure you understand what is required. If you cannot understand the problem then it is best to discover this now so that you can do something about it. You do not have to use the structured Q&A dialogue that I have used previously, but make sure you do write down the answers rather than just making mental notes. Mental notes have a way of not being particularly well formed (as well as slipping away). It is when you try to write something down that you realize how well you understand it. Here is my dialogue with *HTTLAP*.

Understanding the Problem

Q. What are you being asked to do?

A. Load vans with parcels.

Q. What is required?

A. Parcels need to be loaded onto vans until the vans are full. Each van has a maximum capacity (750 kg) and there are no parcels heavier than 120 kg. To decide whether a parcel will fit on a van it is weighed. To report on how many vans were used and which one had the heaviest cargo.

Q. What is the unknown?

A. The number of vans and parcels. I also need to know how to decide whether a parcel will fit. It has something to do with weighing it, and the van's capacity clearly features in the decision. The manager wants to know how many vans are needed and which one had the heaviest load, so I need to find out this information too.

Q. Can the problem be better expressed by drawing a diagram or a picture?

FIGURE 5.3 **A van with some parcels**

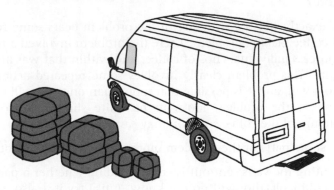

Q. What are the principal parts of the problem?

A. The parcels, their weights, the vans, the maximum payload, a single van load of parcels.

Q. **Are there several parts to the problem?**

A. Yes. Each van needs to be loaded. This involves weighing parcels and calculating whether they will fit. There is also a problem involving reporting back to the manager.

Q. **Have you made any assumptions?**

A. It wasn't spelled out in the problem description, but I am assuming that the physical size of the parcels does not matter. Only the weights of the parcels was mentioned, so is it safe to assume that as long as the van can take the weight of a parcel that there will always be the physical room to accommodate it?

Q. **What can you do about the assumptions?**

A. I should really go back to PPP and get an answer. Here is the question I put to PPP:

"I am working on your van-loading problem and you have not said whether or not the physical size of the parcels is a factor. That is, is it possible that even though the weight of a parcel can be accommodated that it will be too large to fit into the available space?"

And here is their answer:

"Good question. It has never happened before as we tend to deliver mostly consumer electricals which never get too big. Assume it's OK."

Once the problem has been understood we can proceed to devising a plan to solve it.

Devising a Plan to Solve the Problem

Q. **Have you solved this problem before/is it similar to one you have solved before?**

A. Not exactly, but the structure of the problem bears some resemblance to the last coffee making problem. There the problem involved a repeating structure to process individual cups of coffee, and within that was another loop to add sugars. This problem clearly involves some repeated actions to load parcels onto a van, and it is possible that more than one van will be involved, so the shape of the problem looks to be quite similar. Borrowing the outline structure of the coffee solution may save some time here.

Q. **Are some parts of the problem more easily solved than others?**

A. Counting the vans sent out is easy. Deciding whether a parcel will fit sounds more difficult, though I do not know until I try it. I also wonder how to tell which van had the heaviest payload.

Q. **If the problem is too hard, can you solve a simpler version of it, or a related problem?**

A. I think I'll try solving the problem of loading an individual van before tackling the rest of the problem.

Q. Does restating the problem help? Try restating it in a different language.

A. No.

Q. Did you make use of all the information in the problem statement?

A. Yes, I think so.

Q. Can you satisfy all the conditions of the problem?

A. Yes.

Q. Have you left anything out?

A. No, I do not think so.

Carrying Out the Plan

Write down the basic sequence of actions to solve the problem of loading a single van. For now, hide the detail of dealing with multiple vans and concentrate on a single van.

What are the actions and decisions involved? Perhaps as a rough sketch you first came up with something like Figure 5.4.

FIGURE 5.4   **Loading a van**

weigh parcel

if parcel fits on van

  add parcel to van

endif

despatch van

Figure 5.4 reveals some of the structure of the problem. Each parcel needs to be weighed to see if it will fit on a van. If it does, then it is put on the van. I have drawn a line back up to "weigh parcel" to indicate that this is a repeated action (there is more than one parcel). At some point a parcel will not fit so the van can be despatched to make its deliveries. I have drawn another line to indicate that we will likely need more than one van to carry all the parcels, though we are ignoring that complication for now. Although this is not a fully worked out solution it helps me to see the things that need to be done and to recognize that some actions must be repeated. There are some unanswered questions though, such as how do we know if a parcel fits on the van, and are the actions in the right order?

? Think Spot

At this point many beginners have difficulty in writing down the solution. They can find it very hard to move from the conceptual understanding of the problem to being able to express the solution in a clear, precise, well-structured, and unambiguous manner. If you are experiencing this right now, do not worry. It is not that you are stupid, but that you are not used to thinking in this way. Take a step back and think about how we would approach the problem if we were one of the parcel loaders in the warehouse.

You have been tasked with the job of loading parcels on to vans. How do you do it? Consider this for a minute or two. Walk through the process in your mind. Imagine yourself standing at the loading bay taking parcels off the conveyor belt. There is an empty van standing in front of you, and you have just weighed the first parcel. What do you do next, and why? When do you stop loading parcels and tell the van to drive off? When you have a clear picture of the process in your mind, write it down.

I visualized the problem by imagining parcels of different weights coming down a conveyor belt (see Figure 5.5 below).

FIGURE 5.5   **Parcels on the conveyor belt**

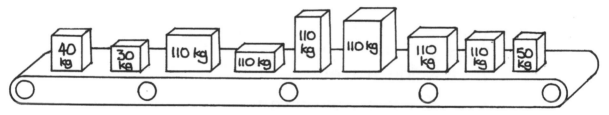

Say the first parcel weighed 40 kg (Figure 5.5). The van is empty, and can carry a total payload of 750 kg, so this parcel will fit. I load the parcel and fetch the next one. This one weighs 30 kg. Will it fit? Yes. Why? Because there is room on the van. How do I know? The van can take 750 kg and it is currently holding 40 kg, which means that there is room for another 710 kg. This parcel is only 30 kg, which will take the van's load up to 70 kg, which is well below 750 kg. The next parcel weighs 110 kg. Adding it to the van will take its payload up to 180 kg, so I know there is room for it, so on it goes. The next five parcels also weigh 110 kg each taking the van's load up to 730 kg. The next parcel weighs 50 kg. That would take the van over its maximum weight so I cannot load it on this van. Therefore, I despatch the van, noting that it went out with a 730-kg load. I bring on the next van, and start the process again with the 50-kg parcel. I have written this down as a sequence of actions in Solution 5.10 below. At this stage I am only thinking of the overall sequence and have not addressed any selections or iterations that may be present.

Solution 5.10 Loading a van

```
 1.   Weigh first parcel (40 Kilos) ;
 2.   Check that parcel will fit (yes) ;
 3.   Load parcel on van ;
 4.   Weigh next parcel (30 kg) ;
 5.   Check that parcel will fit (yes) ;
 6.   Load parcel on van ;
 7.   Weigh next parcel (110 kg) ;
 8.   Check that parcel will fit (yes) ;
 9.   Load parcel on van ;
10.   Weigh next parcel (110 kg) ;
11.   Check that parcel will fit (yes) ;
12.   Load parcel on van ;
13.   Weigh next parcel (110 kg) ;
14.   Check that parcel will fit (yes) ;
15.   Load parcel on van ;
16.   Weigh next parcel (110 kg) ;
17.   Check that parcel will fit (yes) ;
18.   Load parcel on van ;
19.   Weigh next parcel (110 kg) ;
20.   Check that parcel will fit (yes) ;
21.   Load parcel on van ;
22.   Weigh next parcel (110 kg) ;
23.   Check that parcel will fit (yes) ;
24.   Load parcel on van ;
25.   Weigh next parcel (50 kg) ;
26.   Check that parcel will fit (no) ;
27.   Despatch van ;
28.   Make note of van's payload ;
```

Think Spot

That is quite a long list, but notice that after weighing the first parcel (Task #1) there is a repeated sequence of actions: Check the parcel will fit, load it on the van, weigh the next parcel. In other words, as long as parcels will fit on the van keep loading and weighing parcels. When a parcel will not fit on the van, stop the process and despatch the van. *HTTLAP* Step 3 asks whether we have any actions or blocks of actions that must be repeated. Clearly we do, and we saw in the coffee making problem how to express the repetition formally with a WHILE structure. The WHILE causes a block of actions to be followed while (as long as) some condition is met. What is the condition here? We said above that as long as there is room on the van we should keep loading and weighing parcels. We can express this using a WHILE structure.

Solution 5.11 Loading a van with a WHILE

```
 1.   Weigh first parcel ;
 2.   WHILE (room on van)
          2.1.   Load parcel on van ;
          2.2.   Weigh next parcel ;
       ENDWHILE
```

```
3.  Despatch van ;
4.  Make note of van's payload ;
```

Why has the "check parcel will fit on van" action been removed?

Because this check is done by the WHILE. The WHILE says "while parcels will fit on the van, load it and fetch the next parcel". The condition belonging to the WHILE determines whether to carry on loading the van or not. We know we must stop loading when we get a parcel that will not fit, so the condition can be expressed to make this clear....

 **Think Spot**

Looking at Task #2, how do we know if there is room on the van? We solved this problem above when we visualized the process. There is room for a parcel if the weight of the parcel when added to the current load on the van does not take the total van payload over its maximum limit, that is, the parcel's weight + the van's payload is less than or equal to the van's capacity. In the example above, when the van's load was 730 kg the next parcel weighed 50 kg. This gives us the question "is 50 + 730 less than or equal to 750?" The answer is no because 50 + 730 = 780, so we stop loading the van. We could write this out as:

```
WHILE (van payload + parcel's weight less than or equal to capacity)
```

We can use this to refine the solution thus:

Solution 5.12 Adding the condition to the WHILE

```
1.  Weigh first parcel ;
2.  WHILE (payload + parcel weight less than or equal to capacity)
        2.1.  Load parcel on van ;
        2.2.  Weigh next parcel ;
    ENDWHILE
3.  Despatch van ;
4.  Make note of van's payload ;
```

Is this solution sufficient to allow a computer (an idiot) to correctly load a van?

Because we are used to keeping track of things in our heads automatically, you may not have spotted the problem with Solution 5.12. The WHILE loop asks whether the van's current payload plus the current parcel weight is within the van's capacity. How do we know what the van's current payload is? In the visualization above we kept a running total updating the payload by adding the weight of each loaded parcel. If keeping a running total is required to solve the problem, we must write it down. For an empty van the payload will start at zero, so an instruction to initialize the current van's payload is needed. Each time we load a parcel we need an instruction to add that parcel's weight to the payload. That way the condition in the WHILE can be properly tested:

Solution 5.13 Updating of payload

```
1.   Initialize payload to zero ;
2.   Weigh first parcel ;
3.   WHILE (payload + parcel weight less than or equal to capacity)
         3.1.   Load parcel on van ;
         3.2.   Add parcel weight to payload ;
         3.3.   Weigh next parcel ;
     ENDWHILE
4.   Despatch van ;
```

Why has the task "Make note of van's payload" been removed?

Now we can consider what variables are to be used.

Identify and write down the variables needed for Solution 5.13. Remember to write down their names, an explanation of their purpose, and an indicative range of possible values.

Table 5.2 lists the variables I have identified.

Table 5.2   Variables for Solution 5.13

Variables for Van Loading Problem		
Identifier (variable's name)	Description	Range of Values
1. `parcelWeight`	Stores the weight of one parcel	{1 to 120}
2. `payload`	Stores the weight of the total load on the van	{0 to `capacity`}
3. `capacity`	Stores the maximum payload of a van	750

`parcelWeight` is used to hold the weight of a single parcel. We have been told by the company that they do not accept parcels heavier than 120 kg, so the possible range of values is between 1 and 120 kg. We have also been told that no parcel will ever exceed 120 kg,[7] so I have used braces {} to indicate that this is the

---

[7] I have assumed that any weights should be rounded off to the next highest kilogram to avoid parcels of, say 900 g or 400 g, being treated as 0 kg in weight. A better solution, perhaps, would be to deal in grams rather than kilograms. The maximum weight of a parcel would then be 120,000 g, and the capacity of a van 750,000 g and it gets around the problem of dealing with fractions of a kilogram.

range of all possible values for this variable. However, be aware that the requirements of the problem could change in the future to allow heavier parcels so this restriction may need to be revisited. `payload` is used to hold the weight of the total load carried in a van and its value can range from zero (an empty van) up to the maximum `capacity` (in this case, 750 kg). I have used `capacity` in the definition of `payload`'s range of values because `capacity` holds the maximum value of `payload`'s range. Using these identifiers I have rewritten Solution 5.13 as Solution 5.14 below to show where the variables are used.

Solution 5.14 Van loading with variables added

```
1.   Initialize payload to zero ;
2.   Get first parcelWeight ;
3.   WHILE (payload + parcelWeight less than or equal to capacity)
        3.1.   Load parcel on van ;
        3.2.   Add parcelWeight to payload ;
        3.3.   Get next parcelWeight ;
     ENDWHILE
4.   Despatch van ;
```

Assessing the Result

Having produced a solution to the problem of loading a van we should assess it to see if it is correct and that we understand it. One thing to notice is how similar the solution to loading a van is to the solution of adding sugar to a cup of coffee (Solution 4.8). After a while you should start to recognize common problem structures that can be solved with a common solution design.[8] Does the solution work for the problem of loading a single van with parcels? You can simulate the situation by cutting out pieces of paper each with a different weight written on it to represent the parcels (a physical model of Figure 5.5). An envelope or a box can stand for a van. Finally, you could draw a table with the names of the variables as column headings as in Figure 5.6.

Work through the instructions in Solution 5.14 updating the table of variables as you go.

Figure 5.6 shows the table filled in for the first two parcels from Figure 5.5. Each time you take a parcel, ask whether the condition in the WHILE is true. If so, put the parcel (paper) in the van (envelope), and write down the new value of the van's payload. Take the next parcel and go back to the WHILE. Keep going as long as parcels will fit. Once you have worked through the solution shuffle the parcels up and try again to see if the solution still works. Once you are happy with it, give it to your friend, explain the problem and see if they can follow the solution to produce the correct results (a properly loaded van).

---

[8] Both Solution 4.8 and Solution 5.14 use a special structure called a *read-ahead loop*. This (along with other loop constructs) is dealt with in Chapter 6.

FIGURE 5.6   **Table of values for van-loading simulation**

capacity	parcelWeight	payload
750		0
750	40	40
750	30	70

Loading More Than One Van

When devising a plan to solve the problem, I said I would start with the simpler problem of loading a single van. It is time to finish the job and solve the problem of loading all the parcels onto (possibly) multiple vans. How does the problem look now that we have solved the subproblem of loading a single van? The problem statement asked us to load all the day's parcels onto vans and to bring on a new van as soon as a parcel came along that would put the current van over its maximum payload. Furthermore, the manager wants to know how many vans were sent out and which one had the heaviest load.

 **Think Spot**

It is clear that the manager is interested in vans – loading them, counting them, and finding out which is the heavier. We have solved the problem of loading a single van, so now we must look at loading more than one, counting them, and recording their weights. At this point you may like to go back to the coffee-making Solution 5.9 to see how that solution was structured. Does Solution 5.9 give you any clues as to how you might go about dealing with this problem? Questions from *HTTLAP* should help you clarify your thinking.

Q. What are the principal parts of the problem? What is the unknown?

The principal parts of the problem seem to be parcels and vans; we want to know how many vans were used and what their weights are. The unknown each time is how many parcels there are and, consequently, how many vans will be needed. The main ingredient of the problem appears to be the parcel; we must keep fetching and loading vans as long as we have parcels that need delivering.

Devising a Plan to Solve the Problem

We could visualize the overall problem structure thus:

```
WHILE (parcels to be delivered)
Load parcels on to vans, keeping count of the number and weight of
vans used ;
ENDWHILE
Report on number of vans sent out ;
Report on heaviest payload ;
```

That is, load the vans as long as there are parcels to be sent out, tell the manager how many vans were sent, and tell the manager the weight of the heaviest van. We have already solved the problem of how to load an individual van, so we just need to keep repeating this van loading as long as there are still parcels to load.

Write down an outline solution to the problem using the above structure and Solution 5.14. Remember, if you are finding it difficult to start, think about a similar problem you have already solved (Solution 5.9).

How did you get on? Perhaps you have something similar to Solution 5.15.

Solution 5.15 Loading multiple vans – first attempt

```
1.  WHILE (conveyor not empty)
      1.1.  Initialize payload to zero ;
      1.2.  Get first parcelWeight ;
      1.3.  WHILE (payload + parcelWeight less than or equal to
            capacity)
              1.3.1.  Load parcel on van ;
              1.3.2.  Add parcelWeight to payload ;
              1.3.3.  Get next parcelWeight ;
            ENDWHILE
      1.4.  Despatch van ;
    ENDWHILE
2.  Report numberOfVans used ;
3.  Report heaviestVan sent
```

It is not a complete solution and, as we will see in a moment, it has some serious defects. But do you see how the overall structure of the solution fits the problem? The outer WHILE (Task #1) says to keep going as long as there are parcels on the conveyor belt. What do we do when we have got the parcels? We load them onto vans. How do we load them onto vans? We know how to do that – take an empty van and put on parcels until it can take no more then despatch it (Tasks #1.3 to #1.4). But what happens next? The van-loading part ends with Task #1.4 (despatching the van) but then comes the ENDWHILE to close the action block for the first WHILE. We test the first WHILE condition again, that is, we see if there are still parcels on the conveyor belt. If so, we need to bring on and load another van, so we go back into the loop. And so on. Or is it? Can you see how this nested structure allows us to use the solution for loading a single van over and over again until there are no more parcels? Only when there are no more parcels to load do we go on to do Tasks #2 and #3 (reporting back to the manager).

Think Spot

Assessing the Result

I said that Solution 5.15 has some deficiencies. See if you can identify what the defects are. If you need a hint think about:

■ The variables numberOfVans and heaviestVan. How will they get their values?

- The condition for the WHILE in Task #1.3: what happens when loading a van if the conveyor belt is empty?

- The position of Task #1.2 and Task #1.3.3. Task #1.3.3 gets a new parcel. If it will not fit on the van then the van is despatched and the WHILE in Task #1 is begun again which causes Task #1.2 to be obeyed again. What is the implication of this?

 ? Think Spot

Think about these issues for a little while and do not read any further until you have an answer or are completely mystified.

Take the question of Tasks #2 and #3 first. I have introduced new variables to hold the number of vans despatched and the weight of the heaviest van. How should numberOfVans be given a value, that is, how is its value calculated? Each time a van is despatched the number of vans used should go up by 1. So, a simple counting mechanism is needed, but where?

> Identify the point in Solution 5.15 at which **numberOfVans** should be increased by 1. Also, consider whether it needs an initial (starting) value.

Adding a new Task #1.5 "Add 1 to numberOfVans ;" deals with the problem of keeping count of the vans. Each time a van is sent out the counter is increased by 1. In addition, numberOfVans needs to start at zero so that after the first van is despatched its value changes to 1. Therefore, a new instruction is needed before Task #1 to set numberOfVans to zero.

Consider now how to keep track of the heaviest van. It is not as simple a job as keeping count of numbers of vans, so we would do well to treat it as a problem in its own right and use the advice from *HTTLAP*. First then, is to understand the problem.

Q. What is required?

A. We need to record the largest payload that was sent out.

How would you tell which van had the heaviest payload? What would you do? There are several ways we could go about this. We know the weight of a van's load when we despatch it because we store this information in the variable payload. One solution would be to write down each van's payload as it goes out and at the end read down the list to see which one is the larger. Of course, this means storing a number of payload values. If we sent out fifty vans we would need space to write down fifty payload values. In addition, when it comes to writing this solution up as a real computer program we would have to set aside memory in the computer to handle all these values. It is not especially hard to do[9]

---

[9] We do not know in advance how many vans there will be, so we need a way of storing a variable number of values. If we knew the number could never exceed a certain value we could use a programming object called an array. If we do not know the maximum number of van journeys then we would need something more flexible such as a linked list or a vector (Java). These concepts are dealt with in the expanded version of this book (*How to think like a programmer: Problem solving and program design solutions for the bewildered*).

KISS ▶

but there is a cleaner way that needs only the variables already identified in Solution 5.15. A principle I was taught when I first learned programming was the KISS! Rule. KISS! Stands for Keep It Simple, Stupid! and the point is that complex programs are hard to understand (and thus to maintain) while simple programs are simple to understand. We should always strive to keep our solutions as simple and as uncluttered as possible. That makes them easier to understand, and hence makes it more likely that we will find any defects quicker (and probably make fewer mistakes in the first place). Sometimes this means writing code that is not as computationally efficient as it might be, but unless shaving a few microseconds off the execution time is critical the extra comprehensibility of the code is worth the price.[10]

Try yourself to work out what this cleaner solution is. How could you keep track of the heaviest van load without recording the weight of every van? Each time you send a van out you could ask whether it is the heaviest one. You cannot tell until you have dealt with all the vans, but you *can* decide whether it is the heaviest van you have seen *so far*. All you have to do is keep asking of each van whether it is the heaviest one so far. If it is, you write down its weight. If the next van is even heavier then you cross out the earlier value and write in the new one, and so on. When you have sent out all the vans you will have a figure that holds the weight of the heaviest van despatched. Solution 5.15 already has a variable to hold this value: heaviestVan. What is the sequence of actions necessary to find the heaviest van? After carrying out Task #1.4 in Solution 5.15 we know the weight of the current van. How can we tell if it is the heaviest van so far? Think about this yourself now.

Think Spot

If we compare its weight with the heaviest value we wrote down last time we found a heavy van we can tell if this one is heavier. Write down a solution to this problem now.

Because this solution requires asking a question about the weight of a van you should have spotted that we need to use an IF structure. It should look something like this:

Solution 5.16 Finding the heaviest van

```
IF ( payload more than heaviestVan )
    Assign value of payload to heaviestVan ;
ENDIF
```

Solution 5.16 uses the condition in the IF to see whether the weight of the current van is heavier than that of the heaviest van found so far. If it is, then the condition is true so the action block is carried out and the value of heaviestVan is overwritten by the current value of payload. This can be inserted into

---

[10] Of course, processor-intensive applications such as digital signal processing or complex mathematics may just require the most efficient code possible. In those situations the programmer needs to ensure that the hard-to-understand-but-efficient code is **really** well documented with thorough explanations of how it works.

Solution 5.15 after Task #1.4. Is that enough to solve the problem? Not quite. After loading the first van we try to compare its payload with heaviestVan, but what are we comparing it to? There have not been any vans loaded and despatched yet, so heaviestVan will not have a value. This means heaviestVan must be initialized to something before we start loading the vans.

> Decide what value heaviestVan should be initialized to.

A van is the heaviest one so far if its payload is *more than* the value of heaviestVan. After filling up the first van it will obviously be the heaviest one so far as no other vans have been loaded. Suppose the first parcel weighed 1 kg and the second one weighed 750 kg. The second would overload the van so its total payload would be 1 kg. For it to be the heaviest van, its payload of 1 kg must be more than the starting value of heaviestVan. Thus, we can initialize heaviestVan with any value less than 1. Would zero be an appropriate initial value? Where should the initialization instruction go?

The initialization needs to be done before any vans are loaded and the van loading starts with the WHILE in Task #1. Therefore, the initialization of heaviestVan should be the first task in the solution.

Fixing the *WHILE* loop

Earlier I asked you to consider the condition for the WHILE in Task #1.3 (Solution 5.15) – what happens when the conveyor belt becomes empty during the loading of a van? Of course, the conveyor belt must become empty sometime otherwise there would be an infinite number of parcels. The condition for Task #1.3's WHILE is currently only concerned with whether a van is full. If we interpreted the condition literally (which a computer would) we will get into trouble because at some point we will run out of parcels at which point parcelWeight cannot be updated with a new value. Therefore, we need to extend the condition in Task #1.3 to deal with this situation. The outer WHILE (Task #1) has a condition that will be false when the conveyor belt is empty which causes the loop to terminate. We need to add this condition to the one in Task #1.3. We can make a compound (multi-part) condition thus:

WHILE (payload + parcelWeight less than or equal to capacity) AND (conveyor not empty)

Compound ▶
conditions

The keyword "AND" has been used to join two conditions. This means that **both** the conditions must be true if the action block of the WHILE is to be carried out. When either one of them turns false (when a parcel will not fit or we run out of parcels) then the loop will terminate. When a parcel arrives that will not fit we stop the loop and despatch the van. Or, if we are loading a van when the last parcel arrives the loop will also terminate.

There is one final defect in Solution 5.15. I said earlier that there is a problem with the placement of Task #1.2. Task #1.3.3 gets a new parcel. If it will not fit on the van then the van is despatched and the WHILE in Task #1 is begun again which causes Task #1.2 to be obeyed again. What is the implication of this? It means that when Task #1.3.3 fetches a parcel that will not fit on the van we effectively lose that parcel because when we enter the loop again we carry out Task #1.2 which fetches another parcel. Thus, we are not dealing with the parcel that would not fit before getting the next one to start the van-loading process over again. If you cannot grasp this, then trace through the solution with the envelopes and parcels technique from before (Figure 5.6). How can we solve this problem? Think about the purpose of Task #1.2. It is to get the first parcel, that is, the parcel that is needed to start the whole van-loading sequence going. If you think about it there is only one **first** parcel; it is the first one on the conveyor belt at the start of the day. As we only need to fetch the first parcel once all we need to do is move Task #1.2 immediately before the WHILE in Task #1. That way we have the first parcel and go into the loops. After despatching the first van and going back into the loops again we still have hold of the parcel that was fetched with Task #1.3.3. Try it out to see for yourself.

Assigning Values

We are almost ready to write out the revised solution but first I want to introduce a new pseudo-code notation. Up till now we have been writing things like "initialize payload to zero" and "assign value of payload to heaviestVan." It is time to introduce a more formal symbol that represents giving a value to something. It is called the *assignment symbol* and it looks like this:

heaviestVan ← zero ;

Assignment ▶
symbol

The "←" symbol is an instruction to assign the value of the thing on its right to the variable on its left. If we had a piece of paper with a column heading for each variable (as in Figure 5.6) then the instruction would mean we write down a new value for the variable on the left-hand side of the ←. Strictly speaking, what we should do is erase the current value of the variable and replace it by the new one, for that is what the assignment symbol means: it is an instruction to overwrite the value of the variable on its left with the value on its right. The right-hand side could be a simple value like "zero", "2", "20", etc., or it could be the name of a variable, or it could even be an arithmetic expression, such as "2 + 3" or even "payload + parcelWeight." When a variable appears on the right of the "←" symbol, then the value it stands for is used. So, the task

payload ← payload + parcelWeight ;

is an instruction to add the value of parcelWeight to payload. You can read it as "the value of payload becomes the current value of payload plus parcelWeight." That is, the value of the expression on the right hand side of the "←" is calculated and is written into the variable on the left. Below is the complete solution to the van-loading problem which uses this new assignment symbol.

Solution 5.17 Complete van-loading solution

```
1.  capacity ← 750 ;
2.  numberOfVans ← zero ;
3.  heaviestVan ← zero ;
4.  Get first parcelWeight ;
```

```
5.   WHILE (conveyor not empty)
        5.1.   payload ← zero ;
        5.2.   WHILE (payload + parcelWeight less than or equal to
               capacity) AND (conveyor NOT empty)
                  5.2.1.   Load parcel on van ;
                  5.2.2.   payload ← payload + parcelWeight ;
                  5.2.3.   Get next parcelWeight ;
               ENDWHILE
        5.3.   Despatch van ;
        5.4.   numberOfVans ← numberOfVans + 1 ;
        5.5.   IF ( payload more than heaviestVan )
                  5.5.1.   heaviestVan ← payload ;
               ENDIF
     ENDWHILE
6.   Report numberOfVans used ;
7.   Report heaviestVan sent ;
```

If you examine Solution 5.17 you will notice that Tasks #1 to #4 deal with initialization: they set the starting values for the variables that need them and fetch the first parcel weight. Notice an extra task to assign a value to capacity (Task #1). This is done so that the comparison in Task #5.2 can be made; if capacity is not given a value then how will we know whether the van's current load has exceeded that capacity? Task #1 is a simple assignment that moves the value 750 into capacity. Task #5.2.2 updates payload by adding its current value to that of parcelWeight and moving the result back into payload overwriting what was there before. Using the same technique, Task #5.4 adds 1 to numberOfVans. Task #5.5.1 copies the value of payload into heaviestVan.

Assessing the Result

Having produced a solution we must again assess it.

Use the envelopes and paper parcels technique with the set of parcel weights in Table 5.3 to simulate the loading process by following the algorithm in Solution 5.17. At the end of it you should be able to report the number of vans sent out and the weight of the heaviest payload.

Table 5.3   **Sample Parcel Weights**

Parcel Weights for Van-loading Simulation

50, 90, 120, 110, 40,
30, 85, 85, 110, 100,
100, 100, 100, 120, 90,
50, 85, 120, 40

If you followed the solution properly you should have used three vans and found the heaviest payload to be 745 kg (the second van load).

**Limitations ▶
versus defects**

It is useful at this stage to make a note of any limitations in the solution. A limitation is not the same thing as a defect. A defect stops the solution from meeting its requirements. A limitation is simply an acknowledgement of the boundaries of the solution. That means that we can specify under what conditions it should work and, in what situations it will not work. This is very useful to know because if the situation changes (e.g., the parcel size increases) then we can more easily see what aspects of the solution need to be changed.

One limitation is that the solution is written under the assumption that no parcel will ever weigh more than the capacity of a van. There is no reason why this assumption should remain true for ever. It is possible that a number of smaller vans with much smaller capacities could be added to the fleet. In this case the solution would need to be amended so that the capacity of each van is recorded before it is loaded.

Another limitation is that no attempt is made to optimize the parcel loading. As soon as a parcel is encountered that will not fit on a van the van is despatched. A more efficient (and environmentally friendly) approach would be to try and organize the parcels into batches each of which is as close to the van capacity as possible. But this is a different problem and not the one we were asked to solve.

There is one more observation to make about the solution and it is to do with the conditions that test whether the conveyor belt is empty. You may have wondered how the solution works when the last package is fetched off the belt. For instance, take the situation where there is only one parcel on the belt. Task #4 fetches this parcel and then the condition in Task #5 asks whether the belt is empty. If not, the loop will be entered and the parcel is loaded onto the van. Strictly speaking, after we have lifted the parcel then the belt is indeed empty which would mean that the last parcel on the belt is never delivered. I have deliberately left the solution as it is because the way this problem is solved is dependent on which programming language this algorithm is eventually translated into. If the parcel weights were stored on a computer file and a program were written in C to read these weights, then the C instruction that would correspond to Task #5 would not result in the belt/file being deemed to be empty. This is because computer files have a special marker at the end after all the data and it is not until this special marker is read by the program that the file would be judged to be empty. So, the translation of this solution to the computer domain may require some changes, depending on the language being used. For instance, Task #5 could be implemented by a test to look ahead to see if the belt is empty, and if not, the parcel is fetched.

Describing What We Have Learned

It is important to reflect on the lessons learned during the problem solving process, so let's think about what this problem has taught us. Again, *HTTLAP* has some guiding questions.

Q. **What did you learn from this exercise? What do you know now that you didn't know before you started?**

A. I have extended my knowledge of ways to use WHILEs and IFs to control decision making. For example, knowing when to stop loading a van is based on the result of some arithmetic. I'm beginning to see how arithmetic is an important part of solving problems. Also, I have developed my understanding of variables and how they can be assigned values.

Q. Were there any aspects of the problem that caused particular difficulty? If so, do you think you would know how to tackle them if you met something similar in the future?

A. Finding the heaviest van was a challenge. But this technique could easily be applied to problems such as finding the lightest van, or an employee with the most commendations, etc. There was a nasty problem with losing parcels in between the loops. The solution that worked for a single van didn't work when applied to multiple vans; I had to move the instruction to get the first parcel weight. This was a hard defect to spot and it was easiest to find during a dry run. It shows me that what seems to be right on paper often turns out not to work when the strict interpretation used by a computer is applied. Common sense would have made a real person not lose track of the parcels, but a computer can only do exactly what it is told.

Think Spot

You will have learned other lessons from this exercise so take some time to reflect upon them now and write them down.

Documenting the Solution

The final stage in *HTTLAP* is to document the solution. We should produce an annotated solution like we did at the end of Chapter 4. But first we need to document all the variables in the solution. The last time we did this we only had three variables (Table 5.2).

Complete that table now by adding in the remaining variables.

The solution is given as Table 5.4 below.

Table 5.4   **Variables for Van-loading Solution**

Variables for Van Loading Problem		
Identifier (variable's name)	Description	Range of Values
1. `parcelWeight`	Stores the weight of one parcel	{1 to 120}
2. `payload`	Stores the weight of the total load on the van	{0 to `capacity`}
3. `capacity`	Stores the maximum payload of a van	750
4. `numberOfVans`	Stores the number of vans used to deliver the parcels	0 to 20
5. `heaviestVan`	Holds the value of the heaviest payload	{0 to `capacity`}

Table 5.4 has two more variables than Table 5.2: `numberOfVans` and `heaviestVan`. Because we do not know the maximum number of vans that could be sent out (the size of the fleet was never specified, and anyway it could change as vans are bought and sold) I have provided an indicative range of 0 to 20. The range starts at zero because it is entirely possible that on a given day there could be no parcels to deliver and so no vans would be sent out. `heaviestVan` has the same range of values as `payload` because it is used to hold a copy of a `payload` value. We can now produce a documented solution which is given below as Solution 5.18.

Solution 5.18 Annotated van-loading solution

Instructions for loading vans with parcels

These instructions will allow you to load an unspecified number of parcels onto an unspecified number of vans. The load capacity of a single van is 750 kg and no parcel will weigh more than 120 kg. Parcels are taken off the conveyor belt and loaded onto vans. A van is judged to be full when a parcel is encountered that would take it over its maximum payload. At this point the van is despatched and an empty one brought up. A report is required at the end detailing the number of vans used and the weight of the heaviest payload.

```
// ******************************************
// Instructions for loading vans
// Written by Paul Vickers, June 2007
// ******************************************
// Initialize variables
1.    capacity ← 750 ;
2.    numberOfVans ← zero ;
3.    heaviestVan ← zero ;
4.    Get first parcelWeight ;
5.    WHILE (conveyor not empty)
      // Process vans
      5.1.    payload ← zero ;
      5.2.    WHILE (payload + parcelWeight less than or equal to
              capacity) AND (conveyor NOT empty)
                  // Load a single van
                  5.2.1.   Load parcel on van ;
                  5.2.2.   payload ← payload + parcelWeight ;
                  5.2.3.   Get next parcelWeight ;
              ENDWHILE
      5.3.    Despatch van ;
      5.4.    numberOfVans ← numberOfVans + 1 ;
      // Check whether this is the heaviest van
      5.5.    IF ( payload more than heaviestVan )
                  5.5.1.   heaviestVan ← payload ;
              ENDIF
      ENDWHILE
```

6. Report `numberOfVans` used ;
7. Report `heaviestVan` sent ;

5.2 Chapter Summary

In this chapter we looked at some more complicated problems that required the use of arithmetic and keeping track of values. This led us to seeing the need for *variables* and we discussed how to decide the variables needed for a given problem and how to indicate their range of possible likely values. These concepts were applied to a problem of loading and despatching vans which needed nested WHILE loops in the solution.

5.3 Exercises

1. What values do the following assignment statements place in the variable `result`?

   a) `result` ← 3 + 4 ;
   b) `result` ← `result` + 7 ;
   c) `result` ← `result` ;
   d) `result` ← `result` − 7 ;

2. A fairly common programming task is to swap the values of two variables. Because a variable can only hold one value at a time, a common solution is to introduce a temporary variable. For example, assume variable a has the value 7 and variable b the value 4. The following algorithm swaps their values via the intermediate variable `temp`:

   1. `temp` ← `a` ;
   2. `a` ← `b` ;
   3. `b` ← `temp` ;

   All well and good, but suppose you didn't want to use `temp`? Can you find a way to swap the values using only a and b in the solution?

3. Professor Henry Higgins wants to attend a conference in Lincoln, Nebraska in the United States. The conference is being held in June and Professor Higgins wants to know what sort of clothing to take. Coming from northern Europe where temperatures are measured in degrees Celsius, Professor Higgins is unfamiliar with the Fahrenheit scale used in the United States. Therefore, he wants you to design an algorithm that will first convert a temperature in °F to its equivalent in °C, and then recommend clothing based on the result. If the temperature in Lincoln in June is 24 °C or above then Professor Higgins should take summer clothes; if it's less than 24 °C but above 15 °C then spring clothes are in order, otherwise winter clothes should be taken. There is a simple formula to convert from Fahrenheit to Celsius: $c = (F - 32) \times \frac{5}{9}$. Thus, a temperature of $98\,°F = (98 - 32) \times \frac{5}{9} = 33.67$ Celsius. Try your algorithm out with the following Fahrenheit temperatures: 57, 65, 72, 76, and 85.

4. Using the *HTTLAP* strategy design an algorithm that uses repeated subtraction to find out how many times one number divides another. For example, 20 divides 5 four times, 36 divides 7 five times (with a remainder of 1).[11]

5. We are used to seeing times in the form hh:mm:ss. If a marathon race begins at 10:00:00 and the winner finishes at 14:07:41 we can see that the winning time was 4 hours, 7 minutes and 41 seconds. Design an algorithm that takes the start and finishing times of a runner and displays the time it took them to complete the race. If your solution worked using the start time of 10:00:00, does it still work for a start time of, say, 10:59:57?

6. It is usual, when working with times, to convert real-world timings into a figure in seconds as this makes comparisons between two times much simpler. Given that there are 3600 seconds in an hour, write an algorithm that takes the start and finish times of a marathon runner in the form hh:mm:ss, converts them to a time in seconds, subtracts the start seconds from the finish seconds to give an elapsed time, and then converts this elapsed time in seconds back into a real world time of the form hh:mm:ss for display. For example, say I started a marathon at 09:05:45 and finished at 13:01:06, my start time would be $09 \times 3600 + 05 \times 60 + 45 = 32,400 + 300 + 45 = 32,745$ seconds. My finish time would be $46,800 + 60 + 06 = 46,866$ seconds. My race time would then be $46,866 - 32,745 = 14,121$ seconds. This comes to 03:55:21. The real problem here is how did I get 03:55:21 from 14,121? The solution is related to the change-giving problem from Chapter 3.

7. In the solutions to the coffee making problem we have been careful to give precise instructions for how to add the required number of sugars to each cup. If you look closely you may spot that we have not been as careful as we might have been with the rest of the solution. I am referring specifically to the instruction "measure coffee for number required" (Solution 5.8). If you think about it you should realize that this action too needs more detailed instructions. How exactly do you measure the right amount of coffee? How many spoons (or scoops) of coffee do you need? Assume a standard measure of one dessert spoon for each cup of coffee required. Rewrite the task to make the instructions precise. Describe any variables that you need to add to the variable list.

8. I said that it would be hard enough to try and solve the problem on the assumption that the coffee pot is large enough for the required coffee and that I would come back to the more general problem of making coffee for any number of people. You are to tackle that problem now. The capacity of the coffee pot is eight cups. Try to extend the coffee making solution you produced for Exercise 7 to deal with the requirement of being able to make more than eight cups of coffee.[12]

---

[11] Hint: $20 - 5 = 15$ giving 1 subtraction. $15 - 5 = 10$, giving a second subtraction. $10 - 5 = 5$, giving a third subtraction, and $5 - 5 = 0$ giving a fourth subtraction. Hence, 20 divides 5 four times as 4 (the number of subtractions) $\times 5 = 20$.

[12] Hint: If you are having trouble getting started, look at Solution 5.9. The WHILE in Task #2.10 pours a number of coffees from one pot. If ten cups are wanted, then you will have to make two pots of coffee. If more than sixteen cups are needed then you will have to make more than two pots of coffee.

9. *Paul's Premier Parcels* was so pleased with your work that they want you to extend your van-loading solution to incorporate some extra requirements. In addition to the existing reports the manager wants to know the weight of the lightest payload that was sent out. He also wants to know the average payload of all the despatched vans. Using *HTTLAP* draw up solutions to these additional problems and try to incorporate them into Solution 5.18. Think about what extra variables may be needed and how they should be initialized and their values calculated. An average of a set of values is calculated by dividing the sum of all the values by the number of values in the set. Thus, the average of 120, 130, and 140 is $\frac{120 + 130 + 140}{3} = 130$.

10. In 2006, FIFA (the world governing body for international soccer) revised the way teams are allocated points for international soccer matches as shown in Table 5.5. Thus in a normal match the winning team gets 3 points with the losers getting zero. If a match is won through a penalty shootout the winning team only gets 2 points and the losers get 1 point. Both teams get 1 point each for a draw.

Table 5.5 **FIFA Points Allocations**

Result	Points
Win	3
Draw	1
Lose	0
Win (with penalty shootout)	2
Lose (with penalty shootout)	1

Design an algorithm that analyses the result of a match and awards points to the two teams accordingly. For example, given the following score line:

    England 2: Brazil 0, Penalties: No

England would be awarded 3 points and Brazil 0 points. For this match:

    Netherlands 5: Portugal 4, Penalties: Yes

The Netherlands would get 2 points and Portugal 1 point.
Now extend your solution to deal with an unspecified number of matches. The algorithm should stop calculating points when the following score line appears that has a negative goal score for either team. Teams may play more than one match, so each team's points tally will need to be updated as necessary. At the end, the team with the highest points tally should be declared top of the world rankings.

11. Vance Legstrong, a world-class Stocksfield-based cyclist has asked the Department of Mechanical Engineering at the University of Stocksfield to help him out with the selection of gear wheels on his new bicycle. Vance wants to know, for each of 10 gears on his bicycle how many times he must make one full turn of the pedals in order to travel 1 km. A bicycle's gear ratio is given as the ratio between the number of teeth on the chain wheel (the one the pedals are connected to) and the number of teeth on the gear wheel (the one attached to the rear wheel). The rear wheel has ten gear wheels all with

a different number of teeth. The chain wheel has 36 teeth and the gear wheels have teeth as given in Table 5.6.

Table 5.6 **Number of Teeth on Bicycle Gear Wheels**

Gear Wheel	Number of Teeth
1	36
2	34
3	32
4	30
5	28
6	26
7	24
8	22
9	20
10	18

Thus, the ratio of gear 1 is 1 as the chain wheel ÷ gear wheel = 36/36. The ratio of gear 5 is 1.2857, and so on. The diameter of the wheels on Vance's bicycle is 27 inches

a) Design an algorithm to calculate the gear ratios of all ten gears.

b) Extend your solution to tell Vance how many pedal turns are needed to travel 1 km in each gear. You may assume that no freewheeling is allowed. Think about how far the bicycle will travel for each full turn of the pedals.

A sketch of the principal components may be useful. You may like to tackle some of subproblems separately.[13]

5.4 **Projects**

StockSnackz Vending Machine

Up till now we assumed the vending machine had unlimited supplies. It is time to put away such childish notions. Therefore, extend your solution so that the machine now shows a "sold out" message if it has run out of a selected item.

---

[13] Hint: One of the subproblems is finding out how far one turn of the pedals will move the bicycle. In gear 1, turning the pedals one full turn will rotate the rear wheel one full turn as the gear ratio is 1:1, thus the bicycle will travel 27 inches; In gear 5, the rear wheel will make 1.2857 full turns. Another subproblem is finding out how many times the pedal has to turn to move 1 km: how many inches are there in 1 km? You can start off by knowing that 1 inch = 2.54 cm and there are 100 cm in 1 m and 1000 m in 1 km.

For testing purposes set the initial stock levels to 5 of each item (otherwise it will take your friend a long time to work through the algorithm!).

Previously if the buttons 0, 7, 8, 9 were pressed the machine simply did nothing. Now it is time to design a more typical response. The machine should behave as before when buttons 1–6 are pressed but should now show an "Invalid choice" message if the buttons 0, 7, 8, 9 are pressed. For both problems remember to write down all the variables (together with their ranges of values) that are needed.

Stocksfield Fire Service

Look at the algorithm you created in Chapter 4 for the hazchem problem. Identify and write down all the variables you think you may need for this solution. Remember to also indicate the typical ranges of values that each variable can take.

Puzzle World: Roman Numerals and Chronograms

Look at the algorithm you created in Chapter 4 for the Roman numerals validation and translation problems. Identify and write down all the variables you think you may need for your solutions. Remember to also indicate the typical ranges of values that each variable can take.

Pangrams: Holoalphabetic Sentences

Look at the algorithm you created in Chapter 4 for the pangram problem. Identify and write down all the variables you think you may need for this solution. Remember to also indicate the typical ranges of values that each variable can take.

Online Bookstore: ISBNs

Identify likely variables and their ranges of values for:

a) the ISBN hyphenation problem
b) the ISBN validation problem

Write your solution to the ISBN validation problem using an iteration to work through the nine main digits of the ISBN.

6 Extending Our Vocabulary: Data and Control Abstractions

6.1   **Data Abstractions**

6.2   **Sequence**

6.3   **More Selections**

6.4   **Iteration**

6.5   **Applications of the WHILE and DO...WHILE Loops**

6.6   **Chapter Summary**

6.7   **Exercises**

6.8   **Projects**

Learning Objectives

- Understand the ways in which different kinds (types) of data affect the way solutions to problems are designed
- Recognize appropriate operations that can be carried out on different data types
- Identify different ways of carrying out selection and iteration and understand how different specialized control constructs can be used appropriately
- Understand the difference between simple and compound selections, and how complex conditions can be expressed to control the selections
- Understand the difference between determinate and indeterminate iterations and how complex conditions can be expressed to control the iterations
    - Determinate: count-controlled iteration
    - Indeterminate: zero-or-more and at-least-once iterations
- Analyze real-world problems to identify the appropriate selection and iteration constructs to use

In this chapter we will revisit the basic programming ideas of data, sequence, iteration, and selection and look at some of the different ways they can be expressed. From this we will build up a repertoire of standard structures for implementing solutions to common problems.[1]

We came across the idea of sequence, iteration, and selection constructs a few times in previous chapters. These constructs are very important concepts as they are the three fundamental building blocks from which all programs are built.[2] If you examine all the solutions

---

[1] You may come across the term *design patterns* which are standard ways of approaching common problems. There is a bit more to design patterns than that, but they have become very popular in software engineering as they provide tried-and-tested approaches that can be tailored to fit individual circumstances. They are used especially in object-oriented programming projects. If you want to know more, take a look at Shalloway and Trott's (2001) book on the subject.

[2] Well, nearly all. There is a technique called parallel programming in which courses of action that are executed simultaneously (in parallel) on multiple processors are specified. Multi-threading (something you will come across on a C++ or Java course) is a similar concept to parallel programming. Happily, you do not need to know anything about parallel programs to understand this book.

from the previous chapters you can see that they are all just different combinations of sequential actions, repeated actions, and alternate courses of action. When you think about it in these terms, programming is really very simple as there are only three building blocks. Of course, there are only a few notes in a musical scale, but putting them together well to make pleasing music is a valuable skill. One of the marks of a programmer is understanding how to arrange actions in sequences, iterations, and selections to best arrive at the desired outcome. Therefore, in this chapter you will learn about sequential statement blocks (Section 6.2) and the different types of selection (Section 6.3) and iteration (Section 6.4) constructs available in most programming languages. But first, we will take a look at data.

6.1 Data Abstractions

In Chapter 5 we looked at identifying the different variables in a problem and estimating the likely ranges of values they could take. At this point, it is instructive to pause and to see how doing this enables us to begin constructing lower-level abstractions of the data. We have talked much about data. For example, we might talk about bank account data such as the account number, the balance, the account holder's name, and so on. But what exactly is "data"? Data is actually a plural noun (the singular being "datum" from the Latin, meaning "given"), but which is commonly treated as a singular noun. Thus, in texts on programming you will see phrases such as "the data *are* stored in a file" and "the data *is* read into the program." Linguists would, perhaps, prefer us to use the plural, but I think the damage is now done and the singular use so widespread that we can use either. Dictionaries will define data as a set of facts from which other facts can be inferred. For example, given the bank account data "opening balance," "total credits," and "total debits," it is possible to calculate another datum (data item): "closing balance."

In books on computing and information systems, data is commonly defined as unorganized facts. Information is then defined as organized facts, or data with meaning attached. This is a simplistic view and not altogether helpful, for many programs access data files in which the data are highly organized and structured. A more helpful stance is taken by Checkland and Holwell (1997) who define data as facts about the real world that can be verified and checked. In problem solving we then select certain items of data for our attention and organize them in such a way as is helpful for gaining insight into the problem and thus producing a solution.[3] In programming terms, data are usually taken to mean the various items, values, facts, etc. that the program manipulates in order to execute the solution to the problem. For example, in the coffee-making problem we identified the following data (see Table 5.1):

■ The number of coffees to be made
■ The milk preference of a drinker

---

[3] Checkland and Holwell (1997) call such selected data *capta*. They define information as capta (selected data) that has been enriched by having meaningful attributes attached to it. Information that is itself organized into structures is then called *knowledge*.

- The sugar requirements of a drinker
- The number of cups poured so far
- The number of sugars added to a cup so far

Having identified the required data, carrying out the coffee making task simply required us to write down the value of these data on a notepad, or to store them in our head. Notepads and short-term memory are useful for people solving simple problems and computers use an electronic equivalent.

Humans are very good at simplifying complexity and working at high levels of abstraction. For instance, you may not ever have been consciously aware of it when reading your bank statements, but you are able to decode different types of data (such as transaction amount, transaction date, payee name, and so on) with ease. Look at Figure 6.1, which shows a bank statement for Henry and Eliza Higgins.

FIGURE 6.1   **Sample bank statement**

First Bank of **Stocksfield**   Current Account

Date	Details		Withdrawn	Paid in	Balance
1 Jan 2004	BROUGHT FORWARD				1,025.49
3 Jan 2004	Cheque	101	35.00		990.49
10 Jan 2004	ATM Stocksfield		100.00		890.49
25 Jan 2004	Direct Debit	Mastercard	359.99		530.50
27 Jan 2004	Credit no. 101	000002		59.00	589.50
31 Jan 2004	CARRIED FORWARD				589.50

101

Account number 12345678   Professor Henry and Mrs Eliza Higgins
Branch code   00-00-00

The statement contains a number of different kinds of data. The name of the bank is printed at the top together with the account type. These are both textual items. The transaction dates are a mixture of text and numbers. The transaction details also contain text with some numbers in it. The "withdrawn," "paid in," and "balance" columns contain numbers in a currency format. The oval in the bottom left corner has the statement page number which, unlike the currency figures, is a whole number. The account holders' names are clearly textual as are the labels "Account number" and "Branch code." The account number itself is an eight digit number, and the branch code has a "two-digit, hyphen, two-digit, hyphen, two-digit" format.

I am sure that when you looked at Figure 6.1 you did not think about the statement in this kind of detail. You probably just read the statement as a summary of banking transactions. You did not need to know that the currency figures were numeric values with precision to two decimal places, that the names of the account holders are written using a mixture of upper and lower case letters, and so on. Because of this you may never have been aware that data comes in different kinds. But think back to when you started to learn arithmetic. Perhaps at first you were taught to do simple sums using whole numbers, such as $3 + 5$, $11 + 7$, and so on. Subtractions were also simple, and the teacher made sure that the problems always gave a positive answer because five-year-olds find negative numbers a difficult concept to grasp. Perhaps multiplication came next followed by division. Again, problems of division were simplified so as to yield a whole result: fractional numbers come later on in the curriculum. So, a very young child would be able to solve $18 \div 9$, but not $17 \div 9$. Why is $17 \div 9$ so much harder than $18 \div 9$? Because it involves knowing about fractional numbers, decimal points, numbers between 0 and 1, and so on. That is, $18 \div 9$ resides in the domain of whole numbers whereas $17 \div 9$ though composed of whole numbers does not give a whole-number result. Perhaps you first learned to solve problems of this kind by saying that the answer is 1 with a remainder, or leftover, of 8.

When thinking about the problem initially it is fine to consider the data at the high level of abstraction where they are just values. However, eventually our solutions must be translated into programming language code ready for execution by a computer. Unfortunately, computers store different kinds of values in different ways. Each programming language supplies its own set of data abstractions which specify what kinds of values a data item can take, the range of those values, and the actions that can be performed using those values. When you have completed this book and start to learn how to translate your algorithms into a specific programming language you will need to be aware of the different ways the language treats different kinds of data. Because this book is not concerned with detail at that level we do not need to go that far, but it is helpful to begin classifying data into lower-level abstractions than we have been working with up till now.

Consider, for example, the number 7. What can we do with that number? We can add it to another number, subtract it from another number, multiply it, divide it, or even raise it to a power. When we define a data item in terms of the range of values it can take and the different operations that can be performed upon it we have described what a programmer would call an ABSTRACT DATA TYPE or ADT. An ADT describing whole numbers might look like Table 6.1.

Table 6.1 ADT for Whole Numbers

Whole Numbers	
Range	$0 \ldots \infty$
Operations	$+, -, \times, \div$

It is a **data type** because it differentiates between different kinds of values and the operations that can be performed on those values. For example, it makes sense to do

+, −, ×, ÷ on numbers but not on words. For example, what does "Henry" ÷ "Higgins" mean if we take the "÷" symbol to stand for numeric division?

It is **abstract** because we are not concerned (at this point) with how the values are stored inside a computer nor with how the operations are performed. That is, we are interested in knowing that the "×" is an operation that multiplies two values but we are not interested in the details of the algorithm that expresses the solution to the problem of how, exactly, to multiply any two numbers.

Programmers must be aware of the different kinds of data they are dealing with for just as 18 ÷ 9 and 17 ÷ 9 require slightly different approaches, so a computer uses different mechanisms for storing different kinds of data. This is why in Chapter 5 I also asked you to estimate the range of values that could be taken by the variables in a problem (see Table 5.1 on page 99). We need to know what kind and what size of value a variable will take in order to be able to correctly instruct the computer to store and manipulate it.

Data types   ▶   In programming, the classification of data according to its kind is called *typing*. Each data item in a program must belong to a particular data type. Some programming languages (Ada, for example,[4]) are *strongly typed* with very strict rules governing how data of different types can be mixed and manipulated. Other languages, such as early versions of BASIC, are more *loosely typed* and the manipulation rules are less strict. Languages like C, C++, and Java are more strongly typed than BASIC but are less strongly typed than Ada. Whatever the strength of the typing, programming languages have in common that data must be declared to be of a particular type.

Typing is not a sadistic whim of programming language designers to make life awkward for beginners. When you specify a variable as belonging to a particular type you are also implicitly stating what range of values the variable can take and what operations can be performed on those values. For example, we could take a simple view of our bank statement as comprising either numbers or text. If we say that a transaction's value is a decimal numeric type then we know we would expect to be able to perform addition, subtraction, multiplication, division, and other arithmetic operations on that value. We also know that a decimal number can only be formed from the digits 0 to 9 and a single (but optional) decimal point character.[5] If an entry that was supposed to be a number appeared as "hello" we would know something was wrong. Likewise, treating a value as text means that we would expect values to be made up of combinations of letters and other characters. So, on our bank statement, "Credit no. 101" is text,[6] as are "Account number" and "Professor Henry and Mrs Eliza Higgins." Furthermore, we would not expect to be able to add, subtract, and multiply text values in the way that we can with numbers. For instance, what does "XX" + "YY" mean?

---

[4] Named after the nineteenth-century niece of Lord Byron, Lady Ada Lovelace, who is credited with being the world's first computer programmer.

[5] In many European countries the comma is used as the decimal placeholder with the full stop/period being used to separate thousands. Thus the value 1,499.50 (one thousand four hundred and ninety-nine point five) would be written in France as 1.499,50 for example.

[6] Actually, it is probably a combination of the text "Credit no." and the numeric value 101.

Before going on, think about this, and try jotting down two or three possible ways of interpreting "XX" + "YY."

What answers did you come up with? I guess the answer could be "ZZ" or "XXYY." How about "YYXX"? Here is a more subtle problem. What does "A" + "B" mean? If "A" and "B" are text, then the answer could be "AB," or "C," or "BA," etc. But what if "A" and "B" are hexadecimal numbers? In that case "A" + "B" should give 15 in hexadecimal.[7] It is important to know what type of data we are dealing with so that it can be correctly interpreted and only valid operations applied to it. The enclosure of A and B by speech marks may have led you to think that that they were text values rather than hexadecimal digits, but that is only an ASSUMPTION. The typing rules of a programming language will specify what operations are allowed, and how those operations are carried out. In some languages, when applied to text, the "+" operator stands for concatenation (appending one piece of text to another). So, "XX" + "YY" would give "XXYY." The point to note here is that the "+" operator has different meanings for different types of data.[8] Specifying a type tells the computer how to interpret what is required. Strongly-typed languages are very strict and will often not allow data of one type to be combined with data of another type. For example, in a very strongly-typed language, an expression like 15 + "X" may not be permissible as the expression mixes a numeric value with a textual value. However, some loosely-typed languages may allow just such an expression in which case the computer would convert both data items to some common type to allow the operation to be carried out.[9] For example, in the above expression, a loosely-typed language may first convert the "X" to a numeric representation, say 24, as that is X's position in the alphabet. There are other possible conversions that could be done, and as a programmer you need to be aware of how the language you are using stores data types. There is an everyday situation that is analogous to data typing. Cars that run on unleaded fuel have specially shaped filler caps that will only accept unleaded-fuel **Strongly-typed** ▶ nozzles. This is to prevent leaded fuel or diesel being pumped in and ruining the **fuel tanks!** engine. This is an example of strong typing as the tank design prevents fuel of an incompatible type being placed into the tank.

There are many different types offered by the various programming languages. Furthermore, many languages allow you to define your own types as needed. Thus it is impossible in a book that does not focus on a particular language to cover everything that could be said about data types. Therefore, for our purposes all we need to be aware of is that data do belong to different types. When considering the data in our problems it is useful to think in terms of ABSTRACT DATA TYPES, that is, the range of values data of that type can take and the corresponding operations that we might reasonably perform upon that data.

Now we turn our attention to the algorithmic building blocks of sequence, iteration, and selection.

---

[7] A = 10 in decimal, B = 11, so 10 + 11 = 21 decimal, or 15 in hexadecimal. 15, of course, means $1 \times 16 + 5$.

[8] We call this an *overloaded* operator in programming for it has multiple meanings depending on its context of use.

[9] The popular web scripting language JavaScript is notoriously flexible with data types and can catch the unwary programmer out (especially those used to strong typing).

6.2 **Sequence**

The sequence is the simplest of the three programming building blocks, as easy as A, B, C. Think of three actions, say "get up," "get dressed," and "eat breakfast," label the three actions "A," "B," and "C," and write them out in the order you would do them, and you have a sequence:

A. Get up

B. Get dressed

C. Eat breakfast

That is all a sequence is, a set of actions, tasks, or instructions that are carried out in the order in which they're written. You will recall from the *HTTLAP* strategy that writing out a sequence of actions is the first step in writing down the solution to a problem.

6.3 **More Selections**

In Chapter 4 we looked at how to solve problems involving choices and introduced the selection construct IF. The IF allows us to choose whether or not to carry out an action block depending on the value of a condition. At this point you might want to refresh your memory and have another look over Chapter 4.

Simple and Extended Selections

Often tasks or courses of actions only need to be carried out when certain conditions are met. We call this process *selection* because we are telling the algorithm to select between alternative courses of action. All the problems in Chapters 4 and 5 involved making choices and could be solved using an IF that only had one choice to make. That is, we either carried out the action block or we did not. The IF is controlled by a *relational expression*. For example, the coffee making solutions had sections resembling the following:

◄ **Relational expressions**

```
IF (milk required)
    Add milk ;
ENDIF
```

In this example when the condition "milk required" is satisfied then milk is added. When the condition is not satisfied then no milk is added. We can rephrase this more formally as selecting between a course of action and the *null* action.[10]

---

[10] Null is a word that is used much in computing and programming. It means to be void, empty, lacking existence, amounting to nothing. Thus, a null action is one that does nothing at all. A null variable is one that has no value.

You said the selection's null action is carried out. I cannot see any activity labeled "null" in the algorithm. Where is it?

Null means something that is absent or non-existent. Thus, you will not find a null statement – it simply refers to the action that is taken when the condition in the IF gives a false result, i.e., nothing at all.

Extended Selections

However, there are times when the choice is not between an action and the null action but between two positive but alternative courses of action. Take, for example, the case of withdrawing money from a cash machine (ATM). After inserting your card you key in your PIN/security code and choose an option to withdraw cash. If you have enough money in your account (or you are within your credit limit) then the machine should dispense the cash. We could express this in pseudo-code as:

```
IF (funds available)
    Dispense cash ;
ENDIF
```

What if your request for cash would exceed your limits? In this case the ATM should decline your request and display a message such as "Sorry, but you have insufficient funds." The simple IF construct is not able to deal with this situation because its alternative to dispensing cash is the null (non-existent) action, so we would have to resort to something clumsy like this:

```
IF (funds available)
    Dispense cash ;
ENDIF
IF (insufficient funds available)
    Display message of apology ;
ENDIF
```

The above solution does not match how we would phrase such a selection in real life. If you were telling a bank clerk how to handle cash requests you would say something like: "If there are sufficient funds then give the customer the requested cash *otherwise* apologize and explain that their request cannot be satisfied." The key to this is the word "otherwise" which sets out an alternative course of action to be followed if the first action cannot be performed. We can extend our pseudo-code to allow this by adding a new keyword "ELSE" (for some reason, ELSE is used rather than OTHERWISE in most programming languages).

```
IF (condition)
    Action 1 ;
ELSE
    Action 2 ;
ENDIF
```

The "ELSE" enables us to replace the null action with a real action to be carried out when the condition belonging to the IF is false. Here is the cash withdrawal solution rewritten using our new IF...ELSE construct:

```
IF (funds available)
    Dispense cash ;
ELSE
    Display message of apology ;
ENDIF
Return card ;
```

You can read this as "IF there arc funds available then dispense the cash ELSE (otherwise) display the message of apology, and afterwards return the customer's card." The important thing to note is that only one of the two actions blocks is carried out: **either** the dispense cash task **or** the apology task, but not both. If the funds are available the cash is dispensed, the apology task is skipped, and the customer's bank card is then returned. If there are insufficient funds then the dispense cash action is skipped and the apology message is displayed instead, followed again by returning the customer's card.

The reason we would use the IF...ELSE rather than two IFs one after the other is because both action blocks are dependent on the same condition. In the example above where we had two IFs, one to dispense money if funds were available and another to display an apology if funds were not available, we can see that both actions (dispensing cash and displaying an apology) are conditional upon the funds available. Furthermore, the apology is displayed when the opposite condition to the first IF is met. That is, we have two conditions: "funds available" and "funds not available" which are simply opposites. Using two IF constructs leads to a clumsy solution in which we not only have to write out the condition that must be satisfied for money to be dispensed but also to write out the condition to be met when an apology is displayed. We make use of the fact that the apology condition is simply the opposite of the cash dispensing condition by using the IF...ELSE construct.

Write an **IF...ELSE** statement that chooses between wearing sandals or shoes depending on whether it is raining.

Multi-part Selections

The IF...ELSE construct also allows us to solve more complicated problems than the simple either-or example above. Let's go back to the van-loading problem from Chapter 5. The company was so pleased with our work that they have asked us to extend the solution. The van drivers have been complaining that some small parcels were much heavier than they looked and some large ones were lighter than expected. This led to a spate of back injuries when lifting parcels off the vans and the drivers are getting concerned. The management has decided to label each parcel with a sticker. Now, as they are loaded onto the vans at the depot parcels will be categorized as light, medium, or heavy. A light parcel is anything up to 5 kg. Parcels over 5 kg but less than 10 kg are classed as medium-weight and anything weighing 10 kg and over is classified as heavy. We could write a solution to this problem using three separate IF statements as in Solution 6.1 below.

Solution 6.1 Clumsy multiple selection

```
IF (parcelWeight up to (and including) 5 kilos)
    Add 'light' sticker ;
ENDIF
IF (parcelWeight more than 5 and less than 10 kilos)
    Add 'medium' sticker ;
ENDIF
IF (parcelWeight 10 kilos or over)
    Add 'heavy' sticker ;
ENDIF
Load parcel on van ;
```

Think Spot

Solution 6.1 solves the problem but it is not a very good solution. Using a sequence of individual IFs makes it appear that the three selections are separate and unrelated, that is, all three actions could be followed if all three conditions are met. However, we know that the three conditions are mutually exclusive – if any one of them is true the other two must be false.

Do not move on until you understand how the three conditions are mutually exclusive, that is, only one can be true at a time. You can show this by drawing a truth table:

parcelWeight	Condition		
	parcelWeight up to (and including) 5 kilos	parcelWeight more than 5 and less than 10 kilos	parcelWeight 10 kilos or over
4 kg	True	False	False
5 kg			
9 kg			
10 kg			
11 kg			

For each value in the parcel weight column fill in the true or false value for each of the three conditions. How many conditions are true for each parcel weight? The first row has already been filled in for you. A solution is given in Appendix C.

Therefore, the solution is not making full use of what we know about the problem. The IF...ELSE allows us to select between two related courses of action. The problem here is similar except there are three courses of action rather than two. We can represent this situation by extending the IF...ELSE to allow more than two choices.

Rewrite the three separate selections above using a single three-way IF . . . ELSE structure now. Once you have tried to do that, compare your answer with Solution 6.2 below.

Solution 6.2 Using IF...ELSE to add stickers

```
IF (parcelWeight up to 5 kilos)
    Add 'light' sticker ;
ELSE IF (parcelWeight less than 10 kilos)
    Add 'medium' sticker ;
ELSE
    Add 'heavy' sticker ;
ENDIF
Load parcel on van ;
```

Rather than ending the selection after the first ELSE we have added another IF...ELSE structure. You can read this as saying "if it is a light parcel then add a light sticker, otherwise if it is a medium-weight parcel add a medium sticker otherwise add a heavy sticker." The condition for the first IF should be easy to understand. A light parcel is one that weighs 5 kg or less, so the condition is straightforward. When we examine the second condition after the "ELSE IF" it is different from the second condition in Solution 6.1. Solution 6.1 had the condition "parcelWeight more than 5 kg and less than 10 kg" while Solution 6.2 just has "parcelWeight less than 10 kg." Why do you think this is?

A medium parcel is one that weighs more than 5 kg but less than 10 kg, so surely Solution 6.2 is wrong as it only tests to see whether the parcel is less than 10 kg? Wouldn't a parcel of 4 kg therefore be classed as medium weight because it is less than 10?

Think about what the ELSE means. How does it affect the condition? In English we might say "otherwise" rather than ELSE. What does "otherwise" mean?

Solution 6.2 is correct because the conditions are linked by the ELSE keyword. Recall that the IF...ELSE construct says that if the first condition is false then carry out the alternative action. Look at Solution 6.2 to see how this rule is applied. The first IF asks whether the parcel is 5 kg or less in weight. If it is, then a "light" sticker is added, the rest of the selection is skipped, and the next action in the sequence (the one after the ENDIF) is carried out which, in this case, is "Load parcel on van." If the parcel is not 5 kg or less then we follow the ELSE path, which, in this case, has its own condition "parcelWeight less than 10 kg." Why doesn't this condition say "parcelWeight more than 5 kg and less than 10 kg"? Consider how we got to this point. We are only testing this condition because the first one "parcelWeight up to 5 kg" was false, that is, we found a parcel that weighed more than 5 kg. If we already know that it weighs more than 5 kg, to determine whether the parcel is medium weight all we need to do is find out whether it is also less than 10 kg. For example, take a parcel that weighs 7 kg. The first condition will be false because the parcel is not up to five kilos in weight. So we move to the ELSE that has its own IF construct which asks whether the parcel is less than 10 kg. It is, so we have correctly identified a medium-weight parcel.

What happens when the parcel is 10 kg or heavier? This time the second condition would also be false so the next ELSE is followed. At this point we know that we are not dealing with a light- or a medium-weight parcel so, by definition, it must be a heavy one. Therefore, there is no need to test its weight again and we can go ahead with putting on a "heavy" sticker. A mistake many beginners make is to put an "IF (condition)" after the final ELSE in a multi-path selection. If the preceding conditions have been correctly formed, then by the time the final ELSE is reached there should be no need to make another test as all other possibilities for action have been exhausted. In the parcel weighing problem, if a parcel is not light and it is not medium weight then it **must** be a heavy parcel (look back at the truth table you completed earlier).

Writing Selection Conditions

When considering the parcels it is becoming unwieldy to write all the IF conditions in longhand. Table 6.2 lists a set of symbols we will use from now on when making comparisons between different values. These symbols are known formally as **relational operators**.

Table 6.2 The Relational Operators

Operator	Pseudo-code
Less than	$<$
Less than or equal to	$\leq$
Equals (equality)	$=$
Greater than or equal to	$\geq$
Greater than	$>$
Not equal to (inequality)	$\neq$

The relational operators allow us to express real-world conditions in our programs. For example, in many countries you must be at least 18 years old to vote in elections. An algorithm that processes requests to register for the vote might have a section like this:

```
IF (age ≥ 18)
    Statements for issuing a voting card ;
ELSE
    Display 'Sorry, too young' message ;
ENDIF
```

This is much easier to write (and easier to read) than the longhand equivalent:

```
IF (age is greater than or equal to 18)
    Statements for issuing a voting card ;
ELSE
    Display 'Sorry, too young' message ;
ENDIF
```

Now that we are armed with the relational operators we can learn to write selections with properly formed conditional expressions. Take the problem of assigning a grade to a piece of homework. In the University of Stocksfield, grades are calculated on the basis of the percentage mark awarded for pieces of work according to the Table 6.3:

Table 6.3   Grade Calculation

Percentage Mark	Corresponding Grade	Condition
80% or above	A	(mark ≥ 80)
70% to 79%	B	(mark ≥ 70) AND (mark ≤ 79)
60% to 69%	C	(mark ≥ 60) AND (mark ≤ 69)
50% to 59%	D	(mark ≥ 50) AND (mark ≤ 59)
40% to 49%	**E**	(mark ≥ 40) AND (mark ≤ 49)
Less than 40%	**F**	(mark < 40)
Both E and F are fail grades		

The selection for assigning an "A" grade is quite simple: the mark is 80% or above. We could write this in pseudo-code as follows:

```
IF (mark ≥ 80)
    grade ← 'A' ;
ENDIF
```

? Think Spot How would you extend this selection to include the "B" to "F" grades? You could write independent IF statements:

```
IF (mark ≥ 80)
    grade ← 'A' ;
ENDIF
IF (mark ≥ 70) AND (mark ≤ 79)
    grade ← 'B' ;
ENDIF
IF (mark ≥ 60) AND (mark ≤ 69)
    grade ← 'C' ;
ENDIF
IF (mark ≥ 50) AND (mark ≤ 59)
    grade ← 'D' ;
ENDIF
IF (mark ≥ 40) AND (mark ≤ 49)
    grade ← 'E' ;
ENDIF
IF (mark < 40)
    grade ← 'F' ;
ENDIF
```

But, as we saw above, this is a clumsy solution because the different IFs repeat the tests that have gone before.

> Write the above **IF** statements as an extended **IF...ELSE** selection.
>
> If you are finding this exercise a bit tricky, think about each of the grade calculations as a separate problem, but a problem that is related to the one before. What does each previous grade test tell you about the value of the mark? Try thinking of it this way: if the mark is not 80 or above and so does not deserve a grade "A," then what do we now know about the mark's value?

If you managed the above exercise, or you have spent more than fifteen minutes sweating over the answer, look at my solution below.

Solution 6.3 Extended IF...ELSE for calculating a grade

```
IF (mark ≥ 80)
    grade ← 'A' ;
ELSE IF (mark ≥ 70)
    grade ← 'B' ;
ELSE IF (mark ≥ 60)
    grade ← 'C' ;
ELSE IF (mark ≥ 50)
    grade ← 'D' ;
ELSE IF (mark ≥ 40)
    grade ← 'E' ;
ELSE
    grade ← 'F' ;
ENDIF
```

Look carefully at Solution 6.3 and compare it with your own. Was yours the same? If you had >69 instead of ≥70 that is alright because they're logically equivalent. Did you have the ELSE at the end for the "F" grade, or did you include another IF? Why did I not have a final IF? Let's walk through the solution from the top.

> I don't understand why you said >69 is logically equivalent to ≥70.
>
> Is 70 bigger than 69? Yes. Is 70 greater-than-or-equal-to 70? Yes, it is equal to 70. So, 70 is both greater than 69 and it is greater-than-or-equal-to 70. So, the relational expressions >69 and ≥70 evaluate to the same result for any given value.

The first IF asks whether the mark is greater than or equal to 80. If it is, a grade "A" is awarded. That bit shouldn't be baffling you. But how about the first ELSE part? It includes an IF to see whether the mark merits a "B" grade instead. At this point you may have written:

```
ELSE IF (mark ≥ 70) AND (mark ≤ 79)
```

If you did, you were correct to use an ELSE, but not correct to include the second relational expression after the AND. Why not? Think about what we already know about the value of mark. The first IF asked whether it was greater than or equal to 80. If it was then an "A" grade was awarded and the algorithm would then skip to the next statement following the entire IF...ELSE structure. But if the first selection's condition yielded false what does that tell us? It tells us that the mark is **not** greater than or equal to 80 which means it **must** be less than 80. Therefore, because we know it is less than 80 to decide if a "B" grade is warranted we now only have to ask whether the mark is at least 70; if we already know the mark is less than 80 then it is silly to repeat that test. Notice how the remaining IFs all take account of what went before. If the mark is not 70 or above then it must be 69 or below, which means we can award a "C" grade if it is still 60 or above, and so on until we get to the final ELSE.

Why does the final ELSE not have its own IF?

The answer to the above exercise is that by the time we get to this part we know that the mark must be less than 40. As it is less than 40 we know it deserves an "F" grade. Putting another IF there means that that condition could itself yield false, which means that there is yet another grade option. But if the mark is not a grade "A," "B," "C," "D," or "E" then what else can it be other than an "F"? There is no other choice, so we do not need another test on the last ELSE.

If this is at all unclear then take some time now to review Solution 6.3. Try working some data through the algorithm and work through each of the tests by hand to see how the IF...ELSE selection works. Also, convince yourself that taking account of the results of previous selections will only work with an IF...ELSE structure; writing a sequence of separate IF statements with the same conditional expressions as Solution 6.3 would not work.

Sometimes we will have a number of different values of the variable for which we want to take the same course of action, but those values do not lie in a neat range (like they did in the grade calculations above). For example, consider the old rhyme for deciding how many days there are in a month:

Thirty days hath September, April, June, and November.

All the rest have thirty-one,

Except February alone which has twenty-eight days clear,

And twenty-nine in each leap year.

That is, months 4, 6, 9, and 11 all have thirty days, month 2 has twenty-eight or twenty-nine days, depending on whether it is a leap year, and all the other months (1, 3, 5, 7, 8, 10, and 12) have thirty-one days. Figure 6.2 below shows a selection to assign the appropriate value to a variable daysInMonth according to the value held in the variable month.

FIGURE 6.2 **IF...ELSE for days in month calculation**

```
IF (month = 4) OR (month = 6) OR (month = 9) OR (month = 11)
    daysInMonth ← 30 ;
ELSE IF (month = 2)
    Actions to deal with February ;
ELSE
    daysInMonth ← 31 ;
ENDIF
```

Notice how the different months with common actions have been linked using the word OR. There is one problem remaining: how to deal with February.

> How should February be processed? How many days should there be in February? Taking February alone, write an **IF...ELSE** construct that assigns the correct value to **month** depending on whether the current year is a leap year.

Here is my solution to the February problem:

Solution 6.4 Dealing with February

```
IF (isLeapYear)
    daysInMonth ← 29 ;
ELSE
    daysInMonth ← 28 ;
ENDIF
```

For the IF condition you might have written something like "IF current year is a leap year" which is fine: I have just used a variable name isLeapYear as shorthand for this.

> Finally, add the February solution to the overall solution from Figure 6.2.

Solution 6.5 shows the overall solution to the problem.

Solution 6.5 Complete days in month solution

```
IF (month = 4) OR (month = 6) OR (month = 9) OR (month = 11)
    daysInMonth ← 30 ;
ELSE IF (month = 2)
    IF (isLeapYear)
        daysInMonth ← 29 ;
    ELSE
        daysInMonth ← 28 ;
    ENDIF
ELSE
    daysInMonth ← 31 ;
ENDIF
```

? **Think Spot**

I have shaded the IF...ELSE that deals with February simply to make clear that this part of the algorithm is nested within the second IF – you should convince yourself that this nested IF...ELSE is only carried out if month is equal to 2.

6.4 Iteration

The third of our basic programming building blocks is the loop, or iteration. Recall that iteration constructs let us write sections of code that are repeatedly executed.

Determinate Iterations

Iterations can be classified as being either *determinate or indeterminate*. A determinate iteration is one in which the number of times the action block is to be repeated is known in advance or can be calculated at the time the loop is executed. For example, an algorithm that reports the average rainfall for each month of the year would probably use a determinate loop. That is because there are twelve months in the year so we know we must carry out the instructions to display the rainfall for a single month twelve times. That is an example of knowing the number of iterations in advance. A program that calculates the number of leap years between two years chosen by the user would also use a determinate loop. Although the number of iterations is not known in advance, it can be calculated at the time the loop is executed. For example, there is a six-year range between 1999 and 2004 inclusive (1999, 2000, 2001, 2002, 2003, and 2004) but only a three-year range between 2004 and 2006. The number of years that need to be tested for being leap years is not known when we write the algorithm, but the loop is bounded by the chosen start and end years meaning the number of times the loop needs to execute its action block can be calculated.

We have seen an example of a determinate loop in the coffee-making problem. The number of times the instructions for adding sugar to a cup of coffee could be calculated for each cup (see Solution 5.9 on page 101). Here are the instructions for adding sugar which I have taken from Solution 5.9 and renumbered (as well as using the assignment symbol):

Solution 6.6 Determinate loop for adding sugar

```
1.   sugarsAdded ← zero ;
2.   Find out how many sugarsRequired ;
3.   WHILE (sugarsAdded < sugarsRequired)
        3.1  Add spoonful of sugar ;
        3.2  sugarsAdded ← sugarsAdded + 1 ;
     ENDWHILE
```

Look carefully at Solution 6.6 above. Apart from adding the assignment symbols I have also rewritten the condition for the WHILE: Solution 5.9 originally said "sugarsAdded not equal to sugarsRequired." We will get to why I have done that in a moment. First:

Explain why this is a determinate loop.

Notice the structure of the determinate loop. Because it is known how many times the loop must iterate, a *counter* is needed to keep track. In Solution 6.6, the

determinate, ▶
and count-
controlled
loops are
names for the
same thing

counter is the variable sugarsAdded. In a determinate iteration the counter must be initialized to its starting value prior to the loop (Task #1). The counter must then have an increment added to it (or subtracted from it if the loop is counting down through a range) and this is done in Task #3.2. This step is very important because it allows the loop to terminate by eventually causing the condition to become false. The use of a loop counter has led to this type of iteration also being known as a *count-controlled loop*. The common structure, then, of a determinate (or count-controlled) loop looks like this:

```
Initialize counter to starting value ;
WHILE (counter less than finishing value)
    Actions for loop body ;
    Add increment to counter ;
ENDWHILE
```

Of course, there are variations (for example, if the loop is counting down, rather than up, then the condition would be "counter > finishing value") but the overall structure is the same. In fact, this type of loop usually has a special construct dedicated to it which we will look at a little later on.

? Think Spot

Why have I changed the condition from "not equal to" to "less than"? It is a subtle point but it makes the program more correct. For the sake of argument, suppose I accidentally wrote Task #3.2 as

3.2   sugarsAdded ← sugarsAdded + 10 ;

That is, because of a simple typing error when writing the statement I am adding 10 rather than 1 each time a sugar is added. Programmers are no more immune to typos than anyone else and it is very easy to make a mistake of this kind. The mistake has been made and we have not spotted it in our checking. Even a dry run of the solution fails to spot the error because we do not see the "10." Our brains are very good at making us see what we expect to see; we expect to see a "1" because that is what we intended to write, so that is what we see. The error remains and gets incorporated into the eventual computer program. What happens? Say two sugars are required.

Trace through the WHILE loop now adding the two sugars and state at what point the loop terminates.

Tracing through the loop we encounter the WHILE for the first time and the original condition asks whether the number of sugars added is not equal to the number required. At this point we have added zero spoons of sugars so the condition is true. We enter the action block, add a spoonful of sugar and then carry out the defective task #3.2 and add 10 to sugarsAdded. When we go back to the WHILE to test the condition again, this time sugarsAdded has the value 10 and sugarsRequired the value 2. Is the condition true or false? It is still true, of course, for 10 is not equal to 2. The action block is carried out again and now sugarsAdded equals 20. The condition is still true so the action block is executed once more. And again. And again. And again. The algorithm is now stuck in an infinite loop because the condition can never become false as the ever increasing sugarsAdded will never be equal to 2. The loop **never terminates**.

If we change the condition to that shown in Solution 6.6 something different will happen. The first time into the loop sugarsAdded (0) is less than sugarsRequired (2) so the action block is carried out and 10 is added to sugarsAdded. The next time the condition is tested it becomes false because 10 is not less than 2 and so the loop terminates. The wrong number of sugars has been added to the coffee, but the algorithm at least finishes, and the fact that the coffee has the wrong number of sugars might suggest to us that the loop is in error. We need to get into the habit of defining conditions in terms of the absolute minimum required for them to be true. In this case, we only want to add sugars as long as the number added is less than the required value. As soon as the number added equals (or exceeds) the number required then we know we can stop.

Indeterminate Iterations

Indeterminate loops are those in which the number of iterations is unknown in advance and cannot be calculated. We have already seen a loop of this type in the van-loading problem. The first loop in Solution 5.18 said

```
WHILE (conveyor not empty)
```

And the second said

```
WHILE (payload + parcelWeight less than or equal to capacity) AND
   (conveyor NOT empty)
```

In the first WHILE the number of iterations is not known by those loading the vans. They are simply required to keep loading and despatching vans as long as there are parcels on the conveyor belt. Unlike the sugar-adding solution where the number of sugars required is known before entering the loop, here the number of parcels is an unknown quantity. Of course, it would be possible to find out this information by going round to the warehouse and counting all the parcels waiting to go onto the conveyor belt. But there is no need for that as it is not necessary to know the number of parcels in advance – knowing it will not help us to load the vans any better. Anyway, what if after counting the parcels and walking back to the loading bay the company received delivery of another batch of parcels?

Likewise, the second WHILE is indeterminate on two counts. First, it needs to stop when the parcels run out (an unknown quantity), and secondly, we cannot know in advance how many parcels will go on each van unless we weigh them all first and do the sums before bringing on a van. Again, there is little to be gained from doing this and we are quite happy weighing and loading individual parcels, stopping as soon as one will not fit, despatching the van, and bringing up the next one to carry on the process until we run out of parcels.

An order processing program for an online retailer might use an indeterminate/indeterminate loop of the form

```
WHILE (orders to process)
   Fetch details of order ;
```

```
      Calculate order value ;
      Calculate shipping costs ;
      Print invoice ;
   ENDWHILE
```

The number of orders will likely change between runs of the algorithm and there is nothing to be gained from knowing in advance how many times to repeat the invoice printing routine. This is quite unlike the sugar problem where it is absolutely essential to know how many times to execute the sugar-adding action. The alternative would be to specify an indeterminate loop and then, after adding each spoonful of sugar, to ask our guest if more sugar is still required. Think about this now to check that you can see why this would be an unwieldy and unnatural way of approaching the task.

The indeterminate loop used in the van-loading solution has the general form:

```
Get first item ;
WHILE (continuation condition)
   Process item ;
   Get next item ;
ENDWHILE
```

"read-ahead" technique ▶ This structure is commonly known as the *read-ahead loop* as the first item to be processed in the loop's action block is fetched ahead of the iteration construct (before the WHILE). The task to fetch the next item to process then comes at the end of the action block after all the instructions that deal with the previous item. We would typically use the read-ahead technique when the values of the items being processed are needed for testing the iteration condition. For example, in the van-loading problem we must know a parcel's weight before we can decide whether it will fit on the van. Therefore, before the loop condition can be tested for the first time we must already know the weight of a parcel. Contrast this with the *read-and-process* structure:

"read-and-process" ▶

```
WHILE (continuation condition)
   Get item ;
   Process item ;
ENDWHILE
```

The difference between the read-ahead and the read-and-process loops is subtle. Read-ahead is used when information about the items to be processed is needed in order to test the loop's controlling condition. In situations where we do not need to know anything about the items in advance we can use the read-and-process structure. In this scheme the WHILE's condition is tested and if the condition gives a true result then the action body is entered. The first task inside the action block is to fetch an item to process. The remainder of the action block contains tasks to deal with the item.

zero or more iteration ▶ The nature of the WHILE construct means that a loop's action block is carried out zero or more times (there was an example of this in Solution 6.6). That is, if the WHILE's condition gives a false result the first time it is tested then the loop's body will not be entered and so the loop is said to have iterated zero times. For this reason the WHILE is known as a zero-or-more iteration. Sometimes we need to write loops that execute at least once. For example, an ATM asks you for your

PIN before dispensing any cash.[11] Usually an ATM gives you three chances to enter the correct PIN after which it keeps your card. The point is that the loop that keeps asking you for your PIN must iterate at least once. An at-least-once iteration can be built using a WHILE but it requires careful initialization of variables to ensure that the condition is true the first time round.

Another common situation is where we know (or can calculate) in advance the number of times a loop must iterate. Such loops typically have a counter (or *sentinel*) variable to keep track of how many times it has iterated, hence they are often called count-controlled loops. We saw above how to build count-controlled loops with the WHILE in which a counter variable is used to keep track of the number of iterations and which causes the loop to terminate when the counter reaches a defined maximum limit. At-least-once and count-controlled loops are such common features in programs that most programming languages provide specialized iteration constructs to deal with them. Below we shall look at two such constructs using our pseudo-code.

Count-controlled Iterations

Consider the following count-controlled loop built with the WHILE construct. The iteration prompts the user to enter the average rainfall for each month of the year and calculates the running total rainfall for the year:

```
totalRainfall ← 0 ;
month ← 1 ; // Give counter a starting value
WHILE (month ≤ 12) // Specify upper limit for counter
    Display 'Please enter the month's rainfall' ;
    Get monthRainfall ;
    totalRainfall ← totalRainfall + monthRainfall ;
    month ← month + 1 ; // Increment added to counter
ENDWHILE
```

The chief problem with writing count-controlled loops using a WHILE is that it is easy to forget to increase the value of the counter at the end of the loop meaning that the iteration will never terminate. Sometimes programmers also forget to initialize the counter before the loop. Like most programming languages, the *HTTLAP* pseudo-code offers an iteration construct specifically designed for writing count-controlled loops. It is called the FOR loop and Figure 6.3 shows an annotated example:

The FOR loop ▶

FIGURE 6.3   **The FOR loop for count-controlled iterations**

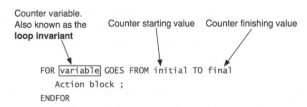

---

[11] PIN? The number you use at cash machines. Why didn't I write "PIN number"? Because PIN stands for Personal Identification Number, and you wouldn't say "Personal Identification Number number" would you?

A count-controlled loop must have a counter variable (known as the *loop invariant*) to keep track of the number of iterations. The loop invariant is so called because it is usually forbidden by programming language rules for any statement within the iteration's action block to change (vary) its value. Initial and final values for the counter are specified in the first line of the loop. By subtracting one from the other the number of iterations can be calculated. The general form of the FOR loop is shown in Figure 6.3. Its starting value is provided by the expression after the keyword FROM and its final value is given by the expression after the keyword TO. The mechanics of the loop are quite simple. Upon entry the counter will be given the value provided by initial. As long as that value is less than or equal to final then the action block is executed. After the last statement in the action block has been performed the counter is **automatically** increased by 1 and its value is again compared to final. At the point that the counter's value exceeds that of final the loop terminates.

To see how this works in practice examine Figure 6.4 which shows the rainfall solution from above rewritten using a FOR loop.

FIGURE 6.4   **FOR loop with simple initial and final values**

```
FOR month GOES FROM 1 TO 12
    Display 'Please enter the month's rainfall' ;
    Get monthRainfall ;
    totalRainfall ← totalRainfall + monthRainfall ;
ENDFOR
```

Reading the first line of Figure 6.4 should make clear what is happening. The counter variable month starts the loop with the value 1. The loop body is then executed. After the statement for adding the month's rainfall to the annual total is carried out the FOR loop *automatically* adds 1 to month making its value 2. This is less than or equal to the final value (12) so the loop body executes again. Work through it by hand and you will discover that month takes the values 1, 2, 3, 4, 5, 6, 7, 8, 9, 10, 11, 12 in succession. When it has the value 12 the loop body is executed once more after which month's value is increased to 13. This is now greater than the final value of 12 and the loop terminates.

There are two things to note. First, month does not need an initial value *prior* to entering the loop as the FOR assigns the value of the expression after GOES FROM to the loop counter. Secondly we do not need to remember to add 1 to the loop counter because this too is taken care of by the FOR construct. Thus, the two principal disadvantages of using a WHILE for count-controlled loops have been overcome by the FOR.

In Figure 6.4, the initial and final values were the values of simple variables. However, you can also use expressions to specify the starting and finishing values of the loop counter. For example, see Figure 6.5 below in which the variable age provides the initial value while the final value comes from an arithmetic expression. Assume that year and age have already been declared and that age has been given a value prior to the FOR.

FIGURE 6.5   **FOR loop with calculated initial and final values**

```
FOR year GOES FROM age TO age + 10
    Action block ;
ENDFOR
```

If the value of **age** were 38 then the loop would iterate eleven times with the counter variable **year** taking the values 38 to 48 inclusive. If **age** were 21, then the loop would still iterate eleven times, but this time the counter would take the values 21 through to 31. In either case, although we do not necessarily know at the time of writing the algorithm what the value of **age** will be, when the algorithm is executed, the number of iterations can still be calculated.

I don't understand why you said in the above example that the loop iterates eleven times when the counter goes from 38 to 48. Thirty-eight plus 10 equals 48, so why do you say eleven times?

Thirty-eight plus 10 does indeed give 48. But if you write down the numbers 38 through 48 inclusive you will find you have written eleven numbers.

We could also write something like the following to display every letter of the alphabet:

```
FOR letter GOES FROM 'A' TO 'Z'
    Display letter ;
    // Other actions that deal with upper-case letters ;
ENDFOR
```

FOR loops should be used when you need a loop that can most easily be controlled by a counter variable. Most programming languages provide a version of the FOR loop, but the exact details and layout vary.

The above **FOR** loop counts through all the uppercase letter characters from A to Z. How would we write the loop so that it works *backward* through the letters? Try it now. Hint: rather than thinking of the loop automatically *adding* to the counter, imagine it *changing* the counter's value to the next appropriate value.

All the FOR loops we have considered so far have counted upward through a range of values. The quick exercise above asked you to write a loop that works downward or backward through a range. Here is my solution:

Solution 6.7 FOR loop that counts backwards

```
FOR year GOES FROM 'Z' TO 'A'
    Action block ;
ENDFOR
```

All you need to do is make the initial value larger than the finishing value and the loop will subtract one from the counter each time around.

At-least-once Indeterminate Loops

We know that the WHILE is a zero-or-more iteration. When you need a loop that will iterate at least once then you should use a DO...WHILE construct. Figure 6.6

shows the layout of the DO...WHILE loop in the *HTTLAP* pseudo-code. Apart from the different keyword, the main difference from the plain WHILE loop is that the condition that terminates the loop is tested after the action block in the DO...WHILE whereas in the WHILE it is tested *before* the action block is executed. This means that before the DO...WHILE can test to see whether the loop should terminate it must first execute the action block. This positioning of the condition means that the DO...WHILE must execute its action block at least once, hence it is an at-least-once iteration construct.

FIGURE 6.6   DO ... WHILE: an at-least-once indeterminate iteration

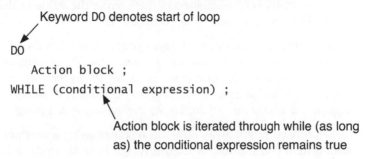

Again, to see how we might use this construct in practice look at Figure 6.7 which shows a DO...WHILE loop for getting a PIN from an ATM user.

FIGURE 6.7   DO ... WHILE loop for getting a PIN

```
DO
    Display 'Please enter your PIN' ;
    Get PIN ;
WHILE (PIN ≠ storedPIN) ;
```

Can you see how the loop works? The program encounters the keyword DO and then proceeds to execute the action block that follows. Immediately after the action block is the keyword WHILE followed by a condition. If this condition gives a true result the loop will iterate back through the action block again. This process carries on until the condition becomes false. This is just like the plain WHILE loop except that the condition is tested at the end of the action block rather than before. So, if the first time through the user does not enter a PIN that matches the one that has been stored on file (i.e., they have entered the wrong PIN) then the condition is true, that is, the PIN entered does not equal storedPIN. As the condition is true the loop will iterate again. It will keep doing this until the condition becomes false (that is, the PINs are equal). We cannot predict at the time we enter the loop how many goes it will take the user to enter the correct PIN, so we can see that this is an indeterminate loop. There is a problem with this example though: it may never finish. When writing loops of this kind it may be necessary to put in some extra logic to terminate the loop if a specified maximum number of iterations is reached. In the case of an ATM you are typically allowed three attempts to enter your PIN correctly before the machine seizes your card.

6.5 Applications of the WHILE and DO...WHILE Loops

Below we shall consider typical applications of WHILE and DO...WHILE loops using *sentinels* which are used to solve many of the typical problems programmers face.

Sentinel-controlled Loops

 **Think Spot**

A sentinel guards a camp or looks for approaching danger and gives warning. In the movie series *The Matrix*, the sentinel robots kept watch for signs of the human uprising. In programming terms a sentinel is a variable that is monitored for a particular value. A sentinel-controlled loop iterates while the value of the sentinel variable is not equal to a terminating value. Consider the following problem:

> *It is required to calculate the average age of a class of children. The program should be able to calculate the average for any number of children (including zero). Children's ages will be entered one at a time. When there are no more ages to enter the user will indicate this by entering an age value of 0. Once all the ages have been entered the algorithm will display the average age of the group.*

I could show you right away how this is solved using a sentinel-controlled loop, but it would help you more to work it through from first principles using the *HTTLAP* strategy.

Understanding the Problem

Q. What are we being asked to do?

A. We need to calculate and display the average age of a class of children.

Q. What is required? Try restating the problem.

A. A collection of children's ages and an age of zero to tell the algorithm we have finished entering age values are required. So, the algorithm must ask for the user to enter ages and must stop accepting ages once an age of zero has been entered. Following that it must calculate and display the average age of those entered by the user. Here is a sketch of the problem situation:

FIGURE 6.8 **Some groups of children and their average ages**

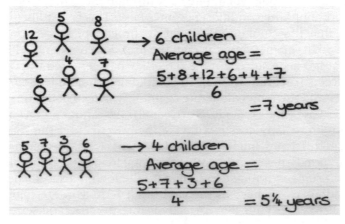

Q. What is the unknown? Have you made any assumptions?

A. For a given set of ages there are two unknowns: the average age, and the total age of all the children. Also, as the size of the groups can vary, the number of children is also unknown. There is one more thing. In my sketch of the problem the first group has an average age of 7 (a whole number) while the second group has an average age of 5.25 years (a fractional value). The problem statement did not specify whether the average should be calculated or reported as a whole number or as a decimal fraction. Without any opportunity to find out I shall assume that a decimal fraction is required.

Q. What are the principal parts of the problem?

A. The principal parts would seem to be the problem data (a set of ages, the total age of the group, the number of ages in the group, and the group's average age), getting the ages into the program, and calculating and displaying the average. Table 6.4 shows the variables we are likely to need in the solution to this problem.

Table 6.4   Variables for the Average Age Problem

Identifier	Description	Range of Values
1. `age`	Holds the age of an individual child (a zero is used as an end marker)	0 to 17
2. `numberOfAges`	Holds the number of individual ages entered Needed for calculation of average	0 to ... ?
3. `totalAge`	Total of all ages added together	0 to ... ?
4. `averageAge`	The average of the ages	0.0 to ... ?

Devising a Plan to Solve the Problem

Q. Have you solved this problem before?

A. Perhaps. Exercise 3 in Chapter 5 required us to calculate the average payload of a delivery van. If you did that exercise then you have solved a problem similar to this one before.

Q. Are any parts of the problem more easily solved than others?

A. Calculating the average is easier than getting the numbers in. Getting the numbers will need some iteration while calculating the average is simple arithmetic.

Q. Can you satisfy all the conditions of the problem? Has anything been left out?

A. We must be careful when calculating the average that the user has actually entered some age values. If the number of ages entered is zero, then we must not attempt to calculate the average as we will be trying to divide by zero which cannot be done.

Carrying Out the Plan

Q. Write down the general sequence of actions necessary to solve the general problem.

A. Solution 6.8 below shows my outline solution to the problem.

Solution 6.8 Calculating the average age: outline solution

```
1.  Get the ages from the user ;
2.  Calculate and display the average age ;
```

Q. Should all actions be carried out in every circumstance?

A. No. I already identified that the average should only be calculated when the user has entered at least one age.

Q. Should some actions be repeated?

A. Action #1 involves iteration as we must allow the user to repeatedly enter age values.

Having identified the need for a selection and an iteration I need to refine my solution:

Solution 6.9 Calculating the average age: expanded outline solution

```
1.  Get first age from user ;
2.  WHILE (ages to process)
    // Process age
    // Get next age
    ENDWHILE
3.  IF (more than zero ages entered)
        3.1.  Calculate average age ;
        3.2.  Display average age ;
    ENDIF
```

Is the above solution sufficient? No – the body of the loop needs to be completed as does the condition and body for the IF in Action #3. This section is supposed to be about sentinel-controlled loops, so let's quickly complete writing Action #3 and get back to focusing on the loop.

Solution 6.10 Age average calculation

```
1.  Get first age from user ;
2.  WHILE (ages to process)
    // Process age
    // Get next age
    ENDWHILE
3.   IF (numberOfAges > 0)
        3.1  averageAge ← totalAge ÷ numberOfAges ;
        3.2  Display averageAge ;
    ENDIF
```

Let us focus on constructing the loop for Action #2. The first question to ask is why have I chosen a WHILE construct rather than a DO...WHILE? Simply because it is possible to enter a zero as the first age. As zero is the value that is used to terminate the loop we have a zero-or-more iteration. Being an at-least-once iteration the DO...WHILE loop would cause the program to treat the zero entered by the user as an actual age value. There is a way round this which we shall look at later on, but for now we will stick with the WHILE as that is the natural zero-or-more iteration.

In this problem we need the WHILE to terminate when the age entered by the user has a value of zero. This means that we must get the user to enter an age value prior to the start of the loop so that its value can be tested in the WHILE's condition. Recall from above that this is known as a read-ahead loop as the value tested in the loop condition is fetched immediately ahead of the loop. As we shall see below when we look at end-of-file-controlled loops, some situations call for a read-and-process structure rather than a read-ahead technique.

The read-ahead ▶ technique revisited

Action #1 can be expanded into two actions: one to prompt the user to enter an age and another to put that value into the age variable. The WHILE loop needs to terminate when the age entered by the user is zero, so the conditional expression needs to be age ≠ 0 – that is, age not-equal-to zero. Within the body of the loop we need to do three things: first add the age entered to the running total; second we must add 1 to the variable numberOfAges which keeps count of the number of ages entered by the user; and third we need to get another age value from the user. Thus we get Solution 6.11 below:

Solution 6.11 Calculating the average age: completed WHILE loop

```
1.   Display 'Please enter an age (zero to finish)';
2.   Get value of age ;
3.   WHILE (age ≠ 0)
        3.1.   totalAge ← totalAge + age ;
        3.2.   numberOfAges ← numberOfAges + 1 ;
        3.3.   Display 'Please enter an age (zero to finish)';
        3.4.   Get value of age ;
     ENDWHILE
4.   IF (numberOfAges > 0)
        4.1.   averageAge ← totalAge ÷ numberOfAges ;
        4.2.   Display averageAge ;
     ENDIF
```

There is one more thing to do – we should complete our solution with the necessary variable initializations.

Solution 6.12 Average age calculation: with variable initializations

```
1.   numberOfAges ← 0 ;  // Initialize numberOfAges to zero
2.   totalAge ← 0 ;      // Initialize totalAge to zero
3.   Display 'Please enter an age (zero to finish)';
4.   Get value of age ;
```

```
5.   WHILE ([age] ≠ 0)
     5.1.   [totalAge] ← [totalAge] + [age] ;
     5.2.   [numberOfAges] ← [numberOfAges] + 1 ;
     5.3.   Display 'Please enter an age (zero to finish)';
     5.4.   Get value of [age] ;
     ENDWHILE
6.   IF ([numberOfAges] > 0)
     6.1.   [averageAge] ← [totalAge] ÷ [numberOfAges] ;
     6.2.   Display [averageAge] ;
     ENDIF
```

Have a look now at the WHILE loop (Action #5) in Solution 6.12. This is an example of a *sentinel-controlled loop*. Notice how the variable age is used here. The loop terminates when the age variable gets a value of zero. For this reason, age is called the *sentinel* for the loop – the variable is like a guard that monitors the incoming data and causes an alert to go out when a particular value is observed (in this case, zero). Of course, no alerts really happen, and the variable does not actually monitor anything, but thinking of the variable as a sentinel is a useful metaphor. Many programming terms are metaphors because grounding concepts in real-world objects and activities can aid understanding.

6.6 Chapter Summary

In this chapter you learned how to construct sequences, iterations, and selections to fit a range of common programming problems. You learned about counter-controlled (FOR) loops and sentinel-controlled (WHILE and DO...WHILE) loops, simple (IF) and extended (IF...ELSE) selections.

6.7 Exercises

1. There are two things wrong with the following IF...ELSE statement. What are they?

```
IF ([mark] ≥ 40)
   Display 'You have passed.'
ELSE IF ([mark] ≤ 40)
   Display 'You have failed.'
ENDIF
```

2. When should you use a FOR loop rather than a WHILE or DO...WHILE loop? When should you use a DO...WHILE rather than a WHILE or FOR loop?

3. As any loop written using a FOR or a DO...WHILE can also be constructed using the basic WHILE construct, what is the benefit of using the FOR and DO...WHILE?

4. State the difference between a determinate and an indeterminate loop.

5. In Stocksfield High School, all the children's work is marked out of 5. An A grade is awarded for work scoring between 4 and 5. A score of at least 3 would get a B

grade, and a C is given for a score of at least 2. Any other score gets an F (fail). For example, scores of 4.0, 4.8, and 5 would get grade A, 3.2 and 3.9 would get a B, 2.9 a C and 1.9 an F. Write an IF...ELSE construct that assigns the appropriate grade to the variable studentGrade depending on the value of the variable studentMark.

6. Stocksfield High School has just changed its grading system. Now an A grade is given for marks between 4 and 5, a B for marks of at least 3.5, a C for marks of at least 3.0, a new pass grade D for marks of at least 2.0, and an F for every mark lower than 2.0. Amend your solution to Exercise 5 to account for this change.

7. Write your solution to Exercise 6 using a sequence of IF statements without ELSE parts. What do you have to do to the condition of each IF statement in order to ensure they work properly?

8. Extend your solution to Exercise 5 to assign to calculate and display the student grades for a class of twenty students.[12]

9. Using *HTTLAP* design an algorithm for a guessing game. The algorithm should choose a number between 1 and 10 and the player has three tries in which to guess the number. If the player guesses correctly, the response "Correct!" should be given. When an incorrect guess is made, the response should be "Hot!" if the guess was one away from the actual number, "Warm..." when the guess is two away, and "COLD!" when the guess is three or more away. Make sure your loop finishes if the player guesses correctly in less than three turns.

10. *Honest Brian's Insurance* sells car insurance policies. The company is owned by Brian who is a cautious type and so hikes the premiums for young male drivers (who are statistically much more likely to make a claim). The basic premium charge is 3% of the value of the vehicle. This figure is raised by 11% for male drivers under 25 years of age, and by 6% for female drivers under the age of 21. A further £/$/€ 250 is added to the premium of any driver who has had any kind of speeding ticket. Design an algorithm to calculate the insurance premiums for the drivers in Table 6.5 (which also shows the premium your algorithm should generate).

Table 6.5   Driver Details and Insurance Premiums

Name	Age	Sex	Car Value	Speeding Ticket?	Premium
Nick	60	M	15,000	No	450.00
Chris	24	M	24,000	No	799.20
Lynne	23	F	8,000	No	240.00
Alf	17	M	35,000	Yes	1,415.50
Shadi	23	M	15,000	No	499.50
Becky	18	F	12,000	Yes	631.60

---

[12] Hint: You will need an iteration construct. Is the loop determinate or indeterminate?

11. The Beaufort scale is used to classify wind speeds. Use Table 6.6 to design an algorithm that declares a variable `windSpeed`, assigns that variable a value representing the wind speed in miles-per-hour (use zero for values < 1) and then displays the corresponding Beaufort number and description. For example, if `windSpeed` had the value 20 the algorithm would display

`Beaufort scale:5, Fresh breeze.`

Table 6.6   **Wind Speeds in the Beaufort Scale**

Beaufort Scale	Wind Speed (miles per hour)	Description
0	<1	Calm
1	1–3	Light air
2	4–7	Light breeze
3	8–12	Gentle breeze
4	13–18	Moderate breeze
5	19–24	Fresh breeze
6	25–31	Strong breeze
7	32–38	Near gale
8	39–46	Gale
9	47–64	Strong gale
10	55–63	Storm
11	64–72	Violent storm
12	≥73	Hurricane

12. You have been asked by an online bookstore to design an algorithm that calculates postage costs. Postage is calculated by adding a fixed weight-based charge to a handling fee for each book in the order. Table 6.7 shows how the charge is calculated.

Table 6.7   **Internet Bookstore Postage Charges**

Weight	Postage Rate	Handling Fee per Book
Up to 200 g	1.75	0.25
Up to 400 g	2.50	0.40
Up to 1000 g	4.00	0.45
Over 1000 g	6.00	0.5

For example, an order for one book weighing 180 g would cost 1.75 + 0.25 = 2.00 to deliver. An order weighing 1500 g total with three books in it would cost 6.00 + 0.5 × 3 = 7.50 to deliver. Using *HTTLAP*, design an algorithm that calculates the postage charge for book orders. The parcel weight and number of books in the order should be provided by the user. The algorithm should calculate postage costs for an unspecified number of orders, terminating when the parcel weight given by the user is a negative number.

13. Stocksfield High School gives e-mail addresses to all its pupils in the form:

    `givenName.familyName@stocksfieldhigh.ac.uk`

    Teachers are given email addresses of the form:

    `firstInitial.secondInitial.familyName@stocksfieldhigh.ac.uk`

    where the second initial may not be present.
    Table 6.8 shows some example teacher and pupil names and the corresponding e-mail addresses.

Table 6.8   Stocksfield High School e-mail Addresses

Teachers	e-mail	Pupils	e-mail
Henry Higgins	`h.higgins@ ...`	Emily Harris	`emily.harris@ ...`
Alfred P. Doolittle	`a.p.doolittle@ ...`	Sarah Jane Smith	`sarah.smith@ ...`
Jennifer P.D. Quick	`j.p.quick@ ...`	John Dobby	`John.dobby@ ...`

Design an algorithm that declares a variable `emailAddress`, assigns to the variable a value provided by the user, and displays the family name of the owner of that e-mail address and whether they are a pupil or a teacher. For example, if the user typed in

`emily.harris@stocksfieldhigh.ac.uk`

the algorithm would display

`Harris:Pupil.`

If the user typed

`a.p.doolittle@stocksfieldhigh.ac.uk`

The algorithm would display

`Doolittle:Teacher.`

Note: The algorithm should be able to handle any valid Stocksfield High e-mail address, not just the ones listed in Table 6.8.

14. Design an algorithm that declares an integer variable `timesTable`, gets a value for this variable, and displays the times table up to 15 $\times$ n. For example, if `timesTable` had the value 12, then the following output would be displayed:

    ```
    1 × 12 = 12
    2 × 12 = 24
    3 × 12 = 36
    4 × 12 = 48
    5 × 12 = 60
    6 × 12 = 72
    ```

$$7 \times 12 = 84$$
$$8 \times 12 = 96$$
$$9 \times 12 = 108$$
$$10 \times 12 = 120$$
$$11 \times 12 = 132$$
$$12 \times 12 = 144$$
$$13 \times 12 = 156$$
$$14 \times 12 = 168$$
$$15 \times 12 = 180$$

6.8 Projects

StockSnackz Vending Machine

Now that you have been introduced to the IF...ELSE construct, revise your previous vending machine solution to deal more elegantly with the problem of dispensing the chosen snack. Using IF...ELSE will also make the problem of dealing with buttons 0, 7, 8, and 9 much simpler.

Now that a proper selection construct has been used it is time to make the vending machine much more interesting. The University of Stocksfield is losing too much money through greedy staff stocking up on free snacks. With the exception of the sales summary (Button 6) all items must now be paid for and cost 10 pence each. If a user presses a button for a snack before sufficient money has been inserted an "insufficient funds" message should be displayed. If the user has deposited sufficient money for an item then the machine will dispense the chosen snack. Assume no change is given. Extend your solution to reflect these new requirements.

Now extend your solution so that if the user has deposited more than 10 pence the machine gives any required change after dispensing the chosen item. You may assume that the machine always has sufficient stock of each denomination of coin to be able to make exact change. The machine accepts (and gives back) the following denominations of coins: 1, 2, 5, 10, 20, 50 pence. Change should be dispensed using the fewest coins possible. Note, you have already solved the change-giving problem (see the exercises for Chapter 3) so see if that solution can be reused (perhaps with some amendments) here. There is a mathematical operator called *modulo* which gives the remainder after division. It often has the symbol %, but our pseudo-code uses MOD. It works like this: $20 \div 7 = 2 : 7$ goes into 20 twice. 20 MOD $7 = 6$: the left over after dividing 20 by 7 is 6. You will find this useful for working out how to give change.

In the United Kingdom and countries using the euro currency, another two denominations of coin are available. The United Kingdom has £1 and £2 coins and the Euro Zone similarly has €1 and €2 coins. Extend your solution to cater for these larger denomination coins. If your machine works on U.S. dollars and you would like to accept the rarer half-dollar and one-dollar coins, by all means go ahead.

Stocksfield Fire Service

In this chapter you learned about alternative iteration and selection constructs. Examine your EAC algorithm and replace IF statements with IF...ELSE constructs wherever possible. What benefits does this bring?

Puzzle World: Roman Numerals and Chronograms

Examine your solutions to the Roman number problems and decide whether you need to use any of the alternative iteration and selection constructs. Update your algorithms accordingly.

Pangrams: Holoalphabetic Sentences

The pangram algorithm needs to be amended so that it allows the test to be run on any number of sentences. The algorithm should keep testing sentences until the user decides to finish. Rewrite your solution to incorporate this feature. What iteration constructs could be used? How will you solve the problem of deciding whether the user wants to continue? Explain why you used your chosen solution strategy. What other loop constructs could you have used? How would that affect the way the algorithm behaves? What other ways could you have tested to see if the user wants to finish? What are the principal advantages and disadvantages of your solution and these alternative solutions?

Online Bookstore: ISBNs

The ISBN validation problem is best suited to using a count-controlled loop for the part which deals with multiplying the nine digits of the number with their respective weights. Update your solution replacing the WHILE construct with an appropriately phrased FOR loop.

You are now in a position to tackle the hyphenation problem. For correct presentation, the ten digits of an ISBN should be divided into four parts separated by hyphens:

- Part 1: The country or group of countries identifier
- Part 2: The publisher identifier
- Part 3: The title identifier
- Part 4: The check digit

To keep matters as simple as possible we will only deal with hyphenating ISBNs that have a group/country code of 0 or 1 (the English language groups). The positions of the hyphens are determined by the publisher codes. To hyphenate correctly, knowledge of the prefix ranges for each country or group of countries is needed. The publisher code ranges in the English group (U.S., U.K., Canada, Australia, New Zealand, etc.) are given in Table 6.9.

Table 6.9   **Hyphenation for Group "0" ISBNs**

Group Identifier "0" Publisher Code Ranges	If Publisher Ranges are Between	Insert Hyphens After		
00—————————————19	00–19	1st digit	3rd digit	9th digit
200——————————699	20–69	"	4th "	"
7000—————————8499	70–84	"	5th "	"
85000————————89999	85–89	"	6th "	"
900000————————949999	90–94	"	7th "	"
9500000—————9999999	95–99	"	8th "	"

Using Table 6.9 develop an algorithm for displaying with correctly placed hyphens any ISBN that starts with digit 0.[13, 14]

For an extra challenge, allow ISBNs with a group code of 1 to be hyphenated. The rules for this group are slightly different than for group "0" and are given in Table 6.10.

Table 6.10   **Hyphenation for Group "1" ISBNs**

Group Identifier "1" Publisher Code Ranges	If Publisher Ranges are Between	Insert Hyphens After		
00—————————————09	00–09	1st digit	3rd digit	9th digit
100——————————399	10–39	"	4th "	"
4000—————————5499	40–54	"	5th "	"
55000————————86979	5500–8697	"	6th "	"
869800————————998999	8698–9989	"	7th "	"
9990000—————9999999	9990–9999	"	8th "	"

This problem is slightly trickier than the group 0 hyphenation because you are not always just testing the first two digits of the publisher code. Use your solution to the group 0 hyphenation problem as a starting point and then work through the *HTTLAP* strategy to help you arrive at a solution to this problem.

---

[13] Hint: You can see that the publisher code takes between two and seven digits. Every ISBN with group identifier of 0 or 1 has a hyphen after the first digit (the group code) and after the ninth digit (i.e., immediately before the check digit). The third hyphen is inserted after the publisher code. For an ISBN in group 0 you can tell from the first two digits of the publisher code how long the rest of the code is. For example, looking at the table above we see that publisher codes beginning with digits in the range 20..69 are three digits in length, while those beginning 95..99 are seven digits long.

[14] Another hint: You need to manipulate the ISBN digit-by-digit. We have not covered how to access individual characters, so when it comes to that aspect use informal *HTTLAP* pseudo-code.

7 Object Orientation: Taking a Different View

7.1   The Procedural Paradigm

7.2   Objects and Classes, Properties and Methods

7.3   Chapter Summary

7.4   Exercises

7.5   Projects

Learning Objectives

- Recognize the difference between procedural and object-oriented problem solving
- Analyze real-world problems to identify the object classes, properties, and methods needed to solve a problem in an object-oriented manner

In this chapter we consider another way of approaching algorithmic problem solving in which the solution is structured around objects which are collections of related data items and their associated actions. Using objects as the basis for algorithms is a very popular programming technique but it is very easy to do badly unless some particular rules are followed very carefully. Because of the very introductory nature of this chapter it is beyond the scope of this book to consider those rules (which can be very subtle) in depth so we will focus instead on the bigger picture which will give you a foundation should you need to learn an object-oriented programming language (such as Java, Eiffel, C++, C#) at a later date.

7.1 The Procedural Paradigm

Up till now we have been designing algorithms by considering what actions need to be performed and what data (variables, data items) are needed to support those actions. We have constructed our algorithms using control abstractions (IF, FOR, WHILE, and DO ... WHILE statements) for the building blocks of sequence, iteration, and selection and data abstractions (numbers and text) for dealing with the values handled in the algorithms. We have been following what is called the *procedural paradigm* for programming. A paradigm is a generally accepted way of doing things within a particular discipline. Programming has a number of different paradigms or ways of viewing problems and expressing solutions to them.

Computers from the 1950s until the present day have been built according to a fundamental design called the VON NEUMANN architecture. In such computers the central processing unit (or CPU – the main part of the computer's processor chip) carries out in sequence instructions that manipulate values stored in the computer's memory. Early programming languages were designed to mimic the operation of a VON NEUMANN machine: the languages had variables to represent values in the computer's memory, instructions were executed sequentially, and assignment statements were used to manipulate the values of the variables. Such languages belong to the procedural (also known as imperative) paradigm. However, this is not the only way that computation can be carried out and different programming paradigms arose to facilitate different ways of solving problems. Besides procedural programming the other main paradigm in use today is *object-oriented programming*, supported by languages such as Smalltalk, Java, Delphi, C#, C++, and Visual Basic.NET. Because even the object-oriented languages use procedural structures inside their objects the approach of this book has been procedural and the *HTTLAP* pseudo-code has followed the procedural model. Of course, today's programmers must be conversant in the object-oriented way of doing things, so in this chapter we will give an overview of the object-oriented way of looking at the world. This serves two purposes. First, you should learn that many of the problem solving skills you have been developing are equally applicable in this object-oriented paradigm. Secondly, this chapter will prepare the ground so that should you need to learn an object-oriented language such as Java or C# in the future, the concepts will not be alien to you.

7.2 Objects and Classes, Properties and Methods

In the procedural approach solutions are constructed by considering the data belonging to the problem and then designing algorithms that manipulate (process) that data to achieve the desired outcome. For example, in the coffee-making problem we identified the following data items:

- The number of coffees to be made
- The milk preference of a drinker
- The sugar requirements of a drinker
- The number of cups poured so far
- The number of sugars added to a cup so far

We then used our understanding of the problem and its data to design an algorithm that correctly manipulated those data items so as to make and pour the required number of cups of coffee each with its own milk and sugar combinations. A computer program is then created by translating the algorithm into programming language code.

Consider the problem of opening and operating an account with an online digital music download service. We might identify key operations such as "open account," "credit account," "spend money," "download track," "query the balance," "query download history," "close account," and so on. We might also identify key data such as account number, amount deposited, amount spent, current balance, customer name, customer address, country in which the account is held, date account was opened, date account was closed, and so on. In our procedural way of thinking we would design a set of algorithms to solve the problem of carrying out these operations and the algorithms would use the variables we identified to store the necessary values.

We can see that some of the data values are associated directly with the music store account, while others are associated with the customer who holds the account. The customer (name, address) pays money into the account while the account receives money from the customer. The account has a balance which the customer may request. The customer may view a history of all recent downloads. Receipts for track downloads are e-mailed to the customer. When discussing the problem sometimes we talk about individual data items, but other times we talk in a more abstract way about the entities/objects/things to which those items belong, such as "my iTunes account," "Customer No. 35478," and so on. In 1967 Alan Kay coined the term Object-Oriented Programming to refer to programming that is focused upon these objects and the actions they perform.

Where procedural algorithms (the kind we have been writing up until now) focus upon data and the operations needed to manipulate that data, an object-oriented solution focuses on the behaviour of *objects*. An object is a mechanism for gathering together into a single package a set of related data items and operations that provide views of the state of those data.

For example, a music downloading system written in a procedural way would have variables to hold customer account details and various algorithms to allow account transactions to be recorded. In an object-oriented approach the account variables and their associated algorithms would be gathered together and stored inside an object. The principle is that data and the operations that manipulate the data are kept together separate from other data and operations. Access to the data is tightly controlled which, in theory, makes it much harder for one part of a program to cause problems in another part.

Consider Figure 7.1, which shows a receipt sent by Brian's Digital Downloads to its customer Professor Henry Higgins. Make sure you do the following exercise before moving on.

Look at the statement and identify the information that pertains to Professor Higgins' account.

FIGURE 7.1   **Receipt from Brian's Digital Downloads (aka BriTunes)**

From: Brian's Digital Downloads
Subject: **Receipt #19298398**
Date: 8 May 2007 14:00:01
To: Henry Higgins

Receipt

Invoiced To:
Prof. Henry Higgins
27a Wimpole Street
London, W1G 8GP

Item	Artist	Title	Price
B1010	Plastic Bertrand	Ça plane pour moi	0.99

Account: 52747   Total: 0.99
Paid by Credit Card •••• •••• •••• 9876
Thanks for shopping with us. Please visit again.

You might have decided that the account number, name of account holder, and the registered credit card are all associated with the account. We might also consider that the receipt number, transaction details, and Professor Higgins' address also belong to the account, but it could be argued that the receipt number and transaction details belong to a transaction and the address belongs to a customer (Professor Higgins). The account, transaction, and customer are all associated with each other, but could be considered to be separate entities. Each transaction itself has an item number (identifying the track downloaded), the name of the artist, the title of the track, and the price paid. All these details relate to the account with the number 52747 belonging to Professor Higgins.

So, we see data belonging to a customer account, data belonging to the customer, and data belonging to a transaction. While an account, a customer, and a transaction are associated, they are not the same thing: a customer possesses characteristics that an account and a transaction do not. Thus, by taking an abstract view we can treat these sets of data as part of a larger entity. In the case of Figure 7.1 we might say these entities are Account #52747, Customer Professor Henry Higgins, and the Transaction for item B1010 (we might also decide Item is something of interest too).

Classes

Because the BriTunes music store will have many accounts, customers, and transactions, we would say that Henry Higgins' account is simply an instance of a more general BriTunes Account class. Higgins himself is an instance of another class of entity called Customer, and so on. There will be many individual accounts each with its own specific details, many customers each with their own name and address, and many transactions. In the object-oriented world we call these different groups of entities **classes**. A class is simply a name given to a kind of object, defining the range of properties and activities associated with that object.

We already use classes in the everyday world. Take the number 7. Seven belongs to the class of numbers known as NATURAL NUMBERS. In mathematics, the natural numbers are all the positive integers from 1 to infinity.[1] Natural numbers have certain properties, the most obvious, perhaps, being that they are whole numbers and possess no fractional parts. They also have certain actions associated with them that may be used to manipulate them. For instance, we know we can add, subtract, multiply, and divide them, we can raise them to a power, and so on. In object-oriented parlance we might define a class called `NaturalNumbers`. Any object belonging to that class would then only be able to take values between 1 and infinity. The class would also provide actions such as +, −, ×, ÷ which could be used to change the property of a natural number object. Does this look familiar? It should, because we have already seen something like this in the form of abstract data types in Chapter 6. We said that an abstract data type, or ADT, is a way of defining the range of permissible values for a data item belonging to that type together with the set of operations that can be performed upon those values. In fact, classes are closely related to ADTs. An ADT defines a set of values together with operations that may be used with those values. A class defines a set of operations that may be used to provide a view onto its properties. At a simplistic level ADTs and object classes look the same.[2]

**Classes ▶
appear
similar
to ADTs**

FIGURE 7.2   **Classes are templates for creating objects**

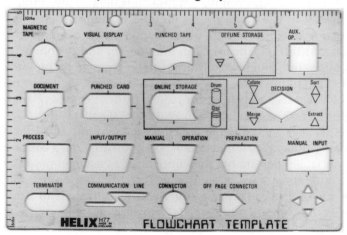

A class, then, is a template for creating objects of a given type. Figure 7.2 is a picture of my old student flowcharting template (circa 1985). Each of the cut outs is a template for drawing an instance of the cut out type. For example, the rectangular cut out labeled "Process" (second from bottom on the left) is used for drawing

---

[1] In Computer Science the natural numbers go from zero to infinity.

[2] At this stage it may be helpful to think of a class as a kind of abstract data type, though they are not the same. The difference between an ADT and an object class is subtle but really quite profound. It is beyond the scope of this book to enter into a discussion of how they are different.

many individual process box objects. The cut out is the template, the object that is drawn with it on the paper is an instance of that template class (see Figure 7.3).

FIGURE 7.3   Objects drawn with the template

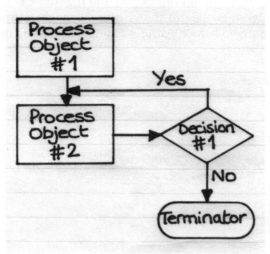

In a banking problem we might have a class called CurrentAccount which we can use to create individual bank account objects such as myAccount, hisAccount, herAccount, and so on.

Because the properties of an account need to be manipulated – balances need to be updated, money needs to be paid in and withdrawn, new statements need to be produced, and so on – a class has a set of behaviours or associated capabilities that define what that class can do, which of its properties may be changed, which may be viewed, and so on. These behaviours are called **methods** as they are the method by which an object manipulates its properties.

To summarize: a **class** brings together a set of data items known as **properties** (also called **members**) and a collection of **methods** which are the algorithms that define how those properties may be manipulated and accessed. An **object** is an individual occurrence or **instance** of the class in which the actual data items for an individual object are stored.

Getting Up in the Morning

To illustrate how we might take an object-oriented view of a problem, let's return to one of the first problems we tackled in Chapter 2, that of getting up in the morning. A rough procedural solution written in pseudo-code might look like this:

Solution 7.1 Procedural approach to getting up in the morning

```
1.   Switch off alarm ;
2.   Get out of bed ;
3.   Wash/shower face, brush teeth, etc. ;
4.   Get dressed ;
```

Of course, the algorithm might differ for you – it's very much geared towards my own routine. In the object-oriented world view we would see our task as building a simulation of the problem situation. That means we need to define classes that represent the principal parts of the problem. Remember that a class defines a set of behaviours that an object (thing) can exhibit and that those behaviours change the properties of the object. Figure 7.4 shows how we might define a `Person` class to represent the person who is waking up, washing, and getting dressed.

FIGURE 7.4 **Class definition for Person**

class Person	
Properties	awake: yes, no ; inBed: yes, no ; needsShower: yes, no ; isDressed: yes, no ;
Methods	WakeUp ; GoToSleep ; GetUp ; GoToBed ; GetWashed ; GetDressed ; GetUndressed ;

We can see that a `Person` object would possess a number of properties. There are data items representing whether the person is awake or asleep, in or out of bed, in need of a shower, and wearing clothes or not. (You might also have decided that a `Person` should have a name). Notice that for each of these properties I have also followed the practice of earlier chapters and have indicated the range of values they can take. Associated with each of these four properties are methods that change the properties' values: `WakeUp` and `GoToSleep` would change the value of `awake` to "Yes" and "No" respectively. `GetUp` and `GoToBed` would change the value of `inBed`, and `GetDressed` and `GetUndressed` would set `isDressed` to the appropriate value. We can also see that `GetWashed` might be used to change the value of `needsShower` to "No," but what would change it to "Yes"? We might decide that a shower is needed every morning, so we could arrange for `WakeUp` to also set `needsShower` to "Yes" to reflect this state of affairs. Clearly there are different ways we could set this out, but the point to note is that an object possesses properties (data items that describe its current state) and methods that are used to view and change these data items. It is a principle of object orientation that only the methods of the object itself should be allowed to manipulate its properties. Looking back at the getting up algorithm in Solution 7.1 we can see that something is missing: what of the alarm? Why is there no `SwitchOffAlarm` operation in the `Person` class?

In the light of what was said above about an object's operations being used to view and change an object's properties, spend a few moments thinking through why it might not be appropriate to have a `SwitchOffAlarm` operation in the `Person` class.

Huh?

You said that the methods would change the values of the classes' properties, but I cannot see where this happens.

Indeed. What we have done is taken an abstract view and have treated the methods as if they will automatically do what we need them to. In fact, a method is just an algorithm and at some point we will need to specify the actions that they must perform in order to have the desired effect. For now we will not be doing that and instead will concentrate on the higher-level problem of identifying the classes involved in the problem and of designing an overall algorithm that will get the object of those classes to do what we need. At the end of this chapter you will find some exercises that get you to try designing the algorithms for the individual methods.

The reason why there is no `SwitchOffAlarm` operation in the `Person` class is that the alarm itself could not reasonably be considered to be a property of a `Person`. A popular tenet of OO thinking is that classes should only possess properties that strictly belong to objects of that class. A person might own an alarm clock, but an alarm clock is not part of the make up of a person. If an alarm is not truly one of the attributes of a person, but it plays an important role in our problem, then we decide that it must be an object in its own right.

Following the way we defined a `Person` class above to guide you try writing out a class definition for an `Alarm` object. Think about the essential properties we need to capture for this problem and then consider what methods will be needed to change those properties.

Solution 7.2 below shows my definition for the `Alarm` class.

Solution 7.2 Possible definition for Alarm class

class Alarm	
Properties	ringing: yes, no ; time: 00:00:00 to 23:59:00 ; alarmTime: 00:00:00 to 23:59:00 ; alarmIsSet: on, off ;
Methods	SetTime: hh:mm:ss ; GetTime ; SetAlarmTime: hh:mm ; GetAlarmTime ; SetAlarm ; UnsetAlarm ; StartRinging ; SwitchOff ; (i.e. stop ringing)

Compare your solution to mine. I don't expect your solution to be exactly the same as mine as you were not given any information about the problem situation, so you have had free rein to be inventive. Also, do not treat my solutions as complete or exhaustive – they are merely indicative. In my `Alarm` class I have identified four properties. `ringing` is simply an indicator of whether the alarm is ringing/beeping or not. The alarm will start ringing at the appointed time by the `StartRinging` method. We can stop the alarm ringing with its `SwitchOff` method. The `time` property is used to make sure the alarm's clock is set. We can set the time with `SetTime` and see what time the alarm is set to with `GetTime`. The reason for the colon followed by an "hh:mm:ss" time specification indicates that the `SetTime` method needs information to work with. The statement that tells `Alarm` to run its `SetTime` method must also provide a time value otherwise `SetTime` will not know what time to set the clock to. `alarmTime` is the property used to specify what time the alarm should go off (say, 7 a.m.). The `alarmTime` is set with `SetAlarmTime` (another method that needs a value to be given to it, hence the colon) and can be viewed with `GetAlarmTime`. I have assumed that the alarm time only needs to be set to the nearest minute hence the lack of an "ss" value in the `SetAlarmTime` method. Finally, we do not want our alarm to go off every morning – perhaps you have a lie in at the weekend? So the `Alarm` has a property `alarmIsSet`: if this is "on" then the alarm will go off at the time specified by `alarmTime` and if it is "off" then it will not ring. `SetAlarm` is used to turn this property "on" and `UnsetAlarm` to turn it "off." Note that this is different from `SwitchOff` which is used to stop the alarm ringing when it has gone off.

Huh?

Is it me, or is this all getting quite complicated? The problem of getting up in the morning seemed quite simple until you started talking about objects. Now it seems needlessly complicated.

No, it's not you. Unfortunately, because of the way we need to think about problems in the OO paradigm, before we can begin to structure algorithms that describe the overall solution we need to expend a lot of effort defining the objects, their properties, and their operations. The getting up in the morning problem is a very simple one that is very easy and quick to tackle with procedural thinking. Alas, object orientation is better suited to larger more complex problems. At the moment we are doing the equivalent of using an 18-wheeler to deliver a pizza. If we had to ship 10,000 pizzas from coast to coast, the truck would become a more attractive option, but for local deliveries of a few pizzas we suffer from a problem of large fixed overheads. The difficulty we face is that using a complex problem of the sort that would really benefit from an OO solution would require a lot of even harder concepts to be faced at once. So, we will continue with this smaller problem in the knowledge that the ideas being learned here will seem much more appropriate when applied to a larger problem. For example, how to manage the morning routines of a dormitory of 200 people with an unknown number of alarm clocks, a limited number of showers, and different getting-up and going-to-bed times.

So far we have managed to identify two classes and define their behaviours. What we need now is some way of getting those classes to actually perform their operations. What we must do is to create new objects that belong to these classes and then instruct those objects to carry out their various methods. For the sake of keeping matters as simple as possible what we will do is design an algorithm that wraps all this up together. In object-oriented terms we will be creating a **controller** that handles the creation of the objects needed in the solution and telling those objects what to do. First of all we need to create an individual `Person` object. Remember that classes are only templates. Just as a cookie cutter is not a cookie, it is a template for a cookie and to get a cookie we must press the cutter into the dough, so we must create a `Person` object from the `Person` template. Let's create a `Person` object called `brian` thus:

1. `brian` ← new Person;

**Object
instantiation** ▶ In object-oriented parlance creating a new object from a class is called **instantiation** as we are creating a new *instance* of a class (just like creating a new cookie

using the cookie cutter). This would set up an object variable called `brian` which would have the associated data items `awake`, `inBed`, `needsShower`, `isDressed` and the methods that also belong to all `Person` objects. In our procedural solution to the problem the first action was

> `Switch off alarm ;`

As the alarm is itself an object we must instantiate it and then tell it to switch itself off. We extend our controller algorithm to give Solution 7.3:

Solution 7.3 First section of the object-oriented controller algorithm

1. `brian` ← new Person;
2. `briansAlarm` ← new Alarm ;
3. tell `briansAlarm` SwitchOff ;

Think Spot

Before we move any further we should inspect Solution 7.3 to see whether it deals fully with ensuring that `brian` is awake and the alarm is switched off. Let us assume for now that when an object is instantiated all of its properties are assigned sensible initial values. In an object-oriented programming language it is necessary to design methods that are carried out whenever an object is instantiated. Such a method (known as a *constructor*) would set the object's properties to their required starting values. For the purposes of this chapter we shall assume that these initializations are done automatically. Taking a `Person` object first, it has four properties: `awake`, `inBed`, `needsShower`, and `isDressed`. Assume for now that when a `Person` object is instantiated its properties are initialized as follows:

Property	Value
awake	No
inBed	Yes
needsShower	Yes
isDressed	No

Why do we tell the alarm to switch itself off? In the real world it would be Brian who turns off the alarm, and you said an OO solution is a simulation of the problem situation. How can an alarm switch itself off?

This is a common difficulty faced by those new to object-oriented thinking. You're right, in the real world Brian would turn off the alarm. However, in the OO world turning off an alarm requires the `Alarm` object to change one of its properties, and properties can only be changed by methods belonging to that object. What we must do is send the `Alarm` object a message asking it to turn itself off. We could, of course, insert a method in a Person object (`TurnOffAlarm`, say) that sends a message to an `Alarm` object asking it to perform its own `SwitchOff` operation. The problem is that the `Person` object then has a method that strictly does not do anything that pertains to a person; recall we said that we should try to store only properties and operations in an object that are essential to the make up of that object. There is a way of establishing a link between two objects to express the real world relationship that Brian has with his alarm (it's called an association class), but that goes beyond the scope of this chapter's brief introduction. For now, we will use a simple controller algorithm to handle all the instructions to request objects to perform their methods.

Looking at Solution 7.3 we see that although Statement #3 switches off the alarm, brian is still asleep. We need to pass brian a message to ask him to wake up:

```
tell brian WakeUp ;
```

The WakeUp method would then set the awake property from its current value of "No" to "Yes." We might reasonably expect brian to wake up before the alarm is switched off, so our algorithm now becomes Solution 7.4:

Solution 7.4 Controller algorithm extended to wake brian up

1. brian ← new Person;
2. briansAlarm ← new Alarm ;
3. tell brian WakeUp ;
4. tell briansAlarm SwitchOff ;

Now that brian is awake and the alarm switched off we can complete the action sequence by sending the brian object messages to perform the other morning methods, as in Solution 7.5.

Solution 7.5 The complete controller algorithm

1. brian ← new Person;
2. briansAlarm ← new Alarm ;
3. tell brian WakeUp ;
4. tell briansAlarm SwitchOff ;
5. tell brian GetUp ;
6. tell brian GetWashed ;
7. tell brian GetDressed ;

Think Spot

Take a closer look at Solution 7.5. We noted previously that the brian object's properties had been initialized upon instantiation to a particular set of values which meant that we had to explicitly tell the brian object to wake up. In Statement #4 we tell the briansAlarm object to switch off its ringer. What we haven't addressed in this algorithm (because we have been concerned with the more abstract problem of the overall sequence) is the question of how the alarm knew what time it was in order to start ringing in the first place. We have not dealt with setting the alarm's clock or the time at which it should ring. Usually, when plugged into a power outlet any appliance with a digital clock starts flashing "00:00" to show that its clock needs setting. What time should an Alarm object show when instantiated? We could take the real-world view and specify that its time and alarmTime properties are both set to "00:00:00" upon instantiation. Assume, then, that when an Alarm object is instantiated its properties have the following values:

Property	Value
ringing	No
time	00:00:00
alarmTime	00:000:00
alarmIsSet	No

We could then send the alarm messages to tell it to set itself to the current time and the desired waking-up time with such statements as:

```
tell briansAlarm SetTime: '10:08:35' ;

tell briansAlarm SetAlarmTime: '07:00:00' ;
```

I have introduced a colon after the operation name to show that the method requires some information for it to carry out its task. SetTime and SetAlarmTime both need time values to be able to update the time and alarmTime properties respectively. I have given the SetTime method the value "10:08:35" to work with because that was the actual time of day at which I wrote that line. We could take a more general-purpose view and write:

```
tell briansAlarm SetTime: currentTime ;
```

where currentTime represents the actual time of day at which the message is passed to the briansAlarm object. This is quite a sensible approach to take because when this algorithm eventually gets translated into programming language code we will find that the programming language we use has some kind of system clock object which can provide the current time.

Extend the controller algorithm in Solution 7.5 to include these messages to the briansAlarm object.

Solution 7.6 Controller algorithm with alarm times set

```
1.  brian ← new Person;
2.  briansAlarm ← new Alarm ;
3.  tell briansAlarm SetTime: currentTime ;
4.  tell briansAlarm SetAlarmTime: '07:00:00' ;
5.  tell brian WakeUp ;
6.  tell briansAlarm SwitchOff ;
7.  tell brian GetUp ;
8.  tell brian GetWashed ;
9.  tell brian GetDressed ;
```

Think Spot

Solution 7.6 shows the controller algorithm with the two new statements to set the alarm's clock and wake-up time. One problem still remains. Look at Statements #4 and #5, or rather, look at what happens *between* statements #4 and #5. Statement #4 passes the message to briansAlarm telling it to set itself so that it will start ringing at 7.00 a.m. Statement #5 then proceeds to tell brian to wake up. How do we know when executing Statement #5 that it really is 7.00 a.m. and that briansAlarm is ringing? This is a problem we are not going to tackle in depth here because its solution requires much lower levels of abstraction than this short introduction can provide. The expanded version of this book (*How to think like a programmer: problem solving and program design solutions for the bewildered*) goes a little deeper into object-oriented programming and considers issues just like this.

For the purposes of this high-level look at objects we can adopt a pragmatic simplification of the problem. The question is: how do we know when it is time to carry out Statement #5? In the real world we would know it is time to wake up because the alarm starts ringing and we are roused from our sleep – our brain listens out for the alarm clock's ring. In essence, what we need between Statements #4 and #5 is some kind of delaying statement (a loop perhaps?) at which the controller waits until briansAlarm starts ringing. Solution 7.7 shows the controller algorithm with such a wait operation.

Solution 7.7 Controller algorithm with wait statement

1. brian ← new Person;
2. briansAlarm ← new Alarm ;
3. tell briansAlarm SetTime: currentTime ;
4. tell briansAlarm SetAlarmTime: '07:00:00' ;
5. **wait until briansAlarm ringing property = 'Yes' ;**
6. tell brian WakeUp ;
7. tell briansAlarm SwitchOff ;
8. tell brian GetUp ;
9. tell brian GetWashed ;
10. tell brian GetDressed ;

Getting Values Out

Statement #5 in the new algorithm (Solution 7.7) tells the controller to wait until the ringing property of the briansAlarm object has the value "Yes." It appears to be accessing an object's property directly which is something we said is not good OOP practice. What we really need is a method that gives us back the value of the ringing property. We have already seen examples of methods that need information to be supplied to them in order to carry out their task (e.g. SetAlarmTime above). Let us introduce a new method to the alarm class called RingingStatus:. Here is its algorithm:

RingingStatus:

1. ← ringing ;

The slightly strange notation appears to assign the value of the ringing property to nothing at all. Imagine that the assignment statement here is passing the value of ringing outside the object and its value will be given to whatever variable is used when the RingingStatus method is used. For example, say our controller algorithm has a variable called answer. We could assign answer a value like this:

tell briansAlarm RingingStatus: answer

What this means is that the assignment statement in the RingingStatus algorithm takes the value of the object's ringing property and assigns it to the variable after the colon, in this case, answer. answer now has the same value as the ringing property of the briansAlarm object. We can now rewrite our solution with a proper loop to deal with waiting for the alarm to ring. The new version of the controller algorithm is found in Solution 7.8 with the new wait loop shown in bold.

Solution 7.8 Controller algorithm with a wait loop added

```
1.   brian ← new Person;
2.   briansAlarm ← new Alarm ;
3.   tell briansAlarm SetTime: currentTime ;
4.   tell briansAlarm SetAlarmTime: '07:00:00' ;
5.   DO
          5.1.  tell briansAlarm RingingStatus: answer ;
     WHILE (answer ≠ 'Yes') ;
6.   tell brian WakeUp ;
7.   tell briansAlarm SwitchOff ;
8.   tell brian GetUp ;
9.   tell brian GetWashed ;
10.  tell brian GetDressed ;
```

If you examine Solution 7.8 now you will see it comprises two principal parts: Statements #1–#5 set up and initialize the simulation of the real world: object instances are created for Brian and his alarm clock, the alarm clock is set to the right time, its alarm is set to 7.00 a.m., and the simulation is put into a waiting state until the alarm goes off. Statements #6–#10 deal with the actual getting up routine. If you look at Statements #6–#10 as a whole they resemble very closely our original procedural solution to the problem which was:

```
1.   Switch off alarm ;
2.   Get out of bed ;
3.   Wash/shower face, brush teeth, etc. ;
4.   Get dressed ;
```

The two may look superficially similar because object-oriented solutions still use the three building blocks of sequence, iteration, and selection. However, the journey we took to arrive at Solution 7.8 highlights the differences. The first part of Solution 7.8 is needed to set up all the objects that the remainder of the algorithm uses. The details of the updating of values are hidden within the objects themselves. In fact, we have completely ignored the issue of designing the algorithms for the objects' operations. You may be thinking that this was a lot of work to arrive a solution that resembles one we had before. It *was* a lot of work and the reason is that object-oriented solutions have a certain overhead associated with them in terms of defining and setting up all the objects that will perform the solution tasks. For very simple problems such as those we have considered in this chapter, the amount of overhead tends to outweigh the algorithms that get the objects doing the right things in the right order at the right time. However, as problems become more complex, the choice to use an object-oriented approach starts to seem more rational and less like using a sledgehammer to crack open a nut.

7.3 **Chapter Summary**

This chapter introduced you to some of the very basic principles and terminology object-oriented programming. We saw how problems are solved by identifying classes of objects which define **properties** and **methods** that individual objects belonging to that class should possess. We saw how object classes are **instantiated** to create an individual **object. Messages** are then passed to the object to instruct it to carry out its methods; an object's methods are the mechanism by which an object's properties are accessed and updated. Finally, we saw how the objects can be coordinated by the use of a **controller** algorithm. There is much more to learn about object oriented programming which is beyond the scope of this chapter. In the expanded version of this book (*How to think like a programmer: problem solving and program design solutions for the bewildered*) the object-oriented approach is considered in more detail with more complex problems in order to cover the remaining core features of object-oriented programming: inheritance, encapsulation, data hiding, and polymorphism.

7.4 **Exercises**

1. Think of a real-world piece of machinery that you use regularly. It could be a VCR, a games console, even a washing machine. Now view the item as if it were a software object: list its methods (the things it can do) and its properties (the information it needs to do its job – some of this might be represented on its display screen/light panel if it has one).

2. Design algorithms for each of the methods for the Person class.

3. Design algorithms for each of the methods for the Alarm class.

4. Assume our Person class has another method, BedStatus, that tells us the value of the inBed property. If we had several instances of the Person class, what would the algorithm look like that counts up how many of the Person objects are still in bed?

5. We defined the Person class to contain methods dealing with going to bed as well as getting up in the morning. Extend the controller algorithm in Solution 7.7 to show the brian object going to bed. Also, assume that the controller is being run on a Friday and that on Saturdays Brian sleeps late which requires his alarm to be reset to the later time of 10.00 a.m.

6. We treated the problem of getting dressed as a single action. If we assume that the task involves putting on underwear, socks, trousers, a shirt, and shoes:

    i) Define classes for each of these different clothing types (Underwear, Socks, Trousers, Shirt, Shoes). Think about what properties and methods each clothing class should have.

    ii) Instantiate the following objects belonging to the different clothing classes: tanPleats (Trousers), whiteBoxers (Underwear), blackAnkles (Socks), brownBrogues (Shoes), whiteLongSleeve (Shirt).

    iii) Extend your solution to pass messages to each of these clothing objects instructing them to be PutOn.

7. Suggest some other methods that could sensibly be included in the Person class and design algorithms for those methods.

7.5 **Projects**

StockSnackz Vending Machine

Look at the vending machine problem through an object-oriented lens. Suppose we decide that there are three classes involved in a vending machine: the Snacks it dispenses, a Vendor mechanism for dispensing the snacks, and the MoneyHandler that receives coins, ensures sufficient money has been paid, and gives change. The MoneyHandler would also have to tell the Vendor mechanism to release a Snack. Try defining the methods and properties for each of these three classes.

Stocksfield Fire Service

No exercise.

Puzzle World: Roman Numerals and Chronograms

No exercise.

Pangrams: Holoalphabetic Sentences

No exercise.

Online Bookstore: ISBNs

No exercise.

8 Looking Forward to Program Design

> The beginning of wisdom for a programmer is to recognize the difference between getting his program to work and getting it right.
>
> *M.A. Jackson (1975)*

8.1   **Algorithms**

8.2   *HTTLAP* **is** not **a Program Design Method**

8.3   **Program Design Methods**

8.4   **Graphical Notations**

8.5   **Exercises**

8.6   **Projects**

Learning Objectives

- Identify different formalized program design methods and their associated graphical notations
- Understand the difference between bottom-up and top-down approaches and between data structure, data flow and object-oriented methods
- Use different graphical notations to highlight different aspects of a given problem

In the preceding chapters we have spent much time looking at how to understand and solve problems. The goal was always to write down solutions to the problems in a structured manner using a semi-formal language. Although we have not written any programming language code, essentially what we have been doing is designing programs or, more properly, *algorithms*.

Sections 8.3 and 8.4 begin to build the bridge between the problem solving of Chapters 1 to 7 and technical programming issues by introducing you to formalized program design methods and associated diagrammatic notations that can be used.

8.1 **Algorithms**

The solutions to the coffee-making and van-loading problems are algorithms because they specify the series of steps necessary to arrive at the desired result. Any computer program is an algorithm or a collection of algorithms. Programming is essentially a two-part process: deriving an algorithm to solve the problem/calculate the answer and expressing that algorithm in a form that can be executed by a computer. The first step we call *program design* and the second step we call *coding* for it is the process of writing down the design in programming language code.

It is evident from the work we did in the earlier chapters that it is difficult to separate the task of problem-solving from that of program design. Indeed, by writing down the solutions to the problems in pseudo-code we have effectively designed an algorithm (or program). The reason I called Chapter 2 *A Strategy for Solving Problems* rather than *Introduction to Program Design* is three-fold. First, I wanted to steer clear of any hint of the panic that can arise in the beginner when faced with writing programs. Secondly, there are actually quite a few different formalized approaches to program design and I wanted to defer discussion of those techniques until after working through the process of real-world problem description, comprehension, and solution. Finally, different people solve problems in different ways. By applying rules and strict notational techniques program design methods in some way constrain the problem-solving activity and may even work against a particular individual's unique way of thinking. Therefore, I thought it a good idea not to present a discussion of program design methods until after we had addressed the discipline of solving problems. I hope that in the future your programming activity will be a mixture of free-form problem solving techniques (such as drawing diagrams, building models, etc.) and using formalized design methods to mould that thinking into a form that can be turned into a good computer program.

8.2 *HTTLAP* is not a Program Design Method

The solutions to the problems in the previous chapters were not always easy to determine. Some parts of the problems were fairly easy to solve but others required some hard thinking. We had to be very careful to challenge our assumptions and to ensure that the algorithms we wrote were sensible, easy to understand, and led to the right results. Designing computer programs is hard to do well though the task gets easier with experience. Something else that can make the process of writing programs easier is to use a program design method. A program design method is a set of steps and guidelines that steer you towards solving the problem in hand. Program design methods typically make use of particular notations or diagramming techniques.

You may be thinking that our *HTTLAP* strategy is a program design method. I would argue that it is not because a good method should be aimed at solving problems of a particular kind. The *HTTLAP* strategy is more of a set of principles that sets out to help you to understand problems generally. It guides you through to writing down a solution, but it does not actually tell you *how* particular problems should be solved. Good design methods, on the other hand, have rules that when followed lead you to a solution whose structure fits well with that of the original problem.

Huh?

Haven't you cheated me by not providing such a program design method in Chapter 2?

Not at all. You see, *HTTLAP* has no particular type of problem in mind, and as such is a general set of guidelines. The trouble with general program design methods is their very generality. As M. A. Jackson observed "if a method offers help with every possible problem, you mustn't expect it to help much with any particular problem" (Jackson, 2001, p. xvii). The focus of this book is the basics of understanding and solving problems with a view to implementing those solutions as a computer program. Having understood the problem you can then progress to using an appropriate program design method to assist with the technical translation.

The *HTTLAP* strategy is a framework for helping you to start thinking about problems generally. It offers a checklist of activities that should help you towards developing skills for analyzing and understanding problems. What *HTTLAP* does not do is provide help with specific types of problem; this is what program design methods are for, or rather, what program design methods *should* be for. Unfortunately, there are very few program design methods aimed at specific classes of problem. By this I mean that many methods offer general guidance on how to solve programming problems. Ironically, the weakness of many design methods lies in their focus on developing solutions. While the goal of any programmer is to develop a solution, to do this correctly he must first understand the problem he is trying to solve. Design methods tend to be good at helping you to describe your solution, but not so good at helping you to understand the principal parts of the problem itself. The goal of *HTTLAP* is to lead you towards greater understanding of the problem, its complexities, and ambiguities, and to assist you with identifying and challenging the assumptions (and simplifications) you make in the process. As programmers, we must understand that the real world is infinitely more complex than any computer program we write. A program is a solution to a problem that lies in the real world, but in order to build the program we must be able to simplify the problem to the extent that it can be solved in a finite number of steps. One of the skills a programmer must learn is where to draw the boundary. If you attempt to solve every little detail and complexity related to your problem you may never finish. In the coffee-making problem, we made a few assumptions and drew a boundary around the problem we were trying to solve. Sometimes we make the boundary explicit, other times we do it unconsciously.

For example, the coffee-making solution only works for situations where there already exists a working coffee machine, where there is coffee in the cupboard, the machine is plugged in to a working electricity outlet, and where there is an available water supply. It also assumes that milk, sugar, and clean cups are to hand and that we have sufficient supplies of each to meet the needs of our guests. If any of these conditions is not met then our solution will not work. You may think that is going to absurd lengths, but it is an important principle to note. A programmer must not only understand what his solution will do, but also what the solution will **not** do. What a program will not do is often more interesting that what it will do. When discussing the coffee-making problem with a colleague, his solution upon considering the many complexities of the problem was to telephone the catering department and order coffee for six people. This is a common practice in industry these days and is known as "outsourcing"–paying somebody else to develop the solution for you.[1] However, as the sign on former U.S. President Harry S. Truman's desk said, *"the buck stops here"* which, for us, means we must learn to develop the solutions.

8.3 Program Design Methods

The purpose of the rest of this chapter is not to provide instruction in the many program design methods that exist. Instead, I want to focus on some of the graphical notations that are used by design methods with a view to showing you how representing a problem (or a solution) in different ways can lead you toward greater understanding of the task. Chapters 2 and 3 looked at some of the ways that real-world problems can be described and modeled, for example using pictures, diagrams, and mathematics. In this chapter, as we move toward considering the computer in which our solutions will eventually reside, we will look at some common representational techniques that are used to describe programs and algorithms. Some of these notations are quite formal and precise allowing ambiguity to be minimized. Others offer a greater degree of vagueness which can sometimes be useful but which can lead to difficulties later on if the unclear aspects are not properly resolved.

Before considering these program design notations, I want first to quickly introduce some of the main approaches to software development. We will not go into these in great detail for that would require a book in its own right. Also, the program design approach to be used is often determined by the language in which you are working or the requirements of a particular college course, and this book is not aimed at solving problems with a particular programming language.[2] If you are using this book as part of a college or university course, you are likely going to be given in-depth training in program design later on and your course will have particular design techniques specified in the syllabus.

Top-down Design: "Dysfunctional Decomposition"

One of the more popular approaches advocated in programming methods and books is TOP-DOWN design, also known as "functional decomposition" or "stepwise refinement." It is popular because it is general and because it makes an appeal to common sense. The premise of TOP-DOWN design is simple: starting with an overall problem

---

[1] Thanks to Rob Davis for that piece of creative thinking. You can tell that Rob used to work in a Business School.

[2] I find this to be an unfortunate state of affairs because it prejudges the solution. The programming language is often picked first and then a design method is chosen that fits with the language rather than one that fits the problem.

statement you decompose it into a set of smaller subproblems. Each subproblem in turn is decomposed into its own smaller subproblems. This process is continued until at the bottom level the subproblems are so small that they can be easily expressed in programming language code. The result is a hierarchy of subproblems (Figure 8.1).

FIGURE 8.1   Top-down hierarchical functional decomposition of a problem

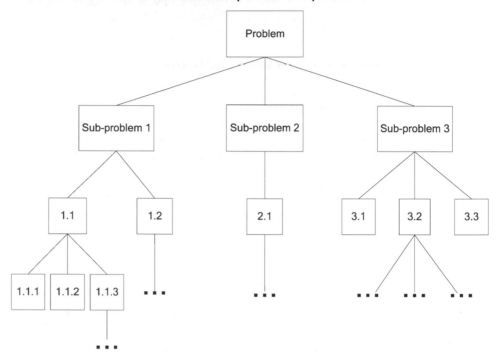

This process of stepwise refinement has psychological appeal as we are led to believe that we are gaining understanding of a problem through breaking it up into simpler subproblems in a kind of divide-and-conquer approach. Indeed, is this not just what *HTTLAP* recommends? Actually, no. In *HTTLAP*, while we are trying to solve the big problem by solving simpler related problems, there was no indication that the set of simpler problems is in any way hierarchically related. Top-down design does not give any advice on *how* to decompose the hierarchy; it merely says that we should keep on decomposing the problems until we arrive at some easily understood level. This division of a problem into separate sub-problems requires that we make the biggest decision (deciding what the first level of decomposition will be) at the start of the process just when we know the least about the problem. To be able to do an effective functional decomposition we must first have already solved the problem in our heads (Jackson, 1983). The top-down design then becomes a description of a problem already solved rather than something that helps to actually solve the problem. There is a more complete discussion of why I do not think top-down is very useful in the Reflections chapter. Because I do not think this method of functional decomposition is helpful I prefer to call it DYSFUNCTIONAL DECOMPOSITION: again, the argument is given in more detail in the Reflections section.

Divide and conquer ►

Dysfunctional ► **Decomposition**

Bottom-up Design

Rather than starting with the problem and breaking it up into smaller and smaller parts, another technique for designing software is to start by considering the small details first. Solutions to the many small problems are worked out and these solutions are then assembled into a hierarchy of functions in a bottom-up manner. Avison and Fitzgerald (1995) claim that it is often difficult to make these separately designed solutions fit together later on as no account has been taken of the overall shape of the problem and its solution.

Data structure Approaches

Many problems involve the processing of structured data. At their most basic level **all** programs process data, but that is not what I mean. It is often the case that the underlying data can be arranged in structured hierarchies. For example, you might be required to write a program that prints invoices for CD purchases made at an online music store. The invoices are to be arranged sorted by album title within artist name, as in Table 8.1.

Table 8.1   **CD Ordering for an Online Store Invoice**

Artist	Album	Catalog No.	Price
Adams, Bryan	18 'til I Die	5405512	9.99
Adams, Bryan	Reckless	3950132	6.99
Adams, Bryan	Waking up the Neighbors	3971642	8.99
Pink Floyd	Dark Side of the Moon	CDEMD1064	7.99
Pink Floyd	The Wall	CDEMD1071	10.99
Pink Floyd	Wish You Were Here	CDEMD1062	7.99
ZZ Top	Afterburner	K9253422	7.99
ZZ Top	Eliminator	7599237742	5.99
ZZ Top	Tres Hombres	K256603	8.99

A data structure oriented approach can be used to design a solution to the problem. The underlying structure of the data is used as the basis for the program's design. Perhaps the best well-known (and well-regarded) data structure design method is Jackson Structured Programming (JSP) (Jackson, 1975). JSP[3] has stages devoted to analyzing and describing the data structures, transforming these structures into a program design, and finally adding the necessary operations and conditions to allow the design to be translated into the chosen programming language. What JSP did was to simplify the program design process for a certain

---

[3] JSP (see ACRONYM) is also the abbreviation for *Java Server Program* – quite a different thing altogether.

class of problems (those that have underlying data structures). It provided a systematic framework that removed much of the guesswork from program design.

One feature of JSP that is especially good is that you know in advance what type of problems it will help you solve. If your problem is not one of transforming structured data then you know JSP will not help you solve it. Why is this a good thing? Because the method knows its limitations and does not offer you false hope. Furthermore, when you do have a problem that JSP fits then you know JSP will lead you towards a good solution. Jackson extended the approach in 1983 to work with designing complete software systems as opposed to individual programs. The newer method is called JSD, or Jackson System Development (Jackson, 1983). Section 8.4 below covers some of the diagrammatic conventions used by JSP (and JSD). Some commentators have incorrectly asserted that JSP and JSD are TOP-DOWN methods, probably because the tree diagrams they use superficially resemble the hierarchical arrangements of TOP-DOWN designs. JSP and JSD are most assuredly **not** TOP-DOWN methods.

Other data structure methods include Logical Construction of Programs (LCP) and Warnier-Orr Methodology which sometimes goes by the name Data Structure Systems Development (DSSD).

Data flow Approaches

Methods that describe the flow rather than the structure of information or data are called data flow oriented methods. For instance, in an invoicing system such a method might concentrate on the passing of orders from the customer to the company, the movement of stock around the company, the delivery of goods to the customer, the transfer of money between the customer and the company, the sending of delivery notes and invoices to the customer, and so on. Data flow approaches attempt to describe the movement of information and thereby the processes that transform the information into various forms. For example, we might define a process that receives an order from the customer and which checks the order to ensure it is correct and which then passes the validated order on to another process that calculates the money owed, and so on. Such methods typically use data flow diagrams (DFD) to assist the developer. Unfortunately, data flow methods often give little real help in the form of systematic rules for deciding how a problem should be partitioned into the various subprocesses that carry out the information processing tasks. In the late 1970s (the early days of so-called structured analysis) DFDs were used in a more formal and rule-based manner that gave the programmer some reasonably clear guidelines to follow. However, in recent years much of the formality has been abandoned in an attempt to be less restrictive. A result of this is that rather than becoming more helpful, such approaches in fact give the programmer even less clear guidance and leave more decisions to clever thinking and intuition. Data flow approaches are generally organized around the TOP-DOWN philosophy.

Two of the better-known methods that employ data flow techniques today are SSADM (Structured Systems Analysis and Design Method) and Yourdon Structured Method (YSM). *SSADM: A Practical Approach* (Ashworth & Goodland,

1989) is a student-friendly introduction to SSADM. Yourdon's method is described in *Modern Structured Analysis* (Yourdon, 1988).

Object-oriented Approaches

Programming languages like C++, Java, and latterly C# have brought into the mainstream object-oriented programming (OOP). Like the structured programming movement of the 1970s, the object-oriented approach gathered force in the 1980s in an attempt to solve the so-called software crisis. Too many software development projects were running vastly over budget and beyond their schedules. Furthermore, many software systems did not work properly and, in extreme cases, were thrown away shortly after installation. Like structured programming before it, OOP was claimed to be the solution to the software crisis because it embodied good practice and reusability. While it is true that many OOP principles are good, the practice did not solve the software crisis.[4] Beware of people who claim that OOP will solve all the ills of the software industry. It may help you to engineer software to a high standard, but if you have solved the wrong problem your efforts will be in vain.

As we saw in Chapter 7 the philosophy of the approach is to build software components that keep the data and the code that processes that data together in a single unit, or object. Because of the focus on engineering individual components, there is an element of bottom-up design in OOP methods. There are quite a few object-oriented design methods and approaches. One that has grown in popularity today is the Rational Unified Process which is based upon the Unified Modeling Language (UML).

8.4 Graphical Notations

We saw in Chapter 3 that different representations can shed light on seemingly intractable problems. By and large, program design methods use diagrammatic notations to assist the programmer. There are many different notations available and the novice can be unsure which one to pick. Often the decision is made for them by a college course that imposes a particular design method. Some say that it does not matter which notation you pick arguing that they all show the same thing and one is as good as another. This is simply untrue: they draw on the same raw material (the principal parts of a problem or program) but they emphasize different aspects. In the following sections we shall look at some of the more common notations to see what they provide and, just as importantly, what they *do not* provide to the programmer. I hope that you will, with practice, begin to see what the different notations are well suited to and thus be able to make informed choices when designing your own programs.

---

[4] This is probably because the design methods still did not help the developers to understand the problems properly. Without a good understanding of the underlying problem even the best tools will not help you to build a good solution.

Flowcharts

FIGURE 8.2   **Basic flowcharting symbols**

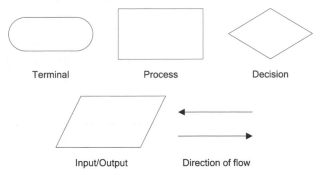

A flowchart is a diagrammatic representation of an algorithm. We have seen some already in Chapter 4 where they were used to illustrate the IF and WHILE constructs. The flowchart is one of the earliest diagrammatic techniques for programming and remains popular today.[5] However, it has fallen out of favour in some quarters because it can be hard to update and it is easy to draw really badly structured algorithms in flowchart notation.[6] Figure 8.2 shows five of the symbols from which basic flowcharts can be constructed (there are more symbols which are not shown here).

The terminal symbol is used to show the start and end of an algorithm. The process box shows tasks performed by the algorithm, such as adding numbers. The decision symbol is used to show points at which the algorithm needs to make a decision. Selections and iterations both use the decision symbol. (Think about why this is so.) A decision symbol has two exits: one for when the condition is true and one for when the condition is false.

Does this mean that selections and iterations are really the same thing?

Almost. What is the essential difference between them, and what is the essential similarity? A selection performs a single course of action if a condition is met while an iteration repeatedly tests the condition and performs the action. An iteration, then, is a selection that repeats. In programming terms, selections and iterations are both *branching* constructs: they represent points at which program flow leaves the purely sequential ordering. A selection branches to a new location (depending on the value of a condition) from which execution continues. A loop also tests a condition and then branches to a new section of code, but when that section finishes, the program returns back to the branch point.

---

[5] A former colleague once told of when he worked as a maintenance programmer in a certain large organization. Each time the main program needed to be updated the team would gather in the corridor and watch in reverential awe as the scroll on which the flowchart was kept was rolled out along the floor. They then walked up and down inspecting the flowchart looking for the bits that needed amending.

[6] Jackson comments that flowcharts can often be obscure and playfully passes on David Gries's name for them–"flawcharts" (Jackson, 1983, p. 43)

The input/output symbol is used to denote any actions that involve getting information into or out of the algorithm, such as getting parcel weights, reporting results, etc. The flow arrows connect the symbols and show which way the algorithm flows.

Using the symbols from Figure 8.2, I have drawn Figure 8.3 which is a flowchart of the van-loading solution. I tried to make the layout of the flowchart match that of the pseudo-code from Solution 5.18 by keeping the main flow running vertically down the page. However, as becomes apparent in this example, even with relatively small algorithms it is hard to keep the flowchart nicely structured **and** on one page. As you can see I have had to move some of the sections horizontally to allow everything to fit. There are symbols to show that part of a flowchart is on a different page, but for such a small solution I wanted to avoid that. Compare Figure 8.3 with Figure 8.4 in which I have redrawn the flowchart to use more horizontal space. Both flowcharts describe the same algorithm, but their layouts are different. One of the drawbacks of flowcharts is that there are no fixed rules governing their layout. Figure 8.3 and Figure 8.4 are only two possible layouts for this solution – I could draw many more. Because programmers can draw flowcharts differently it is not always easy to read and understand somebody else's charts. Because there are no fixed rules for their layout deciding just how to draw a flowchart can be tricky. Furthermore, if the algorithm needs to be amended, the flowchart may need to be completely redrawn in order for its layout to accommodate the changes. Nowadays, many programmers prefer to use pseudo-code over flowcharts as the layout is much more standardized and easier to read.

The above criticisms notwithstanding, a flowchart can sometimes be just the thing for illustrating a point. The small examples in Chapter 4 are easy to understand and help to explain the logic of the IF and WHILE constructs. If you find flowcharts easy to draw then by all means use them, only be careful that you do not end up constructing poorly structured algorithms with them. You can check this by converting a flowchart to pseudo-code. If the pseudo-code starts looking very messy, or it is hard to translate the flowchart into pseudo-code, it is a sign that your flowchart is not very well laid out.

Tree Diagrams

I have found tree diagrams very useful for describing problems and designing and documenting programs. They're used mostly in the JSP/JSD software design methods. As well as describing the structure of programs you can use tree diagrams to describe the structure of data, problems, and objects in the real world. Jackson tree diagrams have strict rules governing their construction which means that their meaning is precise and unambiguous. There is only one way to arrange the boxes in a tree diagram for any given algorithm (allowing for minor differences in relative spatial positioning) and they are always read from top-to-bottom and left-to-right.

There are three component types in a basic tree diagram: sequence, iteration, and selection. An action (or group of actions) is represented by a box. Sequences of actions are shown by placing the boxes left to right as in Figure 8.5.

FIGURE 8.3 **Flowchart for van-loading**

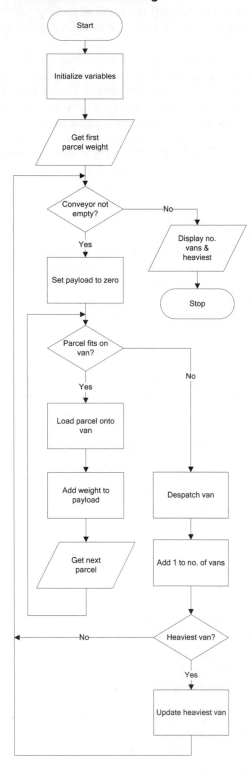

FIGURE 8.4   **Another flowchart for van-loading**

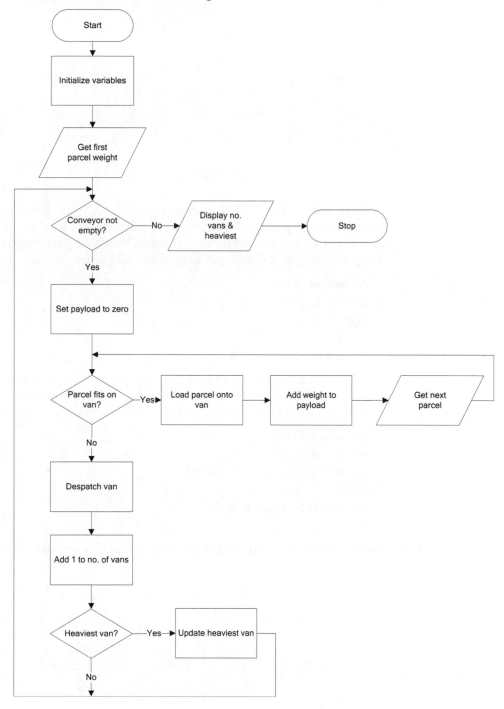

FIGURE 8.5   **Tree diagram for a sequence**

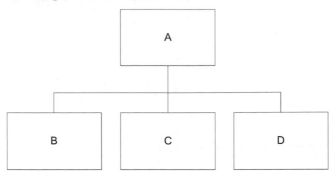

In Figure 8.5 box "A" is a sequence. "B," "C," and "D" are the component actions of the sequence (that is, they comprise the action block of "A"). "A" is not an action itself but a name for the sequence of actions performed by "B," "C," and "D." We could write Figure 8.5 in pseudo-code thus:

// Sequence A

```
Action B ;
Action C ;
Action D ;
```

// End of Sequence A

Selections are represented by Figure 8.6 (a) and (b). In Figure 8.6 the component "A" in both example (a) and example (b) is the selection. Figure 8.6 (a) represents a simple IF construct which would be written in pseudo-code as:

// Selection A

```
IF (condition)
    Action B ;
ENDIF
```

// End Selection A

FIGURE 8.6   **Selection constructs: (a) is a simple selection (b) is a selection with an ELSE path**

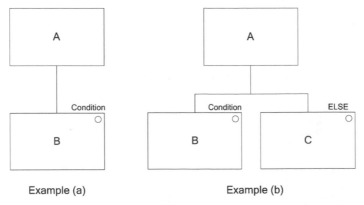

Figure 8.6 (b) gives a compound selection (one with an ELSE path). Its pseudo-code equivalent would be:

```
// Selection A
IF (condition)
    Action B ;
ELSE
    Action C ;
ENDIF
// End Selection A
```

The circle symbol in the top right corners of "B" and "C" of Figure 8.6 denotes the component in which it lies is followed when the condition written above the box is met. Remember the cash machine example from an earlier chapter? We wrote a selection construct that dispensed cash if there were sufficient funds in the account, otherwise an apology was displayed. Figure 8.7 is the tree diagram that corresponds to that selection.

FIGURE 8.7 **Tree diagram for cash withdrawal**

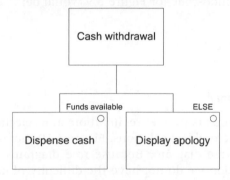

Tree diagrams can also be drawn to show the null action of a simple IF construct (see Section 6.3 in Chapter 6 for a reminder of the null statement). For example, Figure 8.6(a) could be redrawn as Figure 8.8 below. Notice that no ELSE is placed over the null action's box.

FIGURE 8.8 **Selection with *null* action**

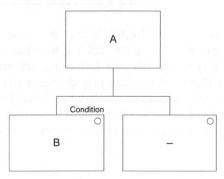

Iterations are shown by putting a star in the corner of the repeated task. Figure 8.9 shows how we could represent the sugar-adding part of our coffee-making problem. The box labeled "WHILE" is the iteration structure, the box "Add Sugar" is the iterated action (denoted by the asterisk in its corner).

FIGURE 8.9   **Tree diagram for iteration**

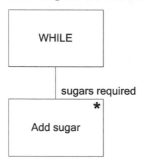

The corresponding pseudo-code for Figure 8.9 would be:

// Adding sugar

```
WHILE (sugars required)
    Add sugar ;
ENDWHILE
```

// End of adding sugar

Using the three components (sequence, iteration, and selection) we can draw tree diagrams for complete problem solutions. Figure 8.10 shows the van-loading solution expressed as a tree diagram. Because tree diagrams have strict rules governing their construction we do not have the difficulty of deciding how best to lay out the solution that we faced with flowcharts.

Compare Figure 8.10 with Solution 5.18 to ensure that you can see how the tree diagram has been derived from the pseudo-code. The vertical sequence of actions in the pseudo-code is reflected in the horizontal sequence of boxes on the tree diagram. The nesting of constructs in the pseudo-code is reflected in the vertical branches of the tree.

Tree diagrams are very good at highlighting the relationships between components. You can easily see what parts belong to what; nested structures are plainly visible and the consequences of following certain selection paths are clear. You can see in Figure 8.10 that processing a parcel is a repeated activity and that it comprises a sequence of three actions. Processing a parcel is done after the van's payload is set to zero and before the van is despatched. Tree diagrams are also known as structure diagrams because they highlight the structure of the solution.

FIGURE 8.10 **Tree diagram for van-loading solution**

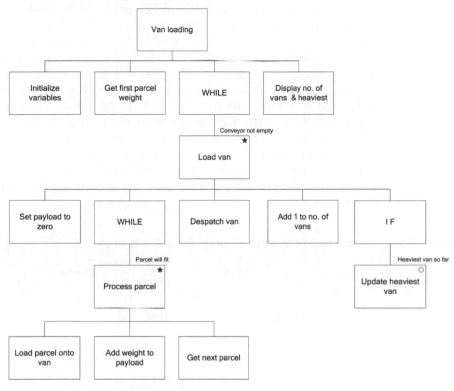

State Transition Diagrams

When it is important to describe a program or an object in terms of the events that happen and the different *states* that those events trigger, it is useful to draw a state transition diagram.[7] Many courses in software engineering and event-driven programming use state transition diagrams (STD) as their preferred diagramming technique. The main focus of the STD is the set of states that a program can be in and the events that cause changes in state. There are several different notational styles used for drawing state transition diagrams, but they share common features. Figure 8.11 shows the basic symbols used in a simple form of state transition diagram.

FIGURE 8.11 **Symbols for basic state transition diagrams**

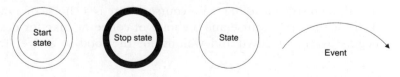

---

[7] Some people call them finite state machines because they show all the possible, but finite, states that a program (machine) can take. The starting and ending states are clearly visible.

The "start state" (with a double border) is the state in which an algorithm begins. The stop state (with the thick border) is its final resting state and the regular "state" is one of the intermediate states. Events cause a program to move from one state to another, and so these are shown as connecting arrows.[8] For example, consider Figure 8.12 which shows a very simple STD for a library book. If we ignore complications such as loan renewals, books being lost and stolen, and the disposal of books when they get to the end of their useful life, we might consider a library book to have two main states: it is either on the shelf or it is on loan. A book begins its life in the library by being catalogued after which it is placed on the shelf. A book remains on the shelf until it is borrowed at which point it is considered to be on loan.[9] It remains on loan until such time as it is returned when it goes back on the shelf. Figure 8.12 shows these different states and the events that cause transition from one state to the next.

FIGURE 8.12   **Simple state transition diagram for a library book**

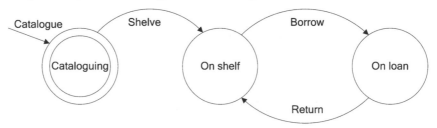

Any state transition diagram can be redrawn as a tree diagram (and vice versa). For example, Figure 8.13 shows the library book redrawn as a tree diagram. Notice how Figure 8.12 and Figure 8.13 give different views onto the same problem. The STD focuses on the resting states in a solution; it brings to the foreground exactly what states are possible to achieve from any other state. It also shows clearly what events can come next. For example, from the "on shelf" state the only possible event that can occur is the "borrow" event. The tree diagram, on the other hand, focuses on the structural relationships of events. Figure 8.13 shows clearly that "borrow" and "return" events come in pairs and that such pairs occur repeatedly throughout the life of a book.

Figure 8.14 shows a more complex STD for someone eating a meal. The meal comprises three courses. The starter is fixed so someone may choose not to have it and to go straight to the main course. There is a choice of a meat or vegetarian dish for the main course and a choice of coffee or cake for dessert. The process begins by sitting down and waiting for the food to arrive. Trace through the

---

[8] Or "graph edges" as a mathematician or a formal computer scientist would know them.

[9] Another complication we are overlooking for now is the fact that a book might very well be off the shelf even though it is not on loan: somebody may simply be reading it in the library.

FIGURE 8.13   **Tree diagram for library book**

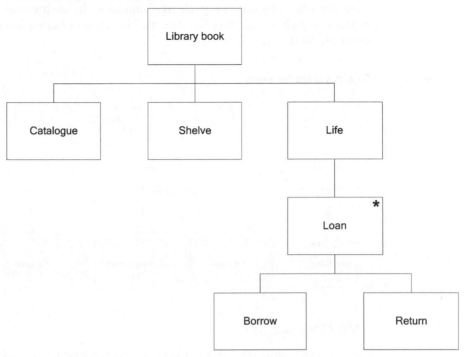

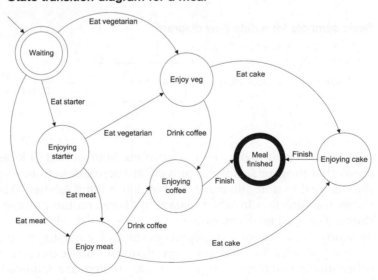

Think Spot   diagram by following the different event/state paths. Notice that you can go from waiting straight to either of the main courses, or from waiting to the starter and then to either main course. From each main course you can go to either the cake or the coffee. The "meal finished" state is achieved after dessert (cake or coffee).

FIGURE 8.14   **State transition diagram for a meal**

Figure 8.15 shows the corresponding tree diagram for the same meal. Notice how the tree diagram very clearly captures the sequential progression from starter through main course to dessert. The choices belonging to each course are also easy to see.

FIGURE 8.15 **Tree diagram for meal**

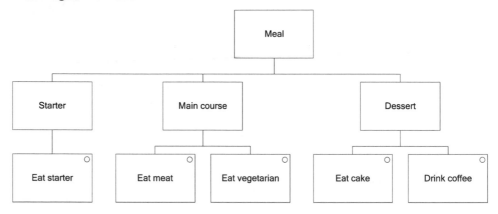

Data Flow Diagrams

Data flow diagrams (DFDs) are a very popular diagramming technique common in many TOP-DOWN design methods and are taught on most systems analysis courses. There are several different styles and notational forms but they have roughly the same ingredients. The main function of a DFD is to show how data flows between the structural units of a program. Figure 8.16 shows the main symbols used in a simple form of DFD notation (the shapes of DFD symbols change according to which notational style is being used, though their meaning is usually the same. (For example, the SSADM method uses boxes rather than circles to denote processes.)

FIGURE 8.16 **Basic symbols for a data flow diagram**

A process is a program or an algorithm. Sources and sinks are people, companies, other programs, etc. that provide or receive data from the processes. A data store is used to store information (a bit like a filing cabinet). The data flow arrow shows the direction in which data flows between the processes, sinks, and data stores. For example, consider Figure 8.17 which shows a data flow diagram depicting the principal components in the coffee making problem.

The "make coffee" process is the algorithm that expresses the solution to the coffee making problem. The guests in the problem are denoted by the box. Guests

FIGURE 8.17   **DFD for coffee making problem**

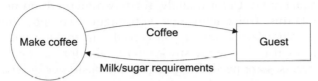

provide the algorithm with their milk and sugar requirements. The algorithm in turn provides the guests with coffee. A DFD does not show task ordering, selections, or iterations like a tree diagram does as its focus is to show what items of data move around the system. Figure 8.17 is a special type of DFD called a context diagram. Context diagrams are used to show the top level of a problem, a program, or a system. The program, system, or algorithm is represented by the process circle. The main data flows in and out of the algorithm are shown as are the principal components or objects with which the algorithm interacts.

context diagram ▶

The next step in methods based on data flow diagrams is to start to functionally decompose the problem in a TOP-DOWN manner. The top-level process of the context diagram is decomposed into subprocesses that correspond to the main functional units. Each subprocess in turn is further decomposed into its own subprocesses. This continues until the various subprocesses can be easily expressed in programming language code. For example, consider Figure 8.18, a context diagram for a company called Stitch in Time. Stitch in Time is a small two-person operation that makes leggings for pregnant women. Knowledge about Stitch in Time came from an interview with the company's two owner-employees.

FIGURE 8.18   **Context diagram for Stitch in Time**

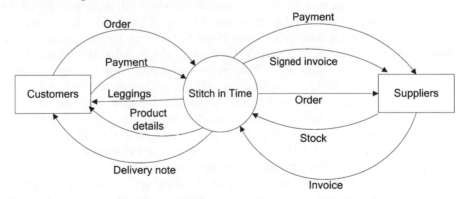

The context diagram shows that the company (represented by the process circle) sends leggings, product details, and delivery notes to its customers from whom it receives orders and payments. Stitch in Time sends orders, payments, and signed invoices to its suppliers who, in turn, send it stock and invoices. The context diagram shows reasonably clearly what interactions the company has with its principal stakeholders.

The next step is to decompose the process in the context diagram into its principal functional areas. Unfortunately, TOP-DOWN methods do not offer much help on how to do this. Think about how you might decompose the main process in Figure 8.18. What factors might you consider in making your decisions? What makes logical sense? If you are stuck, you might, for example, decide that three main subprocesses are needed: one to handle customer orders, one for ordering stock, and one for keeping the accounts.

> Having thought about the problem for a while (at least ten minutes), try drawing a DFD that shows how all the subprocesses you identified are linked by various information flows. This is not a trivial task and requires quite a bit of information about the documents used in the company; as you do not have this information you should make some educated guesses and assumptions at this point.

My own solution is shown below as Figure 8.19. Notice how the DFD in Figure 8.19 shows much more information than the context diagram in Figure 8.18? This is because the context diagram shows the problem solution and the people or objects with which provide information to the solution and receive its outputs. The decomposed DFD in Figure 8.19, on the other hand, shows much more of the internal detail of the problem. It shows the information that flows around the company (orders, stock levels, stock requirements, etc.). Knowledge of this information comes from studying the problem situation (perhaps by carrying out interviews), but the decisions about how to decompose the processes themselves are left to the programmer. You might reasonably ask why it is necessary to have three subprocesses rather than two, or even five or six. That is a good question to which I do not have a very good answer other than it seemed like a good idea at the time. That is one of the challenges of TOP-DOWN design – it does not provide any guidance on how to decompose the processes. If you get it wrong you tend to find out when you have already put in a lot of work which means it takes a lot more effort to redesign the solution.

Looking at Figure 8.19 you may also see that the labels on the diagram are not precise. What does "keep accounts" mean? What does "handle customer orders" mean? Come up with a few definitions yourself. The labels on a DFD can be very precise or very ambiguous depending on how well the designer understands the problem. Too often functional decomposition is used to defer awkward or difficult decisions rather than addressing the main issue which is a lack of understanding. While *HTTLAP* is not a design method and does not give precise instructions about how to solve any particular problem you should still find it helpful. This is because its focus is on problem understanding and resolution of difficulties, ambiguities, and assumptions. This is in contrast to many of the TOP-DOWN methods which do not particularly address the question of understanding the problem.

UML-the Unified Modeling Language

Unified Modeling Language, or UML, has become a standard notation for use in object-oriented system development projects. UML provides a set of notations for

FIGURE 8.19 **First level DFD for Stitch in Time**

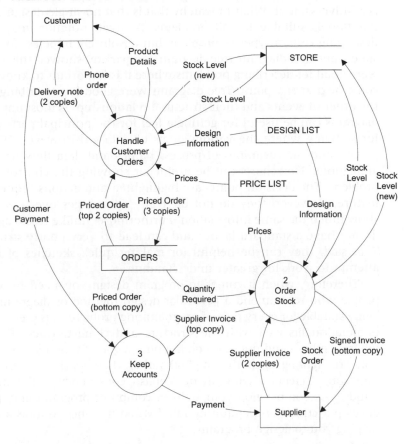

describing different aspects of a system design including object classes, use cases, activity diagrams, sequence diagrams, collaboration diagrams, state diagrams, packages, and implementation diagrams. UML is specifically aimed at object-oriented design and programming languages and is commonly used on many university programming courses. Because of the number of different diagram types in UML and UML's focus on object-oriented design we shall not dwell upon it here.

Summary of Diagramming Techniques

The above notations are all ways of getting different views of a program, a problem, an object, etc. When we discussed solving problems in Chapters 2 and 3 I suggested using a variety of description languages to help you get a proper understanding of the problem. You will recall that some problems were easier to describe with one technique while a different language was needed for other problems. A similar principle holds for program design notations. For example, while tree diagrams and state transition diagrams describe the same things (a tree diagram can be derived from any state transition diagram and vice versa) they each make certain aspects of the problem easy to see while obscuring others.

When picking a program design notation we need to realize that none of them is a universal tool. What I mean by that is that no single design method or design notation is suitable for all problems. A given notation may be excellent for describing certain types of problem, but absolutely hopeless for other types. The state transition diagram/tree diagram comparison showed this very plainly. STDs were good for describing problems where it is important to know about what can come next at any point. Tree diagrams were good for describing problems where the order of events and their structural relationships is most important. Data flow diagrams can be useful for getting a feel for the principal parts of a problem and for showing where the various items of data go. However, DFDs are not very precise and the meanings of process names and data flow names can be quite ambiguous. Flowcharts can be useful for showing the control flow aspects of a problem. The decision points are highlighted and actions sequences are a major feature. However, they do not offer any advantages over tree diagrams which show much the same information. Furthermore, unlike tree diagrams, flowcharts do not have a standard layout and can lead to very poorly structured solutions. That said, they can be helpful for making quick sketches of a problem in an attempt to work for greater understanding.

Therefore, when it comes to program design you need to be very careful of people who recommend a particular design method or diagrammatic notation as being suitable for every type of programming problem. It is great when the method or notation fits well with the structure and characteristics of the problem. But where methods and notations do not offer a good fit then you will continually feel you are fighting with the method rather than working with it. Ralph Waldo Emerson is credited with saying "foolish consistency is the hobgoblin of little minds." As you develop your skills in computer programming, please try also to develop a critical and enquiring mind when it comes to tools and techniques for helping you to design programs.

8.5 Exercises

1. Draw a flowchart for the coffee making solution in Solution 4.9.

2. Draw a tree diagram of the coffee making solution in Solution 4.9.

3. Try drawing flowcharts, tree diagrams, and state transition diagrams for some of the algorithms you have developed in the exercises in previous chapters. Alternatively, use the various algorithm solutions in Appendix C as the basis for your diagrams.

4. Think about buying a book or a CD from an Internet store. Identify what the principal components of the transaction are and then draw a data flow diagram showing how the various data items (including physical objects such as books) flow between the main players in the situation. Do not restrict yourself just to the store and the customer – think about who else might be involved.

5. Find a book on UML in your nearest library. What sort of programming paradigm is it best suited to?

8.6 **Projects**

StockSnackz Vending Machine

Draw a tree diagram and a flowchart of your solution so far. Examine the two representations and decide which one you found a) easier to draw and b) easier to read.

Stocksfield Fire Service

Draw a tree diagram and a flowchart of your solution so far. Examine the two representations and decide which one you found a) easier to draw and b) easier to read.

Puzzle World: Roman Numerals and Chronograms

Use one of the diagramming techniques covered in this chapter to draw a graphical representation of your algorithm for the Roman numerals problem.

Pangrams: Holoalphabetic Sentences

No exercise.

Online Bookstore: ISBNs

No exercise.

This chapter is entirely optional. It contains my own observations and opinions about some current programming practices (e.g., variable initialization, functional decomposition, and others). I have also included more-detailed explanations of some concepts that I felt would have broken up the flow of the main body. All sections in this chapter are referred to at various points in the main text by words in SMALL CAPITAL LETTERS. Feel free to dip into this chapter whenever you like (or even not at all).

Abstract Data Type

The abstract data type, or ADT, is a mathematical specification of a set of data and the operations that can be performed upon that data. The important feature of an ADT is that it is specified *independent* of any particular implementation. Here is an example. We could define a stack (think of a stack of plates), X, onto which a value, n, can be pushed or from which a value, n, can be popped. We can define operations to create a new stack, push an item onto the stack, and pop an item off the top of the stack. The data items belonging to an ADT can only be accessed by the defined operations which means that the internal workings (the implementation) of the ADT can be changed without affecting anything outside it (as long as the changes do not cause it to stop working). ADTs are foundational in the construction of object-oriented programs.

Abstraction

There are two principal kinds of abstraction in programming: data abstractions and control abstractions. Data abstractions are concerned with the properties of data: what values can be stored and what operations can be performed upon those values. Control abstractions are to do with how the flow of control (the execution) of the program is controlled. Sequences, selections, and iterations are all control abstractions. Each programming language implements data and control abstractions in a particular way. When understanding problems we work at quite a high level of abstraction: we think of loops and numbers. When designing algorithms we work at a lower level of abstraction: in this book we dealt with ranges of numbers and three different ways of expressing a loop. When translating algorithms into programming language code we work at an even lower level of abstraction: we differentiate between whole and fractional numbers, letters, strings of letters, and other kinds of data item. We even distinguish between different sizes of whole numbers. What you must learn to do to think like a programmer is manage different abstraction levels, and often *at the same time*.

Acronym

Computing is full of acronyms. BASIC is an acronym as are COBOL and FOR-TRAN. An acronym is a new word made up from or based upon the initial letters or syllables of a compound word or phrase. Thus *laser* is an acronym of **l**ight **a**mplification by **s**timulated **e**mission of **r**adiation, and *radar* of **ra**dio **d**etection **a**nd **r**anging. Many people confuse acronyms with abbreviations which are also rife in computing. CPU is a three-letter abbreviation of central processing unit. There are so many three-letter abbreviations in computing that they are known as TLAs. People mistakenly think this stands for Three Letter Acronym, but it does not, as it does not form a word (well, maybe it is a word in Klingon, but not in English). If TLA is an abbreviation of three letter abbreviation, is acronym itself an acronym? Lawrence Hannay who worked in the IBM Labs at Hursley Park, England, once told me that acronym stands for **a**lphabetically **c**onsistent **r**epresentation of **n**eologically **y**clept **m**agniloquence. That is so good it just deserves to be true, and yes, they are all real words – look them up if you do not believe me.

What is the point of this reflection? The point is that there are many acronyms and abbreviations to learn. Knowing the difference between acronym and abbreviation shows an eye for detail worthy of a programmer.

Assumptions

We make assumptions every day. We assume that we will get to work or to college safely. We assume our home will still be there when we get back. Life would be unbearable if we could not take things for granted. But this can be disastrous for software developers. Manny Lehman estimated that, on average, in every ten lines of program code there lies buried one programmer-made assumption. Assumptions are made when the programmer fails to fully understand the problem, its requirements, and the real world in which it is situated. Software development methods that lead you to question your decisions are more helpful in reducing assumptions than those that do not. See DYSFUNCTIONAL DECOMPOSITION.

The European Space Agency's Ariane 5 was the famously explosive successor to the Ariane 4, and cost more than $7 billion to develop. Much of the navigation control software was reused from the earlier Ariane 4 system (see REUSABILITY). The failure happened when the guidance computer received a horizontal bias value much larger than it had been programmed to deal with. The problem lay in a piece of code that translated a 64-bit floating-point value into a 16-bit integer. The designers of the Ariane 4 calculated that the horizontal bias could never be so large as to require more than sixteen bits to store it. Consequently, no exception handler to trap values larger than the 16-bit limit was included in the software as no such error could occur. (An exception handler is a special section of code that is executed when unexpected values (exceptions) occur – it will trap the rogue value and cause remedial action to take place, for example by either correcting the value, or safely shutting the system down.) This guidance software was copied unmodified into the Ariane 5. It was assumed it would work as well as it had worked in the Ariane 4. The trouble was, the Ariane 5 was a more powerful and faster rocket than its predecessor and *could* generate horizontal bias values larger than could fit in a 16-bit signed integer. The result was that the bias value over-flowed its storage, the software routine failed, the computers crashed, and the rocket self-destructed destroying $500 million worth of uninsured satellites in the process (Quinn, 2004). Ouch. If you are interested, you can read the whole story in the European Space Agency's inquiry board report (Lions, 1996).

Computer Error

There is no such thing as computer error, only programming error. One phrase I hate hearing when something goes wrong is that the fault is due to computer error. There is really no such thing. Computers only produce wrong results because their programs are in error. The only real computer error is if the electronic components break down, the hard drive crashes, etc. The rest are all defects introduced by programmers.

Documentation

Too little and too late. Documentation is the Cinderella of the programming world, for it often gets little attention and, if it does, it is left until the last minute to write it at which point only lip service is paid. There are several reasons for this. First, programmers are busy people who like to write programs, not document them. They are often pressed for time because their project is behind schedule (perhaps because the design and specification documents were not very good) and so do not have time to bother documenting what they have done. Secondly, the documentation that programmers write may never be looked at again (at least, not by the programmers who wrote it) so why bother? Unfortunately, when a poor maintenance programmer is asked to fix a defect or add some new features the documentation he finds does not help him to do his job.

One of the best cases made for documentation that I have seen is in *Introduction to the Personal Software Process* (Humphrey, 1997). In that excellent book, Watts Humphrey shows how a diligent approach to documenting every-thing we do when writing programs actually leads to improvements in the way we, as individual programmers, write programs – a reflective approach makes us better programmers.

Dysfunctional Decomposition

In 1975 Michael Jackson described an iconoclastic program design technique which turned the received wisdom of structured programming on its head (Jackson, 1975). Up until that point the accepted way of doing structured pro-gramming (as opposed to *unstructured* programming, clearly a bad thing) was to use the principles of TOP-DOWN design as espoused by Niklaus Wirth in his classic article *Program Development by Stepwise Refinement* (Wirth, 1971). The central idea of TOP-DOWN design has a very common-sense feel about it. The program being developed is treated as a hierarchy and the first step of devel-opment is to describe the top level of this hierarchy. For example, the coffee making problem might be described in the first step as: "Make and pour coffee for the guests." Clearly, this description is not detailed enough to build the algorithm yet, so we *decompose* the description into the next level. Wirth (1971, p. 221) describes the process thus:

> *In each step, one or several instructions of the given program are decomposed into more detailed instructions. This successive decomposition or refinement of specifications terminates when all instructions are expressed in terms of an underlying computer or programming language, and must therefore be guided by the facilities available on that computer or language.*

That is, we keep decomposing each successive level of the hierarchy until the descriptions can be written in programming language code. This is the guiding principle behind the use of data flow diagrams (see Section 8.3) in methods such as SSADM and Yourdon Structured Method. One of the difficulties is that TOP-DOWN techniques offer no guidance as to exactly how the problem should be decomposed: should the hierarchy be organized this way or that? Jackson (1983, p. 370) says:

> *TOP-DOWN is a reasonable way of describing things which are already fully understood. It is usually possible to impose a hierarchical structure for the purposes of description, and it seems reasonable to start a description with the larger, and work towards the smaller aspects of what is to be described.*

Thus, we might quite easily use a TOP-DOWN approach to describing the structure of the coffee-making problem; we already understand the overall problem quite well and we merely have to finesse some of the details. But, as Jackson points out, this is to confuse the method of *description* with the method of *development*. Using some unwritten scheme we have solved the problem of coffee making in our head and are simply using TOP-DOWN notation to describe the solution. What happens when we turn to a problem that we do not understand clearly? In such a case TOP-DOWN does not help much because it offers no guidance other than the general instruction that we should keep decomposing hierarchic levels until *"all instructions are expressed in terms of an underlying computer or programming language"* (Wirth, 1971, p. 221). Thus, we proceed decomposing the problem into a functional hierarchy that may, or may not, be an appropriate algorithm for the solution. It is only at the end, when we have a thorough understanding of the problem, that we can see whether the chosen hierarchy is a good fit. Alas, it is at the start of the process, when we understand the problem the least, that we make the most crucial and far-reaching decomposition decisions as we define the overall shape of the hierarchy. Surely it is better to make these important decisions when we more fully understand the problem?

Actually, around the same time that this idea of TOP-DOWN "design," or *functional decomposition* was being promoted in the literature, some of its proponents were also, albeit unwittingly, acknowledging its central weakness. In his classic book of essays on software engineering problems, *The Mythical Man Month*, Frederick Brooks (1974, p. 116) offered the following insight:

> *In most projects, the first system built is barely usable. . . . There is no alternative but to start again . . . and build a redesigned version. . . . Hence, plan to throw one away; you will, anyhow.*

When he gave this advice Brooks believed the first version of a system was unusable because of some inherent difficulty in building software. Personally, I am persuaded that it is the use of functional decomposition that leads to this awful state of affairs. It is because TOP-DOWN methods make you take the most risky design decisions when you understand least about the problem and often lead to having to redesign the system that I call it *dys*functional decomposition.

Is there an alternative? After all, even today the majority of programming courses espouse TOP-DOWN as the way to go. Jackson has written a number of excellent books on software engineering that will steer you towards looking at the discipline in a different way. For an easy, light-hearted, and insightful read, have a look at his book *Software Requirements & Specifications: A Lexicon of Practice, Principles and Prejudices* (Jackson, 1995). Jackson's *Problem Frames* (Jackson, 2001) describes a way of decomposing problems, rather than functions, in a non-TOP-DOWN way that, it is claimed, leads to better problem definition and understanding.

Heuristic

Heuristic investigation can be thought of as a process of guided trial and error. The word comes from the Greek word ευρισκω (*heuriskein*) which means "to find out." You may recall the story of Archimedes in the bath. When he discovered the principle of displacement and buoyancy he leapt out of the bath (so the story goes) and ran through the streets of Syracuse yelling "Eureka!", meaning "I have found it!". Pólya's *How to Solve It* (Pólya, 1990) was all about using heuristic investigation to solve mathematical problems. Heuristic investigation is sometimes called "trial and error" though this implies a lack of logic. Heuristic is a rational way to approach problems and search for solutions – it is much more than fumbling around in the dark. A set of common sense rules that aim to increase the likelihood of solving some problem. Heuristic methods typically constitute a process of exploration, investigation, and discovery and may require selecting a solution from several possible alternatives. I hope that this book, which draws upon heuristic method, has helped you by turning the light on, as it were. Once you can see the problem from a number of different view points you have a better chance of finding a way to solve it.

Initialization of Variables

Some programmers (and teachers) think it is a good idea to initialize every variable upon declaration. The argument goes that if you initialize everything then you cannot get caught out later on by wrongly assuming a variable has a value of zero (or whatever it was initialized to) the first time you use it. Others think you should only initialize variables that need to have a particular value upon their first use. I belong to the latter camp. I can see the logic in the initialize everything argument as it offers a degree of safety. However, it is not strictly needed. Consider the following example given in both C and Pascal:

In C	In Pascal
```int counter = 0 ;```	```VAR```
```int numberSugars = 0 ;```	``` counter,```
```scanf ("%d", &numberSugars) ;```	``` numberSugars : Integer ;```
```while (counter <= numberSugars)```	```BEGIN```
``` {```	```counter := 0 ;```
``` counter ++ ;```	```numberSugars := 0 ;```
``` }```	```Readln (numberSugars) ;```
	```WHILE (counter <= numberSugars) DO```
	``` BEGIN```
	``` counter := counter + 1```
	``` END ;```
	```END.```

Note that C allows variables to be initialized upon declaration while standard Pascal does not, so the Pascal program needs two assignment statements to initialize the two variables. counter certainly needs to be initialized at some point as the WHILE loop depends on it having a starting value of zero. However, numberSugars does not need to be initialized as its first value is provided by the scanf/Readln statements. The initialization of numberSugars is, therefore, redundant. So what? Well, blanket initialization can actually get you into trouble. What if the program had two WHILE loops both of which relied on counter having a starting value of zero? The first one would be ok, as counter has been initialized. However, the second loop may not work properly as we cannot say what the value of counter will be. So really variables should be initialized to a starting value at the point at which that value is needed. Furthermore, when you consider how the program has to be coded in standard Pascal, which does not allow initialization of variables at declaration, you can see that needless initialization introduces redundant statements. Apart from cluttering up the program, these initialization statements could, themselves be written incorrectly thus introducing more scope for defects. Yuk.

Natural Numbers

In programming we talk of integers, whereas mathematicians talk more of natural numbers. A natural number is either a positive integer $\{1, 2, 3, \ldots, \infty\}$ (the definition used in *number theory*) or a non-negative integer $\{0, 1, 2, 3, \ldots, \infty\}$ (the definition used in computer science). The set of all natural numbers is called $\mathbb{N}$. The integers are all the natural numbers $\mathbb{N}$ and their negatives $\{-1, -2, -3, \ldots, -\infty\}$, and zero. The name given to the set of all integers is $\mathbb{Z}$. Natural numbers (and by extension the integers) are used for two purposes:

■ Counting things–"There are thirty bedrooms in the hotel" (cardinality).
■ Ordering things–"He graduated second in his class" (ordinality).

A cardinal number, then, is a measure of the size of something, while an ordinal number is a measure of the position of something. In programming we use the ordinal set of integers both to count things:

```
vansDespatched ← vansDespatched + 1 ;   // Add 1 to vansDespatched,
                                         // ie increase cardinality by 1
```

and to order things:

```
Display (employeeArray [2]) ;   // Display element of employeeArray
                                // held in ordinal position 2
```

George Pólya

Strangely, I did not discover Pólya until relatively recently. I guess it is because I did not formally study mathematics beyond age 16. It is a shame because I think I would have benefited from his insights when I was a student. Pólya died in Palo Alto on September, 7, 1985. This was the same day that I received an offer of a place to study for a computing degree. Later, while studying for my Ph.D., Palo Alto, CA was the setting for the first conference paper I presented that came out of my Ph.D. research. As I said, I like to look for the small details.

Reusability

If, in the 1980s, developers hoped the Fourth Generation Languages would be the salvation of the software crisis, in the 1990s as object-oriented languages gained the ascendancy, the focus switched to Software Reuse. Ivar Jacobson was one of the main proponents and the argument goes that with object-oriented languages the programmer does not need to write the same functions for each project he works on, but can reuse functions over and over again. In principle this is a neat idea: the OOP principles of encapsulation, inheritance, and polymorphism, mean that we can build self-contained objects that can be plugged into a variety of different programs. As objects use information hiding to protect their internal data, it is unlikely that any other object can corrupt their data, thus promoting software reuse which, in turn leads to increasing reliability, speeding up development, facilitating compliance with standards, and reducing defects. That is the theory, anyway.

Let's wind the clock back twenty years and consider the software reuse horror story that was the Therac-25 linear accelerator. The Therac-25 used high-energy electron beams and X-ray beams to treat tumours. The Therac-25 was an attempt to build on the success of the earlier Therac-6 and Therac-20 models. To reduce costs some of the safety features were implemented in software on the computer rather than using the hardware solutions of the earlier models. Also, because the model 6 and model 20 machines were so reliable, much of their software was reused in the Therac-25. So far, so good. Unfortunately, the machine was prone to crashing many times each day, and in the case of six patients administered overdoses of radiation (in some cases over 100 times the required dose); three of these patients later died.

The reasons for the Therac-25's failures are complex, but stem mainly from the removal of the hardware overdose-protection features which allowed previously undetected defects in the reused software code to manifest themselves. The Therac-6 and Therac-20 had the same software errors but they simply were not revealed because when the software caused a condition that would lead to an overdose, the hardware fail-safe systems kicked in and prevented the error.

You can read a full account of the problems in Leveson and Turner's (1993) article in the IEEE's *Computer* magazine. Less dramatically, Ian Somerville (2001) enumerates some of the other potential problems that arise from reusing software. As systems that reuse components are changed over time it is possible that the reused components themselves need updating to maintain compatibility. This is fine if the source code is available, but if not, the maintenance costs are dramatically increased as these reused components will need to be rewritten from scratch. Even if reliable components are available for reuse, finding them in the many available libraries can be time consuming and difficult; some programmers may simply prefer to write new components themselves.

What's the moral of this reflection? Simply that reuse is a great idea in principle, but you have to be really careful to do it properly otherwise you can literally end up killing people. The ethics of software development is an interesting area of study that all software professionals should consider. *Ethics for the Information Age* (Quinn, 2004) is a very readable primer and heartily recommended. Quinn discusses the ethical issues that arise from several high-profile software failures, including the Therac-25, the Patriot Missile System, and the Ariane 5 rocket.

Small Capital Letters

OK, so it was only an example of the typesetting that identifies entries in the Reflections chapter. But programmers need to be consistent and not leave anything undone. So what is there to say about small capital letters? Not much except that they provide a useful alternative to hyperlinks in printed books.

Software Maintenance

Software maintenance can be loosely defined as anything that happens to a piece of code after it has been completed or delivered. You might assume that this only involves removing defects, but there are four accepted classes of maintenance activity. First, there is *corrective maintenance* or removing known defects from the program (also known as debugging, and cynically known as the art of replacing one bug by another). It is estimated that corrective maintenance accounts for 17% of all maintenance activity. Secondly, there is *adaptive maintenance*, or modifying a program so that it fits in with a changing environment (such as new hardware, or an updated version of the operating system). This task is reckoned to consume about 18% of the total maintenance activity. Adaptive maintenance is known by cynics as the art of replacing good working code by bugs. Next comes *perfective maintenance*. This is actually the most common type of maintenance encompassing enhancements to both the function and the efficiency of the code. It is carried out when extra features are added to the software or when existing aspects are rewritten to make them faster. Finally comes the lesser known fourth category of *preventive maintenance*. This is the process of changing software to improve its future maintainability or to provide a better basis for future enhancements.

Top Down

One of the more popular approaches advocated in programming methods and books is TOP-DOWN design, also known as "functional decomposition" or "stepwise refinement" (see DYSFUNCTIONAL DECOMPOSITION). It is popular because it is general and because it makes an appeal to common sense. The premise of TOP-DOWN design is simple: starting with an overall problem statement you decompose it into a set of smaller sub-problems. Each subproblem in turn is decomposed into its own smaller subproblems. This process is continued until at the bottom level the subproblems are so small that they can be easily expressed in programming language code. The result is a hierarchy of subproblems:

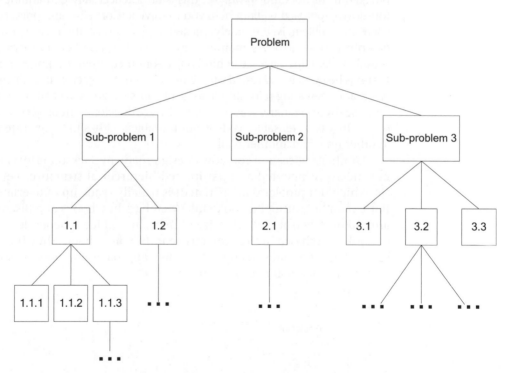

This process of stepwise refinement has psychological appeal as we are led to believe that we are gaining understanding of a problem through breaking it up into simpler subproblems in a kind of divide-and-conquer approach. Indeed, is not this just what *HTTLAP* recommends? Actually, no. In *HTTLAP*, while we are trying to solve the big problem by solving simpler related problems, there was no indication that the set of simpler problems is in any way hierarchically related. TOP-DOWN design does not give any advice on *how* to decompose the hierarchy; it merely says that we should keep on decomposing the problems until we arrive at some easily understood level. This division of a problem into separate subproblems requires that we make the biggest decision (deciding what the first level of decomposition will be) at the start of the process just when we know the least about the problem. To be able to do an effective functional decomposition we must first have already solved the problem in our heads. The TOP-DOWN design then becomes a description of a problem already solved rather than something that helps to actually solve the problem.

Barry Cornelius hints at this in *Understanding Java* (Cornelius, 2001) when he says that a drawback of TOP-DOWN design is that it does not scale well. That is, it does not work very well for large problems that are difficult to understand. Of course, even very small problems can be hard to understand and the TOP-DOWN approach still does not offer any help on how to understand and solve the problem. Consider the "small" problem of finding the next prime number from a given starting point. There is a single requirement and no awkward decisions about milk, sugar, whether the machine is plugged in or not, and so on. Yet this is an intellectually demanding problem and a top-down approach will not help you to solve it. Cornelius also points out that because each subproblem is intimately related to its parent then very little of a solution described in a TOP-DOWN manner can be used in another programming task. Code reusability is a driving force behind object-oriented programming as it means that code that has been built and tested can be used in other projects thus reducing development effort and increasing reliability. This is, of course, a gross oversimplification on my part because there are many reasons why software development projects fail and many reasons why even "reusable" code is not reusable and has to be rewritten. But that is for another time and another book.

Another criticism of TOP-DOWN design made by Jackson (1995) is that it imposes a neatly segmented and partitioned hierarchical structure, yet the real world (in which our problems are situated) is usually made up of overlapping problems. For example, consider a book club. Members buy books at a discount and pay an annual membership fee. The size of their annual fee is dependent on the number of books purchased in the previous year: the more books they buy the lower their subscription becomes. Using a TOP-DOWN approach you may reasonably come up with this functional decomposition.

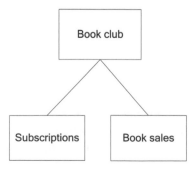

We have decided that there are two main processes needed to carry out the business of the book club: one to deal with members' subscriptions and another to deal with book sales. We could set about decomposing these two processes. The issue here is that the hierarchical decomposition into a subscriptions function and book sales function does not reflect the complexities of the real world of the book club. We know there is a relationship between the number of books purchased and the size of the subscription due, so which process deals with that? In fact, the problem of dealing with book sales overlaps with the problem of dealing with calculating subscriptions. Both subproblems have some unique features yet share some other characteristics. Constraining designs to a functional decomposition description stores up dangers. One of the claimed benefits of TOP-DOWN is that the subprocess separation means that each task (or box on the diagram) can be modified without affecting the other subprocesses. But, as we have just seen, this claim is spurious as it does not reflect the complexities of the real world and instead leads to simplistic abstractions.

For these reasons I like to call the technique *DYSFUNCTIONAL* DECOMPOSITION (see discussion in this chapter) as it does not work as well as it claims on the tin. *HTTLAP*, though advocating looking for simpler problems in an attempt to understand the overall problem does not suggest a TOP-DOWN approach. *HTTLAP* is more of a HEURISTIC approach to problem solving than a function decomposition technique.

John von Neumann

John von Neumann (1903–1957) is credited with developing a workable architecture for a universal computer. He studied under Pólya in Zurich. Pólya said of von Neumann: *"Johnny was the only student I was ever afraid of. If in the course of a lecture I stated an unsolved problem, the chances were he'd come to me as soon as the lecture was over, with the complete solution in a few scribbles on a slip of paper. I was never afraid of my students, but after that, I was afraid of von Neumann."* And, unfortunately (albeit unwittingly) so are many students of computer programming. The third-generation languages like C, BASIC, and Pascal were designed to allow programs to be written that would run on a von Neumann machine. Newer computer architectures have given us new programming paradigms (such as parallel programming) and new languages to support them, but behind it all, in the dawn of computing history, lies the good old von Neumann architecture.

Do not be afraid. Use the principles of *HTTLAP* and conquer your fear. Hooray!

References

Adams, J. L. (2001). *Conceptual Blockbusting: A Guide to Better Ideas*. Cambridge, MA: Perseus Publishing.

Ashworth, C. and Goodland, M. (1989). *SSADM: A Practical Approach*. Maidenhead, UK: McGraw-Hill.

Avison, D. E. and Fitzgerald, G. (1995). *Information Systems Development: Methodologies, Techniques, and Tools*. Maidenhead, UK: McGraw-Hill.

Brooks, F. P. (1974). *The Mythical Man Month and Other Essays on Software Engineering*. London: Addison Wesley Longman.

Checkland, P. and Holwell, S. (1997). *Information, Systems and Information Systems: Making Sense of the Field*. Chichester: John Wiley and Sons.

Cornelius, B. (2001). *Understanding Java*. London: Addison-Wesley.

Dromey, R. G. (1982). *How to Solve It by Computer*. London: Prentice-Hall International.

Humphrey, W. S. (1997). *Introduction to the Personal Software Process*. Harlow: Addison-Wesley.

Jackson, M. (1995). *Software Requirements & Specifications: A Lexicon of Practice, Principles and Prejudices*. Wokingham: ACM Press/Addison-Wesley.

Jackson, M. (2001). *Problem Frames: Analyzing and Structuring Software Development Problems*. London: ACM Press/Addison-Wesley.

Jackson, M. A. (1975). *Principles of Program Design*. London: Academic Press.

Jackson, M. A. (1983). *System Development*. London: Prentice-Hall International.

Ledgard, H. F. (1975). *Programming Proverbs*. Rochell Park, NJ: Hayden.

Leveson, N. G. and Turner, C. S. (1993). An investigation of the Therac-25 accidents. *Computer*, 26 (7), pp.18–41.

Lions, J. L. (1996). ARIANE 5: Flight 501 Failure, Report by the Enquiry Board, European Space Agency.

Pólya, G. (1990). *How to Solve It*. London: Penguin Books.

Quinn, M. J. (2004). *Ethics for the Information Age*. London: Addison Wesley.

Shalloway, A. and Trott, J. J. (2001). *Design Patterns Explained: A New Perspective on Object-oriented Design*. London: Addison-Wesley.

Sommerville, I. (2001). *Software Engineering*. London: Addison-Wesley.

Thompson, S. (1997). Where do I begin? A problem-solving approach to teaching functional programming. *First International Conference on Declarative Programming Languages in Education*. K. Apt, P. Hartel and P. Klint (Eds), Springer Verlag.

Weinberg, G. M. (1971). *Psychology of Computer Programming*. New York: Van Nostrand Reinhold Company.

Wirth, N. (1971). Program development by stepwise refinement. *Communications of the ACM* 14 (4), pp. 221–227.

Yourdon, E. (1988). *Modern Structured Analysis*. London: Prentice Hall International.

Pseudo-code

This appendix summarizes the syntax, meaning, and usage of the *HTTLAP* pseudo-code.

HTTLAP Pseudo-code Elements and Their Meanings

Element	Meaning	Example
;	End of instruction. A bit like a stop in English, the semi-colon terminates an uction or *statement*. It separates instructions to show distinct sequences of actions.	Pour coffee ; Add cream ; Add sugar ;
←	Assign a value. Give a value to something. The value on the right of the ← is given to the thing on the left.	numberSugars ← 2 ;
☐	Denotes a variable. The identifier gives a name to the item. The box is used to show that this is a variable rather than just another word. We can visualize a variable as a box into which a value is placed. The name of the variable, its *identifier* is written on the lid of the box.	sugars ;

Arithmetic operators

+	Addition operator	sum ← 3 + 4 ;
−	Subtraction operator	difference ← 4 − 3 ;
×	Multiplication operator	product ← 4 × 3 ;
÷	Division operator	quotient ← 12 ÷ 3 ;
MOD	Modulus, returns the remainder after integer division	leftOver ← 13 MOD 3 ;

Relational operators

=	Test for equality	IF (a = b)
		    Display ('Equal') ;
		ENDIF

≠	Test for inequality	`IF (`a` ≠ `b`)`
		`   Display ('Unequal') ;`
		`ENDIF`

<	Less than	`IF (`a` < `b`)`
		`   Display ('Less') ;`
		`ENDIF`

≤	Less than or equal to	`IF (3 ≤ 4)`
		`   Display ('Yes!') ;`
		`ENDIF`

>	Greater than	`IF (`a` > `b`)`
		`   Display ('Bigger') ;`
		`ENDIF`

≥	Greater than or equal to	`IF (5 ≥ 4)`
		`   Display ('Yes') ;`
		`ENDIF`

Logical connectives

AND	Logical **AND**. Returns True if both operands are True.	`IF (4 > 3) AND (2 < 4)`
		`   ...`
		`ENDIF`

OR	Logical **OR**. Returns True if either or both operands is True.	`IF (4 > 3) OR (2 < 4)`
		`   ...`
		`ENDIF`

NOT	Logical **NOT**. Returns opposite truth value of its single.	`IF NOT (4 > 3)`
		`   ...`
		`ENDIF`

Constructs

`IF (cond.)`
`   Action ;`
`ENDIF`

The basic conditional. **IF** asks a question the answer to which can be true or false. If the answer is true then the instruction following the **IF** is obeyed otherwise it is not. Parentheses ( ) are used to enclose the question which is called the **condition**. The action, or sequence of actions to be obeyed when the condition is satisfied (true) is written below the **IF** and indented by three spaces and is enclosed terminated by the keyword **ENDIF**. The **IF...ENDIF** brackets are helpful as they distinguish between the following two cases:

`IF (sugar required)`
`   Action ;`
`ENDIF`

Case 1
```
IF (condition)
    Action 1 ;
    Action 2 ;
ENDIF
```
Case 2
```
IF (condition)
    Action 1 ;
ENDIF
Action 2 ;
```
In Case 1 the square brackets indicate that both Action 1 and Action 2 are carried out when the condition is met. In Case 2, only Action 1 is only obeyed when the condition is met, whilst Action 2 comes after the **IF** and so is obeyed regardless of the condition. Here is an example of how you might use it:
```
IF (sugar required)
    Add sugar ;
ENDIF
IF (white coffee required)
    Add milk ;
ENDIF
Pour coffee ;
```
See how the coffee will always be poured whilst milk and sugar will only be added if their conditions are met?

`IF (cond.)`
`    Action ;`
`ELSE`
`    Action ;`
`ENDIF`
	An extension of the **IF** construct. If the condition is True then the action block is executed as in the normal **IF**. However, when the condition is False, the first action block is ignored and instead the one following the **ELSE** is executed.	`IF (`a` > 10)`
		`    Display ('High') ;`
		`ELSE`
		`    Display ('Low') ;`
		`ENDIF`

`//`	A comment. Used to put in explanatory notes that aren't instructions to be coded or carried out.	`// Get the input`

`WHILE (cond.)`
`    Action block ;`
`ENDWHILE`
	WHILE is an indeterminate iteration whose action block is executed zero or more times. The condition is tested and if true then the action block is executed. The iteration continues until	`Get record ;`
		`WHILE (not end of records)`
		`    Process record ;`
		`    Get next record ;`
		`ENDWHILE`

the condition becomes false. The
action block must provide a
mechanism for making the condition
false otherwise the loop will never
terminate.

DO   Indeterminate one-or-more iteration.

```
DO
    Display (ⓐ) ;
    ⓐ ←ⓐ + 1 ;
WHILE (ⓐ ≤ 12) ;
```

FOR   A count-controlled loop.

```
FOR ⓐ GOES FROM 1 TO 10
    Display (ⓐ) ;
ENDFOR
```

Glossary

abstract   The simplification of detail. "Car" is an abstraction for a very complex piece of machinery with many thousands of individual components. Abstraction is a key feature of computing for it allows the construction of data types and operations.

algorithm   A set of procedures or instructions for solving a problem or computing a result. The word is a derivation of Al-Khwarizmi (native of Khwarizm), the name given to the ninth century mathematician Abu Ja'far Mohammed ben Musa who came from Khwarizm (modern day Khiva in the south of Uzbekistan).

Boolean   After George Boole (1815–1864) who devised a system of algebra (Boolean algebra) whose elements have one of two possible values: True and False. Operations on the elements are logical (AND, OR, NOT, etc.) rather than arithmetic (+, −, ÷, ×, etc.).

bug   The commonly used term for a software defect. Defects are errors in programming that cause programs to produce the wrong answers or even crash.

C   A *programming* language. C is a *procedural language*. It has been around for a long time. Its syntax allows for very powerful coding techniques but its flexibility can trip up the unwary novice.

C#   *C#*, pronounced "C sharp" (or "C hash" if you are feeling mischievous) is Microsoft's answer to *Java*. It is a bit like *C++* and a bit like *Java*. You can look the rest up for yourself.

C++   *C++* (pronounced "C plus plus") is an *object-oriented* programming language. It is regarded as a descendant of *C*. Its name is a pun. In *C* the ++ *operator* adds 1 to a variable. Hence *C++* is *C* code for C-plus-one. Hah hah. *C++* *is* very popular today, especially with games programmers.

code, source code   A set of statements or instructions written in a human-readable programming language (e.g., Java). The source code is compiled to produce the machine-executable program.

comments   Strings of text put into program source code that are ignored by the compiler. Comments are used to annotate source code to make it easier to read and understand.

compilation   The process of translating source code understood by humans into the binary form computers can read.

condition   A test of a Boolean relation against which certain processing is carried out depending on the relation's truth value. For example:

```
IF (salary > 20000)
    Display ('High salary') ;
ELSE
    Display ('Low salary') ;
ENDIF
```

data   The values passed into, around, and out of a program.

data types   See *type*

debugging The removal of bugs or defects from a program.

defect Also known as a bug, a defect is something that causes a program to behave incorrectly or to produce erroneous results.

flow The path taken through a program; the progression from one program statement to the next.

flowchart A diagrammatic representation of the set of possible paths through a program.

function A subprogram that processes zero, one, or more parameters and returns a result. For example, we could write a function that takes a number as a parameter and returns the square root of that number.

identifier The name given to a *variable*

input The values that go into a program or subprogram.

iteration A technique for performing the repeated execution of one or more statements within a program.

Java Another *object-oriented* language. It shares many syntactic features with *C* and *C++* but is quite different in many aspects. It is very popular for programming Web-based applications. Unlike C, C++, Pascal, and other languages, Java is not compiled to machine code. Instead the Java compiler creates a higher-level *byte code* which is interpreted and executed by a Java virtual machine (JVM), JVMs exist for most of today's computing platforms such as Windows, UNIX, Linux, etc. This means that a programmer can write a Java program knowing that it will run successfully on all computers regardless of their *operating system*. This is unlike the traditional languages like *C* and Pascal which require a special compiler for each operating system on which the program is intended to be run. One of the drawbacks of Java though is that the byte code is slower to execute than the machine code produced by other language compilers.

JavaScript Do not confuse JavaScript with *Java*. It has a few superficial similarities to Java but that is about it. It was developed by Netscape Corporation and the name is a property of Sun Microsystems. Microsoft has its own version of the language called JScript. JavaScript is a *scripting language* rather than a compiled language which means that programs written in it can only run within a dedicated environment (such as a web page). JavaScript is handy for putting clever features into web pages but is not used for mainstream software development.

Linux A popular operating system developed by Linus Torvalds and based on the well-established UNIX operating system.

loop See iteration.

memory The parts of a computer that retain data. The hard disc is a permanent memory that retains data even when powered down, while the RAM (random access memory) that the computer uses to store running programs is typically *volatile* memory that loses its data when power is removed.

method The name given to the subprograms of a class in an object-oriented program.

Object oriented programming A style of programming that uses the principles of encapsulation, inheritance, polymorphism, and data hiding.

OOP See objected-oriented programming

operand The data manipulated by an operator. The arithmetic expression 3 + 4 has one operator, "+", and two operands, 3, and 4.

operating system The special piece of software that controls a computer's hardware and which manages the basic system operations (such as running programs, copying files, etc.). The most popular operating systems for today's personal computers are Apple's OS X, Linux, and Microsoft Windows (not in that order).

operator   Something that performs an operation on one or more operands (see *operand* above).

output   The data passed out of a program or subprogram.

Parameter   A data item passed to a subprogram (function, procedure, or method). Parameters have three forms:

1. Input: used only to pass values into the subprogram.
2. Output: used by the subprogram for passing values out.
3. Input/Output: a data value passed into a subprogram which is subsequently modified by the subprogram.

problem   What you will have if you do not study hard enough.

procedure   A type of subprogram that performs a series of actions, which may receive zero or more parameters, and which (depending on the calling technique used) may change the values of zero or more of its parameters.

program   A collection of statements representing an algorithm that carry out some specified purpose. Also known as software.

programming language   A set of syntactic and semantic rules that allows a human to write a set of instructions in human-readable form that can be translated by a compiler into a form that is executable on a computer.

pseudo-code   A bit like a programming language, but lacking the formal syntactic and semantic rules. It is used as a general way of writing algorithms without being tied down to any particular programming language.

RAM   Random Access Memory – formally a type of computer storage whose contents can be accessed in any order. Normally we think of RAM as being the memory chips on a computer that store running programs and which, these days, is measured in the hundreds of megabytes. However, formats like DVD-RAM allow random access memory on optical discs. Though most RAM can be written to, strictly speaking the term refers to any memory whose contents can be accessed in any order.

recursion   See page 227.

ROM   Read-Only Memory. A form of computer memory that can be read from (usually in a random access manner) but which cannot be written to. CD-ROMs are of this form.

schematic logic   See *pseudo-code*

selection   See *condition*.

sequence   An ordered set of instructions in a computer program.

source code   See *code*.

statement   An action or command in a computer program.

state-transition diagram   A diagrammatic representation of the different states a system can be in, and the transitions that can occur between states.

structure chart   An ill-defined term that covers a number of diagrammatic representations of the structure of programs and software systems. There are many different notational forms.

structure text   See *pseudo-code*.

structured English   See *pseudo-code*.

syntax   The set of allowable words and symbols and their permitted orderings in a programming language.

syntax error   An error in which a programming language's rules of syntax have been violated resulting in source code that will be rejected by a compiler.

type   A name for a set of values together with the various operations that can be performed on values of that type.

UML   Unified Modeling Language. A set of diagrammatic notations used to design and document object-oriented software.

UNIX An operating system developed in the 1960s which is still widely used today owing to its renowned stability. Popular among middle-aged bearded types with pony tails. The BSD UNIX distribution is the underlying operating system beneath Apple's OS X.

variable A place in memory (with an *identifier* as a name) where a value is stored. Its value can be changed by the program.

Visual Basic One of a stable of Microsoft programming languages beginning with the word "visual." These are not *visual programming* languages in the true sense but are so named because they include sophisticated interface builders that allow the program's graphical user interface (its windows, menus, etc.) to be created by dragging and dropping objects on the screen. The dragging and dropping of graphical objects is the only similarity these languages have with true *visual programming* languages.

visual programming A visual programming language uses a spatial arrangement of special symbols, graphics, and textual elements to define a program. Visual programming languages are typically very graphical and often show connections between components as arrows and lines. Do not confuse with Visual Basic which is not, despite what its name suggests, a visual programming language.

windows A central feature of the graphical user interface. Windows are typically rectangular and contain some interface components (buttons, text boxes, etc.), some graphics, or some text (e.g., a document window in a word processor). The window can be manipulated with a pointer controlled by a mouse or keyboard. Common operating systems that use windowing today are Apple OS, X Window System (on UNIX), and Microsoft Windows.

Solutions to Selected Exercises

Here are solutions to some of the exercises in the book. Some of the solutions are as full as I can make them, others are partial.

In-text Exercises (All Chapters)

In-text Exercise 01 (Chapter 4)

Before you leave home in the morning you check to see whether it is raining; if it is you take an umbrella with you. Write an IF...ENDIF *construct that shows this decision-making process.*

```
1.  IF (raining)
        1.1.   Take umbrella ;
    ENDIF
```

In-text Exercise 02 (Chapter 4)

Write an IF...ENDIF *construct that adds a 10% tip to a restaurant bill and compliments the chef if the service was of a high standard. After the* ENDIF *add a statement to pay the bill and convince yourself that the tip is only added when good service is received.*

```
1.  IF (high-standard service)
        1.1.   Add 10% tip to bill ;
        1.2.   Compliment the chef ;
    ENDIF
2.  Pay bill ;
```

In-text Exercise 03 (Chapter 4)

In the above WHILE *loop, why is there a statement to add 1 to the number of sugars added?*

If the statement were not there then the loop would never terminate. The algorithm would never update its own tally of how many sugars had been added and so the condition controlling the WHILE loop would always be true. The statement comes at the bottom of the loop because only after adding a sugar to the cup should we update the tally.

In-text Exercise 04 (Chapter 5)

Look at Solution 5.1 and identify these two aspects of the problem. State which group of actions deals with making the coffee and which group describes how to process a single cup.

Tasks #1 to #8 deal with making the coffee and Tasks #9 to #14 describe how to *process* a single cup.

In-text Exercise 05 (Chapter 5)

Why has the task "Make note of van's payload" been removed?

Because the new Tasks #1 and #3.2 mean that after despatching the van we already know its payload.

In-text Exercise 06 (Chapter 6)

Do not move on until you understand how the three conditions are mutually exclusive, that is, only one can be true at a time. You can show this by drawing a truth table:

	Condition		
parcelWeight	parcelWeight up to (and including) 5 kilos	parcelWeight more than 5 and less than 10 kilos	parcelWeight 10 kilos or over
4 kg	**True**	False	False
5 kg	**True**	False	False
9 kg	False	**True**	False
10 kg	False	False	**True**
11 kg	False	False	**True**

In-text Exercise 07 (Chapter 6)

Explain why this is a determinate loop.

We do not know until we ask our guest how many times the loop's action body should be executed, and the number would likely vary from guest to guest. But, once we have found out how many sugars are required we can calculate how many times to go through the loop. If two sugars are wanted then the loop must execute twice. If no sugar is required then the loop will iterate zero times, that is, the action block will not be carried out.

Chapter 1

End of Chapter Exercises

1. There are some quite formal definitions, but in layman's terms an algorithm is a set of clear instructions to carry out a defined task.

2. A computer program is an algorithm expressed in a programming language to be carried out by a computer.

3. **High**: black leather. **Medium**: A black leather billfold with a single fastening. Two main currency pockets plus slots for cards. **Low**: A black leather billfold with a single fastening about 5 years old, contains £25 in cash: a £20 note (the old design with Edward Elgar on the back) and a £5 note; 4 debit card receipts, 1 ATM receipt, 1 debit card, 1 credit card, and my Engineering Council registration card ...

6. Well, you might be a history student taking programming as a compulsory course! The answer "the assassination in Sarajevo of Archduke Ferdinand by Gavrilo Princip" is too simplistic and will not receive credit.

Chapter 1 Projects

StockSnackz Vending Machine

No solutions for this chapter.

Stocksfield Fire Service: Hazchem Signs

No solutions for this chapter.

Puzzle World: Roman Numerals and Chronograms

No solutions for this chapter.

Pangrams: Holoalphabetic Sentences

No solutions for this chapter.

Online Bookstore: ISBNs

No solutions for this chapter.

Chapter 2

End of Chapter Exercises

1. Car's range = 840 km (60 × 14). 2000 km ÷ 840 km = 2.38, therefore we must **fill the tank 3 times** (doing it only twice causes the car to stop at 1,680 km).

   How many miles can you travel on 10 gallons of fuel?

   Fuel consumption = 14 km/l = (14 ÷ 1.609344) = 8.699 miles/litre.

   8.699 miles/litre = 8.699 ÷ 0.219969157 = 39.55 miles/imperial gallon = 8.699 ÷ 0.264172051 = 32.93 miles/U.S. gallon.

   Therefore, 10 imperial gallons will get you 39.55 × 10 = 395.5 miles. 10 U.S. gallons will take you 32.93 × 10 = 329.3 miles.

2. Getting dressed in the morning:
   ```
   Put on underwear.
   Put on socks.
   Put on trousers.
   Put on shirt.
   Put on shoes.
   ```

4. Filling a car with fuel:
```
Drive to petrol station.
Unlock fuel cap.
Get out of and lock car (remember to take wallet).
Select correct fuel (diesel or unleaded).
Put nozzle into filler cap.
Pump desired amount of fuel.
Replace nozzle.
Replace fuel cap and secure.
Pay for fuel.
Unlock car, get in, drive away.
```

Chapter 2 Projects

StockSnackz Vending Machine

1. Install the new machine.
2. Turn on power.
3. Load machine with snacks.
4. Dispense snacks.
5. Show dispensing report.

Stocksfield Fire Service: Hazchem Signs

1. Decode first character and give fire-fighting instructions.
2. Decode second character and give precaution instructions.
3. Decode third character and state whether public hazard exists.

Puzzle World: Roman Numerals and Chronograms

No solution provided.

Pangrams: Holoalphabetic Sentences

No solution provided.

Online Bookstore: ISBNs

No solution provided.

Chapter 3

End of Chapter Exercises

Note, for space reasons, documentation is not included.

1. A difficult question until you realize algebra is the way to go. n = Nick, l = Lynne, a = Alf, s = Shadi, c = Chris.

   Nick's computer has three times the memory of Lynne's and Alf's computers put together:

   (1) $n = 3(l + a)$

Shadi's PC has twice as much memory as Chris's:

(2) $s = 2c$

Nick's computer has one-and-a-half times the memory of Shadi's:

(3) $n = \dfrac{3}{2}s$

Between them, Alf and Shadi's computers have as much memory as Lynne's plus twice the memory of Chris's:

(4) $a + s = l + 2c$

Shadi, Chris, Nick, Alf, and Lynne's PCs have 2,800 megabytes of memory between them:

(5) $s + c + n + a + l = 2800$

We know from (1) that $l + a = \dfrac{n}{3}$, so we can rearrange (5) to give:

(6) $c + s + \dfrac{4}{3}n = 2800$

We also know from (2) that $c = \dfrac{s}{2}$, so we can substitute again to change (6) into:

(7) $\dfrac{3}{2}s + \dfrac{4}{3}n = 2800$

We also know from (3) that $n = \dfrac{3}{2}s$, so $\dfrac{4}{3}n = \dfrac{4}{3} \times \dfrac{3}{2}s = \dfrac{12}{6}s = \dfrac{4}{2}s$ which means we can substitute in (7) to give:

(8) $\dfrac{7}{2}s = 2800$

Therefore, $7s = 5600$, $s = 800$, so Shadi's computer has 800 MB. From (2) we can say that Chris's computer has 400 MB. Nick's PC has 1200 MB (from (3)). (4) tells us that Lynne and Alf's computers have the same amount of memory, and between them they have 400 MB from (1), therefore they must have 200 MB each. To double check, we can add these all up: 800 + 400 + 1200 + 200 + 200 = 2800.

Try doing this exercise with words alone!

2. Here is my solution:

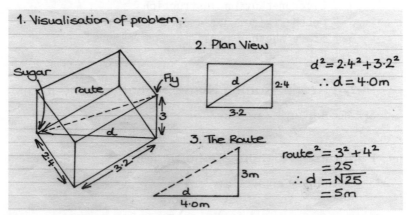

3. Look at the row and column numbers of the white squares. R1C1 is white, R2C2 is white, R1C3 is white, R2C3 is black. What's the pattern?
A square whose row and column numbers are either **both** odd or **both** even is white.

5. It's a problem of repeated division and amounts left over after division. To keep the solution short lets work with U.S. coins because there are fewer of them, but the principle is the same regardless of the number of different coin denominations:

```
// Note we need to do whole number division, so 76 ÷ 25 = 3,
remainder 1.
1.  No. of 25¢ coins needed is amount of change to give ÷ 25 ;
2.  Amount left over = remainder from step 1 ;
3.  No. of 10¢ coins = amount left over ÷ 10 ;
4.  Amount left over = remainder from step 3 ;
5.  No. of 5¢ coins = amount left over ÷ 5 ;
6.  No. of 1¢ coins = remainder from step 5 ;
```

Chapter 3 Projects

StockSnackz Vending Machine

Solution looks a lot like the one from Chapter 2:

```
1.  Install the new machine ;
2.  Turn on power ;
3.  Load machine with snacks ;
4.  Dispense snacks ;
5.  Show dispensing report ;
```

Stocksfield Fire Service: Hazchem Signs

```
1.  Decode first character ;
2.  Give fire-fighting instructions ;
3.  Decode second character ;
4.  Give precaution instructions ;
5.  Decode third character ;
6.  State whether public hazard exists ;
```

Puzzle World: Roman Numerals and Chronograms

See accompanying website.

Pangrams: Holoalphabetic Sentences

See accompanying website.

Online Bookstore: ISBNs

See accompanying website.

Chapter 4

End of Chapter Exercises

1. We use the IF when we want to choose whether or not to perform a single action (or sequence of actions). We use the WHILE when we want to repeatedly perform an action or sequence of actions. Both involve conditionally carrying out an action, but they differ in that the WHILE will repeatedly carry out its action block whereas the IF will only carry out its action block once.

2. When it is raining the hat and shoes are worn. When it is not raining (which could be sunny) then the hat, shoes, and sunglasses are worn. Sunglasses are worn conditionally dependent on the IF construct.

3. What items will be purchased a) on Thursday, b) on Saturday?
   Answer: a) milk and bread, b) milk, newspaper, peanuts, bread
   You might have thought that peanuts were bought on Thursday too, but this is because the buy peanuts action is wrongly indented. The thing which really matters is that the buy peanuts action comes inside the ENDIF keyword. All the actions between the IF and ENDIF keywords are carried out when the condition is true.

4. No stories will be read as the WHILE loop is conditional upon breakfast not being finished but we can see from steps 1 and 2 that breakfast has been eaten before the WHILE loop action is reached.

5. Adding cheese, lettuce and tomatoes:
```
Get cheese, lettuce, and tomatoes requirements ;
IF (cheese required)
   Add cheese ;
ENDIF
IF (lettuce required)
   Add lettuce ;
ENDIF
IF (tomatoes required)
   Add tomatoes ;
ENDIF
```

7. Potency calculator:
```
1.  Start potency at 100% ;
2.  WHILE (potency greater than or equal to 50%)
        2.1.  Display Month & potency message ;
        2.2.  Reduce potency by 6% ;
        2.3.  Move to next month ;
    ENDWHILE
```

10. *Earth's Next Top Professor*

First solution

```
1.  Ask judge for professor's name ;
2.  Get teaching ability score ;
3.  Get humor score ;
4.  Get knowledge score ;
5.  Get good looks score ;
6.  IF (teaching + humor + knowledge + looks is greater than 20)
        6.1.  Display 'scores too high' message ;
        6.2.  Set teaching ability score to 5 ;
        6.3.  Set humor score to 5 ;
        6.4.  Set knowledge score to 5 ;
        6.5.  Set good looks score to 5 ;
    ENDIF
```

Second solution

```
1.  WHILE (professors to judge)
        1.1.  Ask judge for professor's name ;
        1.2.  Get teaching ability score ;
        1.3.  Get humor score ;
        1.4.  Get knowledge score ;
        1.5.  Get good looks score ;
        1.6.  IF (total score is greater than 20)
                1.6.1.  Display 'scores too high' ;
                1.6.2.  Set teaching ability score to 5 ;
                1.6.3.  Set humor score to 5 ;
                1.6.4.  Set knowledge score to 5 ;
                1.6.5.  Set good looks score to 5 ;
            ENDIF
    ENDWHILE
```

Third solution

```
1.  WHILE judges to give scores
        1.1.  WHILE (professors to judge)
                1.1.1.  Ask judge for professor's name ;
                1.1.2.  Get teaching ability score ;
                1.1.3.  Get humor score ;
                1.1.4.  Get knowledge score ;
                1.1.5.  Get good looks score ;
                1.1.6.  IF (total score is greater than 20)
                        1.1.6.1.  Display 'scores too high' ;
                        1.1.6.2.  Set teaching ability score
                                  to 5 ;
                        1.1.6.3.  Set humor score to 5 ;
                        1.1.6.4.  Set knowledge score to 5 ;
                        1.1.6.5.  Set good looks score to 5 ;
                    ENDIF
            ENDWHILE
    ENDWHILE
```

11. Making an omelette.

```
Find out how many people to feed (up to 3) ;
Add (2 × no. people) eggs to bowl ;
Add (pinch × no. people) salt to bowl ;
Add (pinch × no. people) pepper to bowl ;
Add (100 ml × no. people) milk to bowl ;
Add (0.25 × no. people) onion to bowl ;
Add (60 gm × no. people) cheese to bowl ;
Add (knob × no. people) butter to bowl ;
Put pan on heat ;
Mix ingredients in bowl ;
Add mixture to pan ;
WHILE (surface not firming up)
    Cook omelette ;
ENDWHILE ;
Get garnish requirements ;
IF (parsley required)
    Sprinkle parsley ;
ENDIF
IF (parmesan required)
    Sprinkle parmesan ;
ENDIF
Divide omelette by no. people ;
WHILE (portions served not equal to no. required)
    Serve portion on plate ;
    Add 1 to number portions served ;
ENDWHILE
```

13. Constrained hamburger problem:

```
Get cheese requirements ;
IF (cheese required)
    Add cheese ;
ENDIF
IF (cheese NOT required)
    Add lettuce ;
    Add tomatoes ;
ENDIF
```

The IF appears to be missing the ability to automatically add lettuce and tomatoes when cheese is not required.

Chapter 4 Projects

StockSnackz Vending Machine

Pushing Button 1 dispenses a milk chocolate bar, Button 2 a muesli bar, Button 3 a pack of cheese puffs, Button 4 an apple, Button 5 a pack of popcorn, while pushing Button 6 displays on the machine's small screen a summary of how many of each item have been dispensed. Pushing the Buttons 0, 7, 8, or 9 has no effect.

Dispense a single snack:
```
IF (button 1 pressed)
   Dispense milk chocolate ;
ENDIF
IF (button 2 pressed)
   Dispense muesli bar ;
ENDIF
IF (button 3 pressed)
   Dispense cheese puffs ;
ENDIF
IF (button 4 pressed)
   Dispense apple ;
ENDIF
IF (button 5 pressed)
   Dispense popcorn ;
ENDIF
IF (button 6 pressed)
   Print sales summary ;
ENDIF
```

Do this repeatedly:
```
1.  Install machine ;
2.  Turn on power ;
3.  Fill machine ;
4.  WHILE (not the end of the day)
        4.1.  IF (button 1 pressed)
                  4.1.1.  Dispense milk chocolate ;
              ENDIF
        4.2.  IF (button 2 pressed)
                  4.2.1.  Dispense muesli bar ;
              ENDIF
        4.3.  IF (button 3 pressed)
                  4.3.1.  Dispense cheese puffs ;
              ENDIF
        4.4.  IF (button 4 pressed)
                  4.4.1.  Dispense apple ;
              ENDIF
        4.5.  IF (button 5 pressed)
                  4.5.1.  Dispense popcorn ;
              ENDIF
        4.6.  IF (button 6 pressed)
                  4.6.1.  Print sales summary ;
              ENDIF
    ENDWHILE
```

Stocksfield Fire Service: Hazchem Signs

```
// First character
IF character is 1
   Use coarse spray ;
ENDIF
```

```
IF character is 2
   Use fine spray ;
ENDIF
IF character is 3
   Use foam ;
ENDIF
IF character is 4
   Use dry agent ;
ENDIF
// Second character
IF character is P
   Use LTS ;
   Dilute spillage ;
   Risk of explosion ;
ENDIF
 ...
IF character is Z
   Use BA & Fire kit ;
   Contain spillage ;
ENDIF
// Third character
IF character is E
   Public hazard ;
ENDIF
```

Puzzle World: Roman Numerals & Chronograms

See accompanying website.

Pangrams: Holoalphabetic Sentences

See accompanying website.

Online Bookstore: ISBNs

See accompanying website.

Chapter 5

End of Chapter Exercises

1. a) 7 – the expression 3 + 4 gives 7.
    b) 14 – `result` was already 7 from the last assignment so adding another 7 takes it to 14
    c) 14 – we just assigned the value of `result` to itself.
    d) 7 – now we have just subtracted 7 from `result`.
2. Swapping variables. This algorithm will swap any two variables without the use of temporary storage. Try it out for yourself.
    1. a ← a + b ;
    2. b ← a - b ;
    3. a ← a - b ;

4. Division by subtraction.

```
1. Get firstNumber ;
2. Get secondNumber ;
3. counter ← 0 ;
4. remainder ← firstNumber ;
5. WHILE (remainder ≥ secondNumber)
       5.1.  remainder ← remainder - secondNumber ;
       5.2.  counter ← counter + 1 ;
   ENDWHILE
6. Display firstNumber divides secondNumber by counter times ;
```

Note, this solution assumes both numbers are positive.

9. Calculating the lightest and average payload weight. Additions show in bold.

```
// *******************************************
// Instructions for loading vans
// Written by Paul Vickers, June 2007
// *******************************************
// Initialize variables
1.   capacity ← 750 ;

2.   numberOfVans ← zero ;

3.   heaviestVan ← zero ;

4.   lightestPayload ← 751 ;

5.   totalPayload ← zero ;

6.   averagePayload ;

7.   Get first parcelWeight ;

8.   WHILE (conveyor not empty)
         // Process vans
     8.1.  payload ← zero ;

     8.2.  WHILE (payload + parcelWeight less than or equal to
                  capacity) AND (conveyor NOT empty)
               // Load a single van
               8.2.1.  Load parcel on van ;

               8.2.2.  payload ← payload + parcelWeight ;

               8.2.3.  Get next parcelWeight ;
           ENDWHILE
     8.3.  Despatch van ;

     8.4.  numberOfVans ← numberOfVans + 1 ;
           // Check whether this is the heaviest van
     8.5.  IF (payload more than heaviestVan)
               8.5.1.  heaviestVan ← payload ;
           ENDIF
           // Check if this is the lightest van
     8.6.  IF (payload less than lightestPayload)
               8.6.1.  lightestPayload ← payload ;
           ENDIF
```

```
                //Add payload to total payload
        8.7.  totalPayload ← totalPayload + payload ;
      ENDWHILE
// Calculate average payload ;
9.    IF (totalPayload NOT equal to zero) // Can't divide by zero
        9.1.  averagePayload ← totalPayload ÷ numberOfVans ;
      ENDIF
10.  Report numberOfVans used ;
11.  Report heaviestVan sent ;
12.  Report lightestPayload sent out ;
13.  Report averagePayload sent out ;
```

Chapter 5 Projects

StockSnackz Vending Machine

Identifier	Description	Range of Values
chocolateStock	Stock level for chocolate bars	{1..20}
muesliStock	Stock level for muesli bars	{1..20}
cheesePuffStock	Stock level for cheese puffs	{1..20}
appleStock	Stock level for apples	{1..20}
popcornStock	Stock level for popcorn	{1..20}

```
1.   Install machine ;
2.   Turn on power ;
3.   Fill machine ;
4.   chocolateStock ← 5 ;
5.   muesliStock ← 5 ;
6.   cheesePuffStock ← 5 ;
7.   appleStock ← 5 ;
8.   popcornStock ← 5 ;
9.   WHILE (not the end of the day)
        9.1.  IF (button 1 pressed)
                IF (chocolateStock > 0)
                    Dispense milk chocolate ;
                    chocolateStock ← chocolateStock - 1 ;
                ENDIF
                IF (chocolateStock = 0)
                    Display 'Sold out message' ;
                ENDIF
              ENDIF
        9.2.  IF (button 2 pressed)
                IF (muesliStock > 0)
                    Dispense muesli bar ;
                    muesliStock ← muesliStock - 1 ;
                ENDIF
```

```
                        IF (muesliStock = 0)
                            Display 'Sold out message' ;
                        ENDIF
                    ENDIF
         9.3.   IF (button 3 pressed)
                    IF (cheesePuffStock > 0)
                        Dispense cheese puffs ;
                        cheesePuffStock ← cheesePuffStock - 1 ;
                    ENDIF
                    IF (cheesePuffStock = 0)
                        Display 'Sold out message' ;
                    ENDIF
                ENDIF
         9.4.   IF (button 4 pressed)
                    IF (appleStock > 0)
                        Dispense apple ;
                        appleStock ← appleStock - 1 ;
                    ENDIF
                    IF (appleStock = 0)
                        Display 'Sold out message' ;
                    ENDIF
                ENDIF
         9.5.   IF (button 5 pressed)
                    IF (popcornStock > 0)
                        Dispense popcorn ;
                        popcornStock ← popcornStock - 1 ;
                    ENDIF
                    IF (popcornStock = 0)
                        Display 'Sold out message' ;
                    ENDIF
                ENDIF
         9.6.   IF (button 6 pressed)
                    Print sales summary ;
                ENDIF
         9.7.   IF (button 0, 7, 8, 9 pressed)
                    Display 'Invalid choice message' ;
                ENDIF
        ENDWHILE
```

Stocksfield Fire Service: Hazchem Signs

Identifier	Description	Range of Values
fireFightingCode	Fire fighting code	{1,2,3,4}
precautionsCode	Fire fighters' precautions	{P,R,S,T,W,X,Y,Z}
publicHazardCode	Public hazard	{V,blank}

Puzzle World: Roman Numerals and Chronograms

See accompanying website.

Pangrams: Holoalphabetic Sentences

See accompanying website.

Online Bookstore: ISBNs

See accompanying website.

Chapter 6

End of Chapter Exercises

1. There are two things wrong with the following IF statement. What are they?

   ```
   IF (mark ≥ 40)
       Display 'You have passed.' ;
   ELSE IF (mark ≤ 40)
       Display 'You have failed.' ;
   ENDIF
   ```

   First it is ambiguous – what should happen when **mark** is 40 as 40 satisfies both conditions? Second, the ELSE doesn't need the IF: it should just be

   ```
   IF (mark ≥ 40)
       Display 'You have passed.' ;
   ELSE
       Display 'You have failed.' ;
   ENDIF
   ```

2. FOR loop: when you want to implement a count-controlled loop and the number of repetitions is known in advance or can be determined prior to the start of the loop.
   DO...WHILE: When you want to iteratate an undetermined number of times but at least once.
   DO...WHILE is a 1-or-more loop, while the WHILE is a zero-or-more loop.

3. They allow a more precise control abstraction. WHILE offers a general control abstraction that can be used to implement any iteration, but if upon examination the nature of the loop reveals certain characteristics (such as those listed in question 2) then use the appropriate iteration construct. The principle here is use the control abstraction that most closely fits the problem.

5. Calculating grades.

   ```
   IF (studentMark at least 4) // A Grade
       studentGrade ← A ;
   ELSE IF (studentMark at least 3) // B Grade
       studentGrade ← B ;
   ELSE IF (studentMark at least 2) // C Grade
       studentGrade ← C ;
   ELSE //Anything under 2 is a fail
       studentMark ← F ;
   ENDIF
   ```

6. Changed grade boundaries.

```
IF (studentMark at least 4) // A Grade
    studentGrade ← A ;
ELSE IF (studentMark at least 3.5) // B Grade
    studentGrade ← B ;
ELSE IF (studentMark at least 3) // C Grade
    studentGrade ← C ;
ELSE IF (studentMark at least 2) // D Grade
    studentGrade ← D ;
ELSE //Anything under 2 is a fail
    studentMark ← F ;
ENDIF
```

7. Without the **ELSE** paths:

```
IF (studentMark at least 4) // A Grade
    studentGrade ← A ;
ENDIF
IF (studentMark at least 3.5 but less than 4) // B Grade
    studentGrade ← B ;
ENDIF
IF (studentMark at least 3 but less than 3.5) // C Grade
    studentGrade ← C ;
ENDIF
IF (studentMark at least 2 but less than 3) // D Grade
    studentGrade ← D ;
ENDIF
IF (student mark less than 2) //Anything under 2 is a fail
    studentMark ← F ;
ENDIF
```

8. For twenty students:

```
numberGrades ← 0 ;
classSize ← 20 ;
FOR (numberGrades GOES FROM 1 to classSize)
    Get studentMark ;
    IF (studentMark at least 4) // A Grade
        studentGrade ← A ;
    ELSE IF (studentMark at least 3.5) // B Grade
        studentGrade ← B ;
    ELSE IF (studentMark at least 3) // C Grade
        studentGrade ← C ;
    ELSE IF (studentMark at least 2) // D Grade
        studentGrade ← D ;
    ELSE //Anything under 2 is a fail
        studentMark ← F ;
    ENDIF
ENDFOR
```

11. Beaufort scale.

```
Display 'Enter a wind speed' ;
windSpeed ← value typed by user ;
IF (windSpeed = 0)
    Display 'Beaufort scale:0, Calm' ;
ELSE IF (windSpeed ≤ 3)
    Display 'Beaufort scale:1, Light air' ;
ELSE IF (windSpeed ≤ 7)
    Display 'Beaufort scale:2, Light breeze' ;
ELSE IF (windSpeed ≤ 12)
    Display 'Beaufort scale:3, Gentle breeze' ;
ELSE IF (windSpeed ≤ 18)
    Display 'Beaufort scale:4, Moderate breeze' ;
ELSE IF (windSpeed ≤ 24)
    Display 'Beaufort scale:5, Fresh breeze' ;
ELSE IF (windSpeed ≤ 31)
    Display 'Beaufort scale:6, Strong breeze' ;
ELSE IF (windSpeed ≤ 39)
    Display 'Beaufort scale:7, Near gale' ;
ELSE IF (windSpeed ≤ 46)
    Display 'Beaufort scale:8, Gale' ;
ELSE IF (windSpeed ≤ 54)
    Display 'Beaufort scale:9, Strong Gales' ;
ELSE IF (windSpeed ≤ 63)
    Display 'Beaufort scale:10, Storm' ;
ELSE IF (windSpeed ≤ 72)
    Display 'Beaufort scale:11, Violent storm' ;
ELSE
    Display 'Beaufort scale:12, Hurricane' ;
ENDIF
```

Chapter 6 Projects

StockSnackz Vending Machine

Use IF...ELSE:

```
1.  Install machine ;
2.  Turn on power ;
3.  Fill machine ;
4.  chocolateStock ← 5 ;
5.  muesliStock ← 5 ;
6.  cheesePuffStock ← 5 ;
7.  appleStock ← 5 ;
8.  popcornStock ← 5 ;
9.  WHILE (not the end of the day)
        9.1.  IF (button 1 pressed)
                  IF (chocolateStock > 0)
                      Dispense milk chocolate ;
```

```
                              chocolateStock ← chocolateStock - 1 ;
                     ELSE
                        Display 'Sold out message' ;
                     ENDIF
        9.2.   ELSE IF (button 2 pressed)
                  IF (muesliStock > 0)
                     Dispense muesli bar ;
                     muesliStock ← muesliStock - 1 ;
                  ELSE
                     Display 'Sold out message' ;
                  ENDIF
        9.3.   ELSE IF (button 3 pressed)
                  IF (cheesePuffStock > 0)
                     Dispense cheese puffs ;
                     cheesePuffStock ← cheesePuffStock - 1 ;
                  ELSE
                     Display 'Sold out message' ;
                  ENDIF
        9.4.   ELSE IF (button 4 pressed)
                  IF (appleStock > 0)
                     Dispense apple ;
                     appleStock ← appleStock - 1 ;
                  ELSE
                     Display 'Sold out message' ;
                  ENDIF
        9.5.   ELSE IF (button 5 pressed)
                  IF (popcornStock > 0)
                     Dispense popcorn ;
                     popcornStock ← popcornStock - 1 ;
                  ELSE
                     Display 'Sold out message' ;
                  ENDIF
        9.6.   ELSE IF (button 6 pressed)
                  Print sales summary ;
        9.7.   ELSE // we know an invalid button was pushed, no
               need to test for it.
                  Display 'Invalid choice message' ;
               ENDIF
     ENDWHILE
```

Checking for sufficient money (only partial solution given for effect):

```
9.   priceOfChocolateBar ← 10 ;
10. WHILE (not the end of the day)
       10.1.  IF (button 1 pressed)
                 IF (money > priceOfChocolateBar)
                    IF (chocolateStock > 0)
                       Dispense milk chocolate ;
                       chocolateStock ← chocolateStock - 1 ;
                    ELSE
```

```
                            Display 'Sold out message' ;
                        ENDIF
                    ELSE
                        Display 'Insufficient funds' message ;
                    ENDIF
        10.2.  ELSE IF (button 2 pressed)
                ...
                ...
                ...
```

Giving change

Algorithm for giving change:

```
1.  leftover ← money - priceOfSnack ;
2.  numberFifties ← leftover ÷ 50 ;
3.  leftover ← change MOD 50 ;
4.  numberTwenties ← leftover ÷ 20 ;
5.  leftover ← leftover MOD 20 ;
6.  numberTens ← leftover ÷ 10 ;
7.  leftover ← leftover MOD 10 ;
8.  numberFives ← leftover ÷ 5 ;
9.  leftover ← leftover MOD 5 ;
10. numberTwos ← leftover ÷ 2 ;
11. numberOnes ← leftover MOD 2 ;
12. FOR count GOES FROM 1 TO numberFifties
        Dispense 50p coin ;
    ENDFOR
13. FOR count GOES FROM 1 TO numberTwenties
        Dispense 20p coin ;
    ENDFOR
14. FOR count GOES FROM 1 TO numberTens
        Dispense 10p coin ;
    ENDFOR
15. FOR count GOES FROM 1 TO numberFives
        Dispense 5p coin ;
    ENDFOR
16. FOR count GOES FROM 1 TO numberTwos
        Dispense 2p coin ;
    ENDFOR
17. FOR count GOES FROM 1 to numberOnes
        Dispense 1p coin ;
    ENDFOR
```

Using change algorithm:

```
9.  priceOfChocolateBar ← 10 ;
10. WHILE (not the end of the day)
        10.1.  IF (button 1 pressed)
                IF (money > priceOfChocolateBar)
                    IF (chocolateStock > 0)
                        Dispense milk chocolate ;
```

```
                              chocolateStock ← chocolateStock - 1 ;
                                 Insert change algorithm here...
                              ELSE
                                 Display 'Sold out message' ;
                              ENDIF
                           ELSE
                              Display 'Insufficient funds' message ;
                           ENDIF
        10.2.   ELSE IF (button 2 pressed)
                   ...
                   ...
                   ...
```

Stocksfield Fire Service: Hazchem Signs

Using IF ELSE

```
// First character
IF fireFightingCode is 1
   Use coarse spray ;
ELSE IF fireFightingCode is 2
   Use fine spray ;
ELSE IF fireFightingCode is 3
   Use foam ;
ELSE
   Use dry agent ;
ENDIF
// Second character
IF precautionsCode is P
   Use LTS ;
   Dilute spillage ;
   Risk of explosion ;
ELSE IF...
...
ELSE
   Use BA & Fire kit ;
   Contain spillage ;
ENDIF
// Third character
IF character is E
   Public hazard ;
ENDIF
```

What about dealing with an invalid code letter?

```
// First character
IF fireFightingCode is 1
   Use coarse spray ;
ELSE IF fireFightingCode is 2
   Use fine spray ;
ELSE IF fireFightingCode is 3
   Use foam ;
```

```
ELSE IF fireFightingCode is 4
   Use dry agent ;
ELSE
   Invalid fire fighting code ;
ENDIF
// Second character
IF precautionsCode is P
   Use LTS ;
   Dilute spillage ;
   Risk of explosion ;
ELSE IF...
...
ELSE IF precautionsCode is Z
   Use BA & Fire kit ;
   Contain spillage ;
ELSE
   Invalid precautions code ;
ENDIF
// Third character
IF publicHazardCode is E
   Public hazard ;
ELSE IF publicHazardCode is blank
   No hazard ;
ELSE
   Invalid public hazard code ;
ENDIF
```

Puzzle World: Roman Numerals and Chronograms

See accompanying website.

Pangrams: Holoalphabetic Sentences

See accompanying website.

Online Bookstore: ISBNs

See accompanying website.

Chapter 7

End of Chapter Exercises

2. The Person class outline was like this:

class Person	
Properties	awake: yes, no ; inBed: yes, no ; needsShower: yes, no ; isDressed: yes, no ;

Methods	WakeUp ; GoToSleep ; GetUp ; GoToBed ; GetWashed ; GetDressed ; GetUndressed ;

Method Algorithms
WakeUp
1. awake ← Yes ;
2. needsShower ← Yes ;

GoToSleep
1. awake ← No ;

GetUp
1. inBed ← No ;

GoToBed
1. inBed ← Yes ;

GetWashed
1. needsShower ← No ;

GetDressed
1. isDressed ← Yes ;

GetUndressed
1. isDressed ← No ;

3. The Alarm class outline was like this:

class Alarm	
Properties	ringing: yes, no ; time: 00:00:00 to 23:59:00 ; alarmTime: 00:00:00 to 23:59:00 ; alarmIsSet: on, off ;
Methods	SetTime hh:mm:ss ; GetTime ; SetAlarmTime: hh:mm ; GetAlarmTime ; SetAlarm ; UnsetAlarm ; StartRinging ; SwitchOff ; (i.e. stop ringing)

Method algorithms
SetTime: hh:mm:ss
>   1.   `time` ← hh:mm:ss ;

GetTime
>   1.   Display `time` ;

SetAlarmTime: hh:mm
>   1.   `alarmTime` ← hh:mm ;

GetAlarmTime
>   1.   Display `alarmTime` ;

SetAlarm
>   1.   `alarmIsSet` ← on ;

UnsetAlarm
>   1.   `alarmIsSet` ← off ;

StartRinging
>   1.   `ringing` ← yes ;

SwitchOff
>   1.   `ringing` ← no ;

4. Algorithm for counting sleeping people.

>   1.   `stillInBed` ← 0 ;
>   2.   WHILE (Person objects to look at)
>   2.1.   tell Person BedStatus: `answer` ;
>   2.2.   IF (answer = 'yes')
>   2.2.1.   stillInBed ← stillInBed + 1 ;
>   ENDIF
>   2.3.   Move to next Person object ;
>   ENDWHILE
>   4.   Display `stillInBed` ;

6. i) Clothing classes.

class Socks	
Properties	beingWorn: yes, no ; dirty: yes, no wholePair: yes, no // **one sock may be missing**
Operations	PutOn ; TakeOff ; Wash ; Dispose ; // **if one sock is missing**!

class Underwear	
Properties	beingWorn: yes, no ; dirty: yes, no ;
Operations	PutOn ; TakeOff ; Wash ;

class Trousers	
Properties	beingWorn: yes, no ; dirty: yes, no ; Belt ; (class)
Operations	PutOn ; TakeOff ; DryClean ; ThreadBelt ; RemoveBelt ;

class Shirt	
Properties	beingWorn: yes, no ; dirty: yes, no ; wrinkled: yes, no ;
Operations	PutOn ; TakeOff ; Wash ; Iron ;

class Shoes	
Properties	beingWorn: yes, no ; dirty: yes, no ; wholePair: yes, no Laces ; (class)
Operations	PutOn ; TakeOff ; Polish ; ThreadLaces ; RemoveLaces ; Dispose ;

ii) Instantiation of objects.

```
tanPleats ← new Trousers ;
whiteBoxers ← new Underwear ;
blackAnkles ← new Socks ;
brownBrogues ← new Shoes ;
whiteLongSleeve ← new Shirt ;
```

iii) Calling methods.

```
tell tanPleats PutOn ;
tell whiteBoxers PutOn ;
tell blackAnkles PutOn ;
tell brownBrogues PutOn ;
tell whiteLongSleeve PutOn ;
```

Chapter 7 Projects

No solutions for projects.

Chapter 8

End of Chapter Exercises

1. Flowchart for coffee making problem

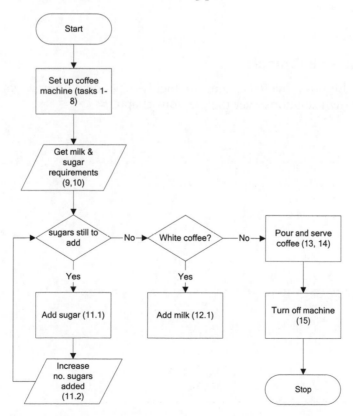

2. Tree diagram for coffee making problem

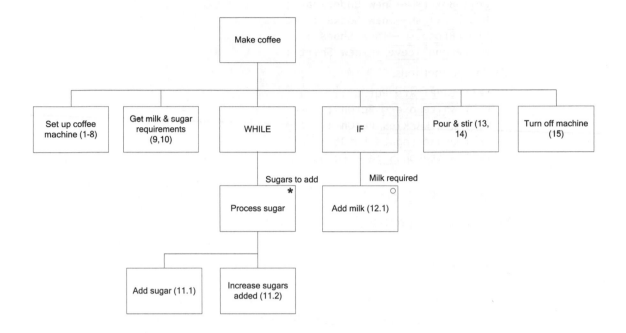

Chapter 8 Projects

No solutions provided as they are highly dependent on how you have structured your own solutions over the previous chapters.

Index

A

abstract data type (ADT), 131, 168, 207
abstraction, 9–10, 207, 225
  control abstraction, xiv, 9, 165, 243
  data abstraction, 9, 129–133, 165
  levels of, xiv, 10, 129,130–1
  misinterpretation, caused by, 46, 217
  precision, unambiguity, 13
  useful for simplifying problems, 42,130
Abu Ja'far Mohammed ben Musa *see* Al-Khwarizmi
action *see* task
action block, 64, 147, 150, 223, 224
  conditional execution of, 67, 134, 136
  in tree diagrams, 194
  repetition of, 144
acronym, 208
Ada, 132
Adams, James, 40, 232
  on the habit of problem solving, 50
  on viewpoints, 51
addition operator +, 221
ADT *see* abstract data type
algorithm
  building blocks (sequence, iteration, selection), 133
  definition, 8, 225
  diagrammatic representation, 190–201
  design from pseudo-code, xiii
  general pattern, 77
  in the program design process, 183
  in functional decomposition, 209–10
Al-Khwarizmi, 225
  Abu Ja'far Mohammed ben Musa, full name of, 8
  inventor of the algorithm, 8
AND, 100, 115, 140, 142, 222, 225
ant and sugar problem, 43–7
Ariane, V 52, 98, 208, 214, 219
arithmetic, 15, 225, 227
  difficult with Roman numerals, 16
  effect of data typing upon, 131
  expressions of in variable assignment, 116
  operators, 221
  problems involving, 23, 47, 102
  thinking in terms of leads astray, 43
assignment operator, ← 116, 221

assignment statements, 165, 176, 212
assignment
  in the procedural paradigm, 165
  of variables, 86
  pseudo-code operator, 116
association class, 173
assumptions, 26, 27, 52, 58–9
  cause of failure, 52
  deliberate, 60
  hidden, 31
  identification of, 34–5
  incorrect, 42, 45
  showing in pseudo-code, 59
  sometimes seem reasonable, 30
  unjustified, 26
at-least-once *see* iteration

B

BASIC, 10, 132, 208, 217
Boole, George 100, 225
Boolean, 100, 225
  see also Boole, George
bottom-up, 187, 189
braces {}
  to denote full range of values of a variable, 99, 109
branching, 190, 196
Brian Wildebeest, 4
Brooks, Fred, 211, 219
  on 'throwing one away', 210
bugs, 29, 214–5, 225
  see also defects
Byron, (Augusta) Ada, countess of Lovelace, 132
Byron, George Gordon, Lord Byron, 132

C

case sensitive, 98
  see also identifier; variable
C, 98, 99, 212, 225
C#, 164, 165, 189, 225
C++, 98, 99, 128, 132, 165, 189, 225, 226
camel casing, 98
  see also identifier
capta, 129
  vs knowledge, information data, 129
central processing unit (CPU), 165, 208
chessboard and dominoes problem, 41–3
choice *see* selection; iteration

class (object orientation), 165, 167–70, 203, 226
  discovering properties, 171
  methods, xiv
  see also association class; object
COBOL, 99, 208
coding, xiii, 10, 12, 19, 39, 183, 225
comment symbol //, 89
compiler, xi, 21, 35, 225, 226, 227, 228
compilation, 13, 21, 225
computer error, 72, 209
conditional action, 62, 73
conditions, 52, 64, 223, 225
  construct for testing *see* IF; IF . . . ELSE
  compound, 115, 195
  in iterations *see* iteration
  multiple, testing of, 140–2
  restricting courses of action, 61
  true or false, 66
  underlying a problem, 27–8, 30, 35
  writing selection conditions, 139
construct, 50, 52, 128, 190, 222
  branching, 190
  DO . . . WHILE *see* DO . . . WHILE
  FOR *see* FOR
  IF *see* IF
  IF..ELSE *see* IF . . . ELSE
  iteration, 65, 144–151
  nesting, 91
  selection, 62, 134–143
  WHILE *see* WHILE
construct nesting, 91
  example of, 112, 143
  shown in tree diagrams, 196
constructor, 165, 173
  see also object
context diagram, 201–2
control abstraction *see* abstraction
controller, 172, 173–7
Cornelius, Barry, 216, 219
CPU *see* central processing unit
cucumber, 39

D

data abstraction *see* abstraction
data flow approaches, 188–9
data flow diagram, 188, 200–2, 204, 210
data hiding, 227

data, xi, 9, 10, 128–134, 165–6, 226
  allowable operations performed
    upon, 131, 166
  as a parameter, 227
  as input to algorithm, 26, 156
  belonging to objects, 167–9
  corruption of, 213
  definition of, 129
  different types of, 100, 130
  flow of, 201
  identification of, 129
  in object orientation, 189
  mechanisms for storage, 132
  represented by variables, 86
  vs capta, information,
    knowledge, 129
  see also data flow diagram
data structure approaches, 187–8
data structure, xiii, 164, 187–8
  represented by tree diagrams, 191
Data Structure Systems Development
  (DSSD), 188
data type, xi, 100, 130–3, 168,
    225, 226
  not sadistic, 132
  strong & weak, 132–3
  see also abstract data type
datum, 129
  see also data
debugging, 214, 226
decomposition
  of problems, 47, 217
  of functions, 185–6, 201–2,
    209–11, 215–7
defect *see* bug
defects, 29, 112, 212, 225, 226
  caused by assumptions, 30
  caused by imprecise
    specifications, 94
  caused by programmer mistake,
    72, 209
  corrected during maintenance,
    76, 214
  reduced by simple programs, 114
  reduced by software reuse, 213–4
  vs limitation, 118
  see also bugs
Delphi, 165
Deming, W. Edwards, 83
design patterns, 128, 219
diagrams, 39–47
  better than words, 51
  for understanding a problem, 34
  not always useful, 43
  misinterpreting, 46
  shed light on problem, 25
  see also tree diagrams; data flow
    diagrams; state transition
    diagrams; flowcharts
division operator ÷, 221
DO . . . WHILE, 151
  applications of, 152
  pseudo-code for, 151

documentation, 25, 209
  how to write it, 75–7
  importance of, 30
  purpose of, 76
DSSD *see* Data Structure Systems
  Development
dysfunctional decomposition, 185–6,
    208, 209–11, 215, 217

E

Eiffel, 164
ELSE *see* IF . . . ELSE
Emmerson, Ralph Waldo, 204
ENDFOR *see* FOR
ENDIF *see* IF
ENDWHILE *see* WHILE
equal to =, 139, 221
error
  computer *vs* programmer, 72
  see also bug
Errors of the Third Kind, 39
  example of, 47
Euclid of Alexandria, xii
event, 198

F

false *see* condition
FIFA, 123
Finite State Machine (FSM), 197
  see also State Transition Diagram
flawchart, 190
flowchart, 63, 67, 190–1, 196, 204, 226
  for the IF statement, 63
  for van loading problem, 192–3
  template for, 168
FOR, 148–150, 224
  invariant: initial and final values
    of, 149
  pseudo-code for, 148
Francis of Assisi, Saint, 39
FSM *see* Finite State Machine
function, 226
functional decomposition, 185, 186,
    202, 209–11, 215–7
  see also dysfunctional decomposition;
    top-down

G

graphical notations, 189
greater than >, 139, 222
greater than or equal to ≥,
    139, 222

H

heuristic
  art of invention, xii
  guided trial and error, 211
  problem solving approach, 9
  vs functional decomposition, 217
How To Solve It, 24, 34, 211, 219
Humphrey, Watts, 30, 209, 219

I

identifier, 97–98, 101, 221, 226, 228
  naming conventions, 98–99
  put in boxes in pseudo-code, 101
  see also variable
IF, 62–64, 134
  control flow diagram for, 63
  execution of action block, 64
  multi-part, 136
  pseudo-code for, 222
  simple *vs* extended, 134
  writing condition for, 139–142
  vs iteration, 65–66
IF . . . ELSE, 135–142
  multi-part, 136–142
  no final IF, 141
inequality *see* not equal to
information
  about the problem, 35
  data stores, 200
  hiding, 213
  loss of owing to abstraction, 42
  vs capta, data, knowledge, 129
initialization, 77, 101, 115
  of variables *see* variable
input, 26, 191, 226
input parameter, 227
instance *see* object
instantiation, 172, 173, 178
  initialization of object properties
    upon, 174
integer, 168, 208, 209, 212, 213, 221
invariant *see* FOR
iteration, xi, xiv, 35, 56, 65, 95, 128,
    144–56, 177
  as a control abstraction, 207
  at-least-once, 150
  count-controlled, 144, 148–50
  determinate, 144
  DO . . . WHILE *see* DO . . . WHILE
  FOR *see* FOR
  indeterminate, 146
  in flowcharts, 190
  non-terminating; infinite, 146
  not shown in data flow diagrams,
    201
  read-ahead, 147, 155
  read-and-process, 147
  sentinel-controlled, 152
  tree diagram for, 196
  WHILE *see* WHILE
  zero or more, 147

J

Jackson, Michael A
  books by, 211,
  on flowcharts, 190
  on Pólya, xiii
  on problem solving & programming
    languages, 27
  on program design methods, 184
  on structured programming, 209

on top-down, 210, 216
on wisdom, 181
see also Jackson Structured
Programming; Jackson System
Development; tree diagrams
Jackson Structured Programming
(JSP), 187, 188, 191
Jackson System Development (JSD),
188, 191
Jacobson, Ivar, 213
Java, xiv, 10, 189, 225, 226
case sensitive, 98
object-oriented language, 164,
165
strong typing, 132
threading, 128
variable names in, 99
vectors, 113
Java Server Pages, 187
JavaScript, 133, 226
Johnson, Samuel, 39
JSD *see* Jackson System
Development
JSP
see Jackson Structured
Programming
see Java Server Pages

K

Kay, Alan, 166
keyword, 50, 64, 71, 115, 135, 138,
149, 151, 222, 235
KISS!, 114
knowledge
gained through study, 202
incomplete, 23
of problems, 24
prior knowledge, 74
vs information, capta, data, 129

L

laser, 208
LCP *see* Logical Construction of
Programs
Ledgard, H. F., 19, 219
Lehman, Manny, 208
Leibnitz, H. Gottfried, xi, xii
less than <, 139, 222
less than or equal to ≤, 139, 222
limitations, 8
of program design methods, 188
vs defects, 118
Linux, 226, 227
logical connectives, 222
see also AND; OR; NOT
Logical Construction of Programs
(LCP), 188
loop, 66, 69, 110, 190
see also iteration
loop counter, 145, 149
Lovelace, Ada *see* Byron, (Augusta)
Ada

M

Matrix, The, 152
maintenance *see* software maintenance
mathematics
fear of, 47
for describing problems, 47–8
in problem solving, 34
variables, 86, 99
methods, 169, 170–1, 178, 226
constructor, 173
requiring data, 176
see also object
MOD, 160, 221
multiplication operator ×, 221
music, 7
Mythical Man Month, The, 210, 219

N

natural language, 12, 39, 48
natural numbers, 168, 212
see also integer
NOT, 100, 117, 146, 222, 225
not equal to ≠, 139, 155, 222
null, 134
null action, 134–136
in tree diagrams, 195
null variable, 134

O

object, 164–178, 213
behaviour, 166, 169–72
belongs to a class, 167
constructor method, 173
created through instantiation, 172
has properties (data) and methods,
170, 178
invoking methods of, 173
message passing, 173–175
operation by a controller, 172, 178
reporting property values, 176
setting property values of, 173
see also class; instantiation
object-oriented programming
(OOP), xiv, 11, 128, 164–173,
207, 225, 226
design approaches, 189
procedural building blocks
within, 177
supported by UML, 202–203, 228
supports reusability, 213, 216
OOP *see* object-oriented programming
operator, 133, 139, 160, 225, 227
arithmetic operators, 221
logical operators, 222, 225
overloaded, 133
relational operators, 139–140,
221–222
OR, 100, 143, 222, 225
OS, X, 227, 228
output, 26, 191, 202, 227
output parameter, 227

P

Pappus of Alexandria, xii
paradigm, 204
object-oriented, 172
procedural, 164, 165
parameter, 227
Pascal, 212, 217, 226
PDL *see* Program Design Language
Personal Software Process, 209, 219
physical models, 34, 48–9, 110
pictures *see* diagrams
plan, 26–7
Pólya, George
and John von Neumann, 217
died, 213
foolishness, 24
How To Solve It, xii, 24, 34, 211
precise thinking/expression, 50
precondition, 30–31
problem, 21–2
understanding, 25–6
problem frames, 26, 211, 219
problem solving
confused with coding, 10
is habitual, 50
strategy for, 24–31, 34–35
procedural, xiv, 166, 169, 172, 173,
177, 225
see also paradigm
Program Design Language (PDL) *see*
pseudo-code
program design, xiii, xiv, 50,
194–205, 209
program, xi, 19, 25, 30, 55, 181, 227
acting out, 49
an algorithm, 183
a solution description, 12
badly constructed, 21
different views of, 203
identifying limitations of, 118
like a musical score, 7
maintaining, 25
providing with input, 26
top level, 201
translating into code, 166
what is it?, 6
programming, xi–xiv
approached with awe, 6
declarative, 219
developing a repertoire, 29
errors, 72
functional, xiii
is fun, ix
keep it simple, 114
object-oriented, 163
perceived as hard, 10, 21
problem solving is the essence
of, 13
procedural, 165
process of, 10
structured, 209
techniques, 5
why do it?, 6

programming language, 227
  Ada, 132
  C, 225
  C++, 225
  C#, 225
  COBOL, 99, 208
  defer consideration of, 27
  Delphi, 165
  difficulty in understanding, 3
  distinguishing between data types, 100, 132
  do not use before understanding the problem, 8
  Eiffel, 164
  FORTRAN, 208
  implementation of abstractions, 207
  Java, 226
  JavaScript, 226
  mimic operation of computer, 165
  object-oriented, 164
  problems introduced by, 22–3
  resembled by pseudo-code, 52
  SmallTalk, 165
  syntax, xiii
  used late on in the process, 9
  Visual Basic, 228
property *see* object
pseudo-code, 6, 12, 49–52, 227
  aka Program Design Language, 50
  aka structured English, xiii, 50
  algorithmic language, 12
  assigning values in, 116
  for the DO . . . WHILE construct, 151
  for the FOR construct, 148
  for the IF construct, 64
  for the IF . . . ELSE construct, 136
  for the WHILE construct, 65–66
  preferred over flowcharts, 191
  relational operators, 139
  syntax of, 221–224

R

radar, 208
read-ahead *see* iteration
read-and-process *see* iteration
real-world
  conditions, 139
  domain, 8
  infinitely complex, 184
  problems, 11, 57
relational expression, 134, 141, 142
relational operators *see* operator
repeated action *see* iteration
reuse *see* software reuse

S

selection
  conditions, writing, 139–143
  extended, 135–6
  multi part, 136–139
  pseudo-code for, 222–223

simple and extended, 134
  tree diagram for, 194–196
  vs iteration, 65–66
semi-colon ;, 51, 222
sentinel *see* iteration; variable
sequence, 194
  tree diagram for, 194
sleep
  an aid to problem solving, 28, 34, 35
small capital letters, 6, 214
SmallTalk, 165
software maintenance, 25, 75, 190, 214–215
  adaptive, 214
  corrective, 214
  easier with good documentation, 30
  perfective, 215
  preventive, 215
software reuse, 26, 90, 213, 214
  inappropriate use of, 208
Somerville, Ian, 55, 214
SSADM *see* Structured Systems Analysis and Design Method
state, 198
  paths, 199
  start and stop states, 198
  waiting state, 177
statement *see* task
State Transition Diagram (STD), 197–200, 203, 204
  see also Finite State Machine
STD *see* State Transition Diagram
stepwise refinement, 185, 186, 209, 215, 219
structure diagrams *see* tree diagram
structured English *see* pseudo-code
Structured Systems Analysis and Design Method (SSADM), 188, 200, 210
subproblem, 23, 93, 111, 186, 215–217
  identification of to simplify the task, 90
  in 'functional decomposition', 186
  in 'top down', 215
  introduced by language, 23
  problem decomposed into, 47
  programming tasks comprised of, 26
  partitioning a problem into, 27
  relationship of to parent problem, 216
  some easier to solve than others, 27
  thinking reveals existence of, 74
  unique features of, 217
subtraction operator –, 221
syntax, xiii, 23, 221, 227
task
  aka statement; action
  in pseudo-code, 51
  null task, 135
  underlined to show assumption, 59
  see also construct
Therac-, 25 213, 214, 219
think spot, 4

top-down, 185–6, 187, 200, 201, 202, 209–11, 215–7
  see also functional decomposition; dysfunctional decomposition
tree diagrams, 188, 191–7, 203–4
  complete algorithm, 197
  for iteration, 196
  for selection, 194–5
  for sequence, 194
  vs State Transition Diagrams, 199–200
true *see* condition
Truman, Harry S, former US president, 185
type, 227
  see also data type
typing (data), xiv, 132–133
  see also data type

U

UML *see* Unified Modeling Language
underscore character _, 98
Unified Modeling Language (UML), 202, 227
Upper case letters, 99
UNIX, 226, 228
variable, 84, 86, 98, 165, 221, 226, 228
  as an object, 173
  as a sentinel, 152, 156 assignment of values, 86, 116
  case sensitive, 98
  discovery of, 97
  estimating magnitude of, 98, 109, 129, 132
  initialization of, 70, 117, 148, 155, 211–212
  in pseudo-code, 221
  kinds of, 100
  memory taken up by, 98
  naming conventions, 98–99
  null, 134
  purpose of, 98
  see also identifier

V

Visual Basic, 14, 228
Visual Basic.NET, 165
visualization
  of ant's path, 46, 47
  of chessboard, 43
  of problems, 39, 41, 44
  of a variable, 221
  through diagrams, 51
  through imagination, 106
von Neumann, John, 165, 217
von Neumann architecture, 165, 217

W

Warnier-Orr Methodology, 188
WHILE, 65–67

applications of, 152
control flow diagram for, 66
resembles IF, 66
vs DO . . . WHILE, 155
Windows, 226, 227, 228
windows, 228
Wirth, Niklaus, 209, 210, 219

wisdom, 181, 209
working storage, 84, 85
   see also variable

YSM *see* Yourdon Structured Method

Yourdon Structured Method (YSM), 188, 210

zero-or-more *see* iteration